SMASHING GLASS & KICKING ASS

LESSONS FROM THE MEANEST WOMAN ALIVE™

LINDA SMITH, ESQ.

Hardback ISBN: 978-0-9978106-0-8
Paperback ISBN: 978-0-9978106-1-5
Digital ISBN: 978-0-9978106-2-2

Cover Design: Dino Marino
Interior Design: Christina Gorchos, 3CsBooks.com

“Teach your daughters to worry less about fitting into glass slippers and more about shattering glass ceilings.”

—MELISSA MARCHONNA
Digital Marketer for the New York Jets

Dedication

To All Women Who Are Ready To Unleash Their Power

To My Parents Who Always Thought Girls Could Do Anything They Wanted To

Contents

PART I

PREFACE

WOMEN, LISTEN UP!

We have the power, as women, to run the world. This isn't hypothetical. It's not wishful thinking. *We already have the ability to do it.* As women, we have unique advantages that make us ideally suited to lead—and to lead *more* effectively than men.

Despite decades of superficial change in the ranks of business, today's women remain stalled in their quest to advance their careers. Across every level of work, in every industry, women still struggle to earn the same level of pay, to receive equal access to opportunity and promotion, and to do the work they were hired to do without fear of harassment or the discrimination of pervasive gender bias.

Men, meanwhile, act in countless ways that perpetuate these very biases, secure in the belief that this is the natural order of things. Men still think they run the world, and still think they dictate the rules.

Not anymore. We have the power to change this right now.

I'm going to rock the boat—hell, *capsize* the boat—by showing you how we can harness our natural talents *as women* to dominate in business. Not by "leaning in" or "outmanning the men" or "beating men at their own game," but by capitalizing on the very things that make us different.

Women need to jettison the societal norms perpetuated by male domination and use an entirely different playbook—one written by a woman, for women. You are holding that playbook. I have succeeded for decades in a cutthroat, male-dominated profession specifically by using my skills as a woman; I'm here now to guide you on your own quest for success. Your journey will be much easier, not to mention more fun, knowing how to avoid the pitfalls, roadblocks, and dead ends.

It's possible you think none of this applies to you. But, before you make that judgment, do me –and yourself—a favor and answer these questions honestly:

- *Do you feel like men call the shots at your company? Do you compete according to the rules of a male playbook?*
- *Do you feel like you're stuck in your job with no clear path for advancement? Are you so tired of being stalled in a midlevel job that you are thinking of just quitting? Does it feel like your colleagues or your boss are trying to push you out? Would you like an effective way of moving forward?*
- *Do men routinely underestimate you? Do you under-estimate yourself?*
- *Do men make sexist comments, engage in male bonding rituals, and feel no shame in showing you unwanted attention? Would you like to know how to eliminate that behavior?*
- *Do you engage in self-sabotage, allowing self-doubt, risk aversion, and the fear that you're a fraud prevent you from stepping forward for the best projects, speaking your mind boldly, and taking credit for your accomplishments? Would you like to learn techniques for gaining the confidence to take risks and seize opportunities?*
- *Do you feel like men confidently voice their opinions, brush off slights, interrupt you in meetings, joke around with the bosses, and brag about their successes? Would you like to do away with the old boys' network?*
- *Do your male colleagues expect to take the lead when your boss hands out assignments, while you remain just another member of the team? Would you like to lead a team?*
- *Do you overthink things, try to please everyone you work with, and have a hard time shaking off criticism and moving on? Do you hold yourself back from acting forcefully or*

competitively? Would you like to learn how to conquer those instincts and take charge?

- *Do you feel that men are so entrenched as the dominant sex in our social hierarchy that you feel like that's just the natural order and will never change? Do you want to join other women in shaping a new social order?*

You may be afraid to rock or capsize the boat. But if your answer to any of the questions above is *yes*, read on. Today's women do not have to put up with this bullshit any longer. We have the talent and the smarts. It's time to change the gender rules by using our unique advantages as women to advance our careers and shine as the leaders we're meant to be.

Together, let's seize the moment and get this done.

CHAPTER 1

YOU ARE A FORCE TO BE RECKONED WITH

"If you ask me what I came into this life to do, I will tell you: I came to live out loud."

—ZOLA

IN THE FALL OF 2005, MY LAW FIRM decided to hold its first-ever women's retreat.

It was, I hoped, a sign of changing times. As a newly-minted lawyer, I had arrived at O'Melveny & Myers in downtown Los Angeles in 1977 to find a firm with one foot still in the gender-divided workplace of the 1950s—there was only one female partner, and the firm had only just done away with the steno pool. Back then, if you were a woman in the company, you were either a secretary or a receptionist.

The profession outside of O'Melveny at the time was even bleaker. There were no women federal judges, only a handful of women state judges (most of those in family court), no women general counsel and no functioning networks of women lawyers. The legal profession was a gender desert, and I had arrived thirsty, with no oasis in sight.

Fast forward some twenty-eight years, and we were drawing female partners (now totaling 5 percent of the partnership) and other senior women from our fifteen global offices, along with some of our eminent female clients, to a three-day event honoring what, not many years before, hadn't even existed. This event, I felt, would be a celebration. A victory not just for women in law, but for all of us.

I arrived at the venue that day to a flurry of preparation. The event organizers had pulled out all the stops, and the schedule boasted an impressive lineup of speakers, including a senior executive from a global oil conglomerate and a best-selling author who wrote about how women could better succeed in business. The schedule also included *me*—I'd come a long way since those steno pool days, and I was the opening-day keynote speaker.

Before the event kicked off, however, I was to help record a segment for a video honoring the monumental contributions made to the practice of law by female attorneys. Many partners and clients were recording short pieces for the video, which would be shown to the entire delegate assembly.

Among those to be recorded, unfortunately, were some of the leading senior partners.

Once upon a time, O'Melveny & Myers had thrived under a consensus-building management style. There was an unspoken spirit of contribution and teamwork, and a drive to find the best solution, not just the solution at the top of a hierarchy.

That all changed when there was a shift in management at the top. On the outside, some of the new managing partners may have looked like the august leaders of an international prestigious law firm, but on the inside, they were little more than Neanderthals.

One of these leaders in particular, for all his obvious caveman barbarism, still fancied himself an emperor. Like a little Napoleon, one of his first decrees had been to commission a special conference room for his private use. He had his own limousine and driver, and an entourage that traveled with him to cater to his needs, the largest of which was his ego.

When the time came to record my video segment, it so happened that the Neanderthal was scheduled just ahead of me in the queue. The videographer was running late, so they were only beginning to film this leader's segment when I arrived for my appointment.

I watched him in action as he stared square-jawed into the camera. The interviewer asked him a stock question about the value of female lawyers. I remember every beat of his response.

"If Darwinian principles applied," he said, "there would be no women partners."

When he finished, he turned to me confidently and asked what I thought of his remarks. I couldn't believe what I was hearing. *He's expecting praise*, I realized.

It was unbelievable. I could think of a few things I'd like to have given him, but praise was the last thing on my mind. At the time, I was bringing in twenty-five to thirty million dollars a year in fees from clients who had come to the firm specifically to hire me. I was leading several large teams of attorneys and support staff. Other female partners had been making similar contributions in their own fields of practice.

I told him all of this in no uncertain terms. I explained (slowly, so he'd understand) that the firm could not open its first women's leadership conference with one of its most senior leaders telling the assembled group of highly successful women that no woman would make it if partnership was a true test of survival of the fittest. He had managed in just one sentence to demonstrate his disdain for female attorneys and to minimize all of their demonstrable successes. His remarks, I told him, suggested that the real reason the firm made an effort to hire woman partners was for the sake of appearances.

Then I turned to the cameraman and said, "I'm ready to record my segment now."

The look on the Neanderthal's face was priceless, and something I've always wanted in a frame on my desk.

////////////

My encounter with the caveman illustrates two important principles, and they form the core thesis of this book.

The first is that *the world hasn't changed as much as many would like to believe.* Despite innumerable women's empowerment books and articles, and endless corporate diversity training courses, today's women are stalled in their quest to advance their careers. While the media showcases the women who have managed to run the gauntlet and become CEOs or flourishing entrepreneurs, those women stand out because their numbers are still so few. Only 6.4 percent of the Fortune 500 have female CEOs—a record high, by the way.

What's more, despite graduating from college and professional schools and entering the workforce in equal numbers with men, females fail to make the same progress in their jobs as their male counterparts do, and that phenomenon repeats itself throughout the leadership pipeline. The number of women shrinks by about half at the middle-management level and dwindles to a fragment when it comes to promotion to the C-suite. Throughout the workforce, women get fired, get discouraged and quit, or settle on jobs for which they are overqualified. And men act in countless ways that perpetuate this cycle, secure in the belief that this is the natural order of society.

It shocks me today that talented, fantastic women are still not making it to the top. While women enter many careers in the same numbers as men, they don't advance like men do. Too many of them fall off, get pushed off, settle for positions for which they are overqualified, or burn out along the way. That's why only one in six equity partners in law firms are women; there are only twenty-one women in the United States Senate, and only *four* state governors.

The problem is not only that the glass ceiling still exists, but that there are *many* glass ceilings, and they tend to get thicker the higher you climb. *Men like the Neanderthal still run the world, and still dictate the rules.* The first purpose of this book is to describe to you that reality, which certainly no one ever explained to me, and to show you the techniques for breaking through the barriers that will be in place for as long as men continue to dictate the rules.

The second principle of this book is apparent in the great irony of my showdown with the Neanderthal. He believed that men had a natural advantage in the world of work. He'd no doubt be distressed to discover that, in fact, it's quite the opposite, Darwinian principles, it turns out, favor *us*—it's women, not men, who have the remarkable advantage when it comes to the modern workplace. With our superior emotional intelligence, we have the edge in crucial business skills like analysis, connection, and leadership.

This isn't grandstanding. Thanks to research findings that have been exhaustively validated by business leaders, the media, and a phalanx of consultants, the corporate community has finally recognized something vital: based on the new sine qua non of business success—emotional intelligence—*women's leadership skills are superior to men's.* Women score higher than men on all but one of the emotional intelligence competencies proven to impact business performance. What's more, multiple studies have confirmed that companies with more women in their executive ranks and on their boards of directors significantly outperform companies with fewer or no women in these positions. These empirical studies show *companies will actually make more money if they have more women on their boards and in senior executive positions.*

Money talks. Unlike 1977, today, we have new and potent ammunition in the fight to establish our leadership prowess. The hard facts of capitalism are on our side. We are superior leaders—we need only harness our higher abilities as women to take command.

Even though tough challenges await, we are mighty, and we will conquer.

I wrote this book to show you how.

MEET THE MEANEST WOMAN ALIVE

Bitch.
Vixen.
Wolf.
Mother, leader, mentor, friend.

I've been called all of these things, and I own them. I'm all of them. My enemies run for cover when they hear my high heels coming their way, but my friends have no better ally. I've conquered my own field and helped open the way for other women to ascend to rarefied heights.

It's the type of life that tends to generate a few labels along the way. But perhaps my favorite came from clients of mine.

In the world of trial law, it's common practice to carefully prepare witnesses. Faced with the pressure of a jury and audience, and the stern presence of a judge, even the toughest person can crumble—or at least stumble—under the scrutiny of opposing counsel. The best way to prepare witnesses is through mock cross-examination—to ask them questions in as realistic and difficult a way as possible so that they aren't rattled into making a mistake during the real thing.

I defend my clients' interests with the ferocity of a mother bear guarding her cubs. I know all the weaknesses in the cases I take on, and I ask questions in the practice sessions that place maximum pressure on my clients. I would make them sound like fools as I challenged their responses. Since it was counterproductive to leave them in that sorry state, the linchpin of my technique was to then rebuild them, showing them how to deflect even the toughest onslaught with confidence and fortitude. After sparring with me, they would find the real cross-examination a breeze.

When *Corporate Board Member* magazine—the industry publication for Fortune 500 companies—did a profile on me, a client was quoted as calling me "The Meanest Woman Alive," and it stuck. My clients love it, knowing that I will rip the heart out of anyone who tries to hurt them or our case.

The Meanest Woman Alive profile highlighted how far I had traveled. I came from a lower middle-class family in Vermont—an upbringing that did not include any built-in privileges. My dad was a traveling salesman and my mom was an elementary school teacher. With three girls to feed and clothe, money was tight. Back-to-school shopping meant a trip to the thrift store. Fine dining and birthday celebrations happened at the local McDonald's.

Nobody handed me anything. And I never had a female mentor in my profession—because there were none to be found. But I persevered, using the innate talents that all women share. Eventually, I went from a lowly first-year lawyer to the only woman of my entering class to make partner after the smoke had cleared. Today, the name Linda Jane Smith strikes fear into the hearts of opposing counsel. Now I'm one of the top five female litigators in the United States. Women from all over the country tell me that I've inspired them to keep fighting for themselves: to never surrender, to honor their aspirations, to ascend to the apogee of their careers. Over 350,000 of them follow "The Meanest Woman Alive" on social media.

Given my petite, curvy frame, men have tended unconsciously to label me as a blonde bimbo. Big mistake. I am fierce in defense of my clients and my positions. And if the other side lies about the facts or the law, or mistreats my witnesses or mischaracterizes my position, God help them. I am my clients' gladiator. To them, I truly am The Meanest Woman Alive, and they love it.

In the years since I received my moniker, I've run with the brand, achieving wondrous things in both my professional and my personal life. I have litigated cases where many billions of dollars hung in the balance. Men who control the levers of power have been brought to tears by my relentless cross-examinations. I am respected by friend and foe alike, for my victories on the battlefield and my camaraderie during peacetime.

The lesson, however, isn't that I became successful. The real lesson—the one I wrote this book to teach you—is this: I didn't become successful *despite* being a woman. I became successful *because* of it.

My job is to teach you how to do the same thing.

WHO WILL YOU BECOME?

I don't expect—or even suggest—that you become the meanest woman alive. What I do insist is that you understand that you have the potential, the promise, and the genetic birthright to become *whatever kind of woman you want.*

Corporate researchers' studies have validated what women have known all along—we have superior emotional intelligence (EI), now the universally recognized marker for leadership success. Using that superior ability and its recognition by the business community, women can confidently move up the corporate ladder.

In this book, I focus on three of the factors grounded in EI that bestow stunning advantages: women's empathy-driven abilities to read minds, play well with others, and understand how emotions influence decisions. These factors—the marriage of intelligence, empathy, and emotions—enable women to excel as leaders.

In the next chapter, I'll address how to deploy these unique abilities to greatest effect in your quest to succeed. Then I'll arm you with the lessons you'll need to avoid the traps, barricades, and detours you will encounter in your journey.

Those lessons include the need for resilience. When I graduated at the top of my law school class at UCLA, I thought I was hot shit. Out in the real world, I had to get over myself quickly. I learned that no one but your parents cares if you think you're special, and that it's only by consistently delivering excellent work and taking your lumps that you prove your worth. There are plenty of people ready to take your place if you falter or show weakness.

I'll show you how to diagnose the onset of self-sabotage and how to negate its effects. Even the most successful women in the world have to confront that harshly critical voice in their heads that says, *You're not good enough* or *You can't.*

After learning my field-tested methods for putting assholes in their place, you'll know how to establish your own rules of engagement. Then you can decide how to communicate (sweetly, matter-of-factly, or forcefully) what you will put up with, what you won't, and what the consequences will be for assholes who cross the line.

Those methods become even more important—and trickier—when you're dealing with sexual bullying from a boss or a client with the power to damage your career. Once in a while, a woman may have to take serious action, by using verbal judo that defuses the situation or by confronting her harasser head-on and unleashing her inner badass. Having done both in my own career (I once had to tell Mick Jagger to go fuck himself, and I'm glad I did), I'll coach you step by step through the process. You'll learn to set the agenda and reinforce everything you say with a strong, confident, no-bullshit demeanor.

I'll also spend more than a few pages explaining the danger of snipers—not only men, but also rival women who use gossip and rumor to sow doubt within the old boys' network about your competence, morals, or leadership. I'll teach you the fine art of self-defense, so you can dodge sabotage as you take your career to the next level. Once there, you will be in a position to take on a mentorship role and make it easier for the women who follow.

This book is a road map to the essentials. Women must be bold and speak up with confidence and be fearless and take charge of difficult situations. They must show grit under pressure and in the face of uncertainty and push back against those who deny them what they need. For decades, courage and a willingness to stand up to challenges have propelled me forward in a man's world. They've enabled me to break glass ceilings and kick ass all along the way. Now, it's your turn.

Ultimately, the only power women have is what we can conjure from within. If doing that was easy, every talented woman out there would have a fair shot at the executive suite. Unfortunately, that's *not* what's happening. But it can change; cultivating inner confidence in the face of entrenched male dominance is the foundation for achievement—and also one of the most difficult things for a woman to do. It took me a lifetime of experience to build this persona and to develop a rock-solid sense of self-worth.

You can do the same, and I promise you, it's well worth the effort.

ANY WOMAN CAN BECOME A BADASS

This book is for any woman—whether you're starting out in the workforce or stuck somewhere on the ladder to the top, no matter what career you've chosen, and whether you're a student or an entrepreneur or a middle manager. I learned these lessons and perfected my formula for success in Big Law and the corporate world, but they apply across the board, anywhere people organize themselves to pursue a line of work together. In the chapters that follow, I'll demonstrate exactly why women are superior leaders and how to harness our higher abilities as women to break through the barriers that will be in place for as long as men continue to dictate the rules. You'll discover:

- **A clear understanding of women's emotional intelligence,** and how to use those unique talents to your best advantage.
- **An "eyes wide open" discussion of the need to slay two demons.** First, the external demon: the traditional gender stereotyping hierarchy of the business world. Second, and just as dangerous: the demon that lives inside us, spawned from the internalization of those gender stereotypes and breeding self-doubt and fear.

- **How to augment the best female traits with the best male traits.** You must aggressively use the best parts of being a woman, while discarding those diffident feminine qualities that cripple you. You'll also learn to draw on the best qualities traditionally attributed to men while trashing stereotypical alpha male behavior.
- **Proven techniques for dealing with specific challenges.** You're going to face many types of male domination, so you'll need specific methods for combating them. I'll teach you how to shape a confident persona so you can "fake it til you make it," how to infiltrate the old boys' network, how to speak truth to power, how to neutralize assholes, and how to deal with men who think with their dicks.
- **How to lead as a woman, in an enlightened way.** As a female leader, you need to understand how to lead with gusto, establish your dominance, and maximize your effectiveness as a "benevolent dictator" so you can enjoy the kind of fierce loyalty my subordinates have shown for me—all while feeding your soul.

I know what's holding women back, and I know how to get past it. Every woman is entitled to set her own path for her career, just like men do. It's not a privilege; you *deserve* it.

I am not going to advise you to lean in, or to accept that women still can't have it all. Instead, I'll share with you what I've learned about how to succeed, and prove to you that having a pair of ovaries far surpasses growing a pair of balls.

CHAPTER 2

EMBRACE YOUR DESTINY TO LEAD

"What I have learned is that people become motivated when you guide them to the source of their own power..."

—ANITA RODDICK, founder of The Body Shop

FOR THOUSANDS OF YEARS, MEN HAVE ASSERTED dominance and dictated the rules of society, with women expected to take subordinate roles—nowhere more strikingly than in the workplace. With the exception of a few noteworthy and much-remarked-upon female CEOs or entrepreneurs, male supremacy has always defined the business world.

Although equally bright and talented, women have generally accepted their fate, albeit with occasional encouragement from self-help books telling them how to better compete with men. Sadly, advice on how to outman the men does little to improve our chances of success or create a less biased society.

The social stratification of the genders has its origins in early human development. Men were the hunters, traveling far and wide in search of big game, while women bore the children and tended the hearth. Surprisingly little has changed. The modern multinational corporation may be more complex and requires knowledge, analytical talent, and people skills more than brute strength or aptitude with a spear, but the power dynamics of the workplace still remain rooted in those ancient patterns.

Over the past decade, a body of serious research has upended these traditional assumptions. Not because men have finally recognized that in the modern business world women are equally competent and deserve a shot at success on the grounds of simple fairness. Fat chance of that. Instead, change has been driven by empirical studies analyzing the factors that increase corporate productivity and management effectiveness. The data-driven result of these studies is both simple and powerful: *promoting women to senior positions makes companies more money.*

Based on their research, social scientists developed a matrix of the measurable competencies most important for overall leadership effectiveness. (In the original 2012 study, sixteen competencies were identified; in the 2016 follow-up study, the competencies were refined, resulting in a total of twelve competencies.) Unsurprisingly for women, *we rate higher than men in eleven of those twelve competencies.* And, contrary to what you might assume, the higher scores are not just in so-called "soft" skills, such as dealing with people's feelings. In fact, two of the traits in which women outscored men to the highest degree—taking initiative and driving for results—have long been perceived as particularly male strengths.[1]

Despite how some men see it, women's ability to lead should hardly be a groundbreaking revelation. Still, the recognition of women's superior leadership skills, as chronicled in research studies, media reports, and now the recommendations of management consultants and efficiency experts, gives us an empirical basis to effect change. When *Forbes,* McKinsey & Company, the *Harvard Business Review, Business Insider, Fortune,* and the *Wall Street Journal* talk, men listen. The time is ripe for us to act boldly.

No longer will women with demonstrably superior leadership skills meekly carry out men's bidding. No more will we allow male bosses to disrespect us or belittle highly accomplished women. It's time to flex our freshly-accredited competencies to prevent men from stepping on or over us in their quest for success.

THE END OF FUTILITY

During our annual worldwide partner outings, the women partners at my law firm would pry one free hour out of the organizing committee so we could enjoy a cocktail party just for ourselves. The female partners (there were a mere 20 of us, out of 350 total partners) would gather in a small room, have a glass of wine, and talk. The men passionately resented this event. They seemed convinced that it was an opportunity for our tiny minority to foment revolution. Or perhaps they simply feared we would compare notes about them. In any case, their paranoia was laughable.

You can guess who was unable to stay away for that one long hour: the same "caveman" senior leader. He would hang around outside the door of our meeting room like a cat waiting to pounce.

One year my law firm won the award for best litigation firm in the United States from no less an authority than *The American Lawyer*. This was a hotly contested honor for which each firm submitted a list of its accomplishments. As the victor, my firm was featured on the cover of the magazine and in a multi-page spread. The piece ran accompanied by a full-page picture, presumably of our best litigators. That photo featured six white male litigators standing tall in all their glory. Perched next to them on a stool was a young Asian woman.

This was puzzling, because the woman was not a litigator, not a partner, and, as it turns out, not even a member of the firm. Clearly, someone involved in taking the photo noticed the astounding lack of diversity the image suggested and shoved a random woman into the frame. Why not kill three birds with one stone by choosing a woman who was also young, attractive, and Asian?

The women partners were appalled, and rightly so.

The same senior managing partner I mentioned earlier picked that year to actually wander into our cocktail party uninvited. I said to him, "Please explain why there are no women partners in *The American Lawyer* picture. We've earned the right to be featured based on the cases we've brought into the firm and the millions of dollars those cases have generated. Our contributions far exceed those of some of the men in the picture." He stood there, coolly appraising all the female rainmakers and achievers in the room, and then replied, "Because none of you deserved it."

Once again, that pompous ass had intentionally insulted every woman in the room and negated our contributions. While we stood dumbfounded, he sauntered back out.

Back then, we let him. He wielded great power in the firm, and had a well-earned reputation for vindictiveness when crossed. Failure to play by the rules at that time meant a demotion at the least or outright dismissal at worst. We had no choice but to go along. Besides, continued protest would have been an exercise in futility. That issue of *The American Lawyer* had been published before the outing.

History cannot endlessly repeat itself. Women must rise up and wrest control from these kinds of unenlightened and boorish men. The business world has changed, and so must the role of women in it. We can't allow ourselves to be held back by men who have ignorantly made camp on the wrong side of history. As women, we are already authoritatively endorsed by top business researchers, consultants, and leaders for our higher competencies of leadership; let that give you more confidence and more credibility to seize command opportunities and kick ass in them.

THE IMPORTANCE OF EMOTIONAL INTELLIGENCE

Let's define these special assets possessed by women and address how to deploy them to greatest effect. I'd call them "superpowers," because they are, but with so many comic book superheroes filling our movie screens and tablets, including our own Wonder Woman, that term just doesn't capture the unique combination of our superior assets and an ability to use those assets to kick ass.

Those *kick-assets* are our true superpowers.

What are these kick-assets? The answer has been right in front of us for decades, but was largely ignored until psychologist and *New York Times* journalist Daniel Goleman's landmark 1995 book, *Emotional Intelligence*. In the book, Goleman described a theory of emotional intelligence, referred to as EI or EQ, that trumps more traditional measures of intellect such as IQ when it comes to business leadership. In the decades since the book's publication, Goleman's theory has gained immense social currency.

Harvard Business Review has hailed emotional intelligence as "a ground-breaking, paradigm-shattering idea." In January 2017, it published an article finding that "thousands of academic studies have demonstrated the predictive power of scientific EQ assessments vis-à-vis job performance, leadership potential, entrepreneurship, and employability."[2]

There is a debate about the specific definition, characteristics, and measurement of EI, but simply stated, emotional intelligence is the ability to monitor one's own emotions and perceive those of others, to discriminate among different emotions and identify them accurately, and to use emotional information to guide thoughts and behaviors.

It's not your college degrees, a high IQ, or even specific expertise in your field that makes you an outstanding leader. Those attributes unquestionably help your chances, and they may even be a mandatory baseline for success, but it's emotional intelligence that distinguishes great leaders from others.

Using the Emotional and Social Competence Inventory (the "ESCI"), the most validated and widely used behavioral measure of emotional intelligence, Daniel Goleman and Richard Boyatzis analyzed the results of 360-degree ratings of 55,000 men and women across ninety countries and all levels of management. Their analysis determined that, of the twelve emotional intelligence competencies proven to impact business performance, women outperform men in eleven of them.[3]

Combining intelligence, empathy, and emotions magnifies our capacity for analysis and our comprehension of interpersonal dynamics. These are qualities we are born with; later, we learn to exhibit them effectively through societal norms and interactions. The result is that women have more highly developed EI, which gives us a springboard to excel as leaders.

Contrast this with how alpha males typically lead in an office environment. Studies suggest that the stereotypical "strong" male leader is often inflexible and lacks the ability to innovate or to inspire real loyalty from his team. Establishing and maintaining dominance is his touchstone. Spurred by his arrogance and narcissism, the alpha boss doesn't just want to beat the opposition; he wants to destroy it.

Unflinchingly confident in his decisions, the alpha boss gives no time or value to kicking around ideas or listening to other viewpoints. Lacking emotional intelligence, rigidly analytical in his cognitive style, the alpha boss may be eager to learn about business, technology, and "things," but he has little curiosity about people or feelings.

This single-minded focus, hard-driving competitiveness, and belief that results are the only metric for success often leads to team disunity and breakdowns in interpersonal relationships. People working for an alpha-male leader frequently suffer from low morale, high stress, and total burnout.[4]

Ironically, the more executive authority an alpha boss gets, the more pressure he experiences and the more pronounced his faults become. A boss with a domineering management style often makes for a perfect midlevel manager, where his primary role is to oversee operations. But as he approaches the CEO level, he's suddenly expected to become an inspirational people manager. Good luck getting *that* leopard to change his spots.

There is a stark contrast between how an alpha male leads teams of subordinates and how an alpha female manages her staff. While many men lead in command and control mode, female leaders tend toward a participatory style that includes more conversation and listening, and tends to foster cooperation. This approach often takes more time (another reason it's unpopular among impatient alpha male types), but it also makes team members feel more valued, and improves overall efficiency and task-oriented results. It's worth noting again that women on average outscore men when it comes to taking initiative and driving for results.

AS GOOD AS, OR *BETTER*?

My own experience has shown me that women use three aspects of EI that make them uniquely suited for leadership roles:

- *We can read minds.*
- *We play well with others.*
- *We understand how emotions influence decisions.*

I've proven time and again in my own career that each one of these traits gives women an advantage over "tough-guy" leaders because they inspire the best performances in everyone they work with—subordinates, peers, and even superiors. These same traits also allow women to deal effectively with third parties, especially those with whom they have a continuing, even if adversarial, relationship. Since women possess these three aspects of EI *innately*, it's no surprise that women are effective as leaders.

What's important to note is that this should represent a shift in the way we see the role of women in business. After decades of struggling to demonstrate our equal value—to little avail, it seems—we have empirical proof that we're not *as good* as men. We're *better*.

And this goes beyond the superior leadership skills of women as measured by our emotional intelligence. There is also a growing body of research that reveals that businesses don't just perform *as well* when women join the ranks of leadership—they perform better.

In 2016, a study from the Peterson Institute for International Economics and Ernst & Young reviewed the business performance of almost 22,000 publicly traded companies in ninety-one countries around the world. They found that having women in the top ranks was tied to better overall profitability. In fact, increasing the number of women in company leadership roles from zero to 30 percent correlated with a 15 percent increase in profits.[5]

Similarly, an older study by Catalyst found that the Fortune 500 companies with the most women on their boards of directors performed significantly better financially, on average, than the companies with the lowest representation of women. Companies with three or more female board directors performed even better than that. Companies with the most women on their boards outperformed those with the least in three crucial financial metrics: return on equity (53 percent higher), return on sales (42 percent higher), and return on invested capital (66 percent higher). The correlation was also found across many industries, from consumer goods to IT.[6]

Many other studies support the same conclusion: Companies *simply perform better* when they have more women in leadership positions. To take just one example from a large body of research, in 2012 McKinsey

& Company published the results of a study that surveyed more than 58,000 employees at 101 companies. Their work showed that companies with three or more women in senior management scored higher in each of the consultancy's nine criteria for organizational excellence (leadership, accountability, innovation, work environment, and so on) than companies with no women in top roles. They noted that "performance increases significantly once a certain critical mass is attained: at least three women in a corporate board."[7]

The Leadership Research Institute boiled down the issue by asking this question:

If there was a proven strategy that could triple your company's revenue, double its profitability, and increase the engagement of half your workforce, would you do it?[8]

To summarize, accepted empirical studies have shown that women have superior leadership skills, based on their higher emotional intelligence; these studies have shown that companies with women on their boards (preferably three or more) or in senior leadership positions significantly improve company profitability.

I hate to say, "I told you so" to alpha bosses ... Well, no, actually, I don't hate it. In fact, I'm gleeful that women's prowess in leadership is finally receiving the attention—and rigorous research—that it deserves. It's time to accept the facts.

Let's turn to discussing each of these three qualities of women that contribute to our greater leadership skills to see how we can consciously harness them to our advantage.

QUALITY #1: READING MINDS

I can read people's minds. No, not literally—but like all women, I have the inherent ability to decode what's called the *perceptual screen* of those around me. A perceptual screen isn't just one belief or attitude, like political affiliation or religious orientation. It refers to someone's subjective consciousness, a summation of their experiences, beliefs, opinions, and personality traits. How they view the world is inherently influenced by these factors—the perceptual screen is a filter for how we see everything.

When I'm interacting with a man, I'm evaluating how he thinks and what he cares about. Does he value impeccable integrity, or feel like the end sometimes justifies the means? Would he rather talk it out, or see it written down in black and white? Can he laugh at himself, or is he humorless and arrogant? Is this someone who categorizes people by their status in the social hierarchy, so that a secretary or junior staffer is considered less worthy? Does he believe that he has *no* equals? We all view the world through perceptual screens like these, occasionally consciously—but far more often subconsciously.

Once you figure out someone's screen, you can adjust your approach to complement it. I don't mean that you compromise your personality or values to act in accordance with their beliefs or thinking. It's a question of modulating your approach so you avoid triggering a negative reaction or misunderstanding.

While many women do this intuitively, you can significantly hone this ability by paying attention to the subtle references and mannerisms of the people you interact with. *Business Insider* summarized Wall Street executive Cara Fleisher's view on this: "Successful women often learn to be 'multilingual' within their language, meaning being observant and learning to communicate with different people in ways that make them feel comfortable."[9]

By the time I joined my firm O'Melveny & Meyers, I'd honed my own multilingual skills to a much finer edge. This was fortunate, because I needed to put them to use right away.

The men I worked with cut me very little slack, and a lot of them had no idea how to deal with a woman as a professional. I *had* to read their minds, because they certainly weren't going to try to figure out what *I* was thinking. In general, they tended not to care what anybody else thought.

On my first big case, Transamerica's antitrust lawsuit against our client, IBM, I was assigned to help prepare and present several witnesses at trial with a senior partner named Patrick Lynch. Working with Pat was challenging. To his credit, he's a brilliant trial attorney, and I soaked up invaluable knowledge working with him. But he did have his quirks. (It seems like the more brilliant the lawyer, the more idiosyncratic they are.) Pat was famous for one particular behavior whenever he asked an associate to prepare a draft of a brief. The associate would labor over that draft for days, working long, stressful nights, only to have Pat look at the draft and then dismiss it, saying, "That's not what I asked for!" He'd then use the draft as scratch paper on which to prepare his own brief.

I saw this happen repeatedly. Whatever we junior attorneys would submit to him never matched up with his expectations. I decided I was no longer going to fall into the trap of wasting my time or his.

The next time he gave me an assignment and had already turned to something else, I simply stayed in his office until he looked up at me, clearly wondering why I was still standing there.

I said, "I understand you are looking for this and this."

"No, that's not right," he would say.

Then I would begin the process again, always in a non-combative way.

"Did you mean that you wanted this and this instead?"

"No. That's not right."

After several rounds, we'd eventually reach an understanding of what he actually wanted. The key was to get inside that brilliant but idiosyncratic legal mind to understand the very particular way it worked. I used my intuition to assess his perceptual screen and determine that an analytical back-and-forth exchange like that wouldn't exasperate him. By contrast, other men I've worked for would have barked at me the moment they noticed me standing my ground, and they wouldn't have been able to tolerate any such back-and-forth.

Once I started asking Pat questions, he was willing to keep clarifying his request until I managed to hit upon the exact approach he wanted. That way, I could pin him down and spare myself the grief of burning the midnight oil to write a brief that he would then ignore—which would have exasperated *me*.

Pat could be prickly, but my efforts to understand him from his own perspective vastly improved our working relationship. During the same trial, we used a sleazy, pay-by-the-hour hotel next to the federal courthouse in downtown San Francisco as a staging area. It was a home base, where we could prepare our witnesses, hold strategy meetings, and eat lunch.

One day I was a few minutes late returning to court, and Pat read me the riot act. I was appropriately contrite. Several days later, Pat was late, so then *I* read *him* the riot act. Because I refused to let him treat me as a useless subordinate and had worked tirelessly to clearly understand and complete the assignments he assigned me, I had established a level of rapport with him beyond that of my peers. I believe that over time he developed a higher sense of respect for me. Because I didn't push it too far, I think he also enjoyed my feistiness.

The kind of mindreading I'm outlining flows directly from *empathy*, or one's ability to understand and share the feelings of another. In recent years, empathy has at long last begun to be recognized as a crucial management skill, one sought after by top companies worldwide. The new gold standard of effective leadership skills—emotional intelligence—has empathy at its core.

In the Information Age, success is predicated on building and maintaining relationships, and that requires today's leaders to be people-focused and diplomatic—it's what helps them to effectively work not just with those in the next cubicle, but to manage people across multiple offices or even countries. Without the ability to understand and identify the feelings and motivations of others, leaders will never get the most out of their people—or fully understand their competition.

The Center for Creative Leadership analyzed data for 6,731 managers from thirty-eight countries to understand if empathy influenced a manager's job performance.[10] Not surprisingly, the study found that empathy does in fact positively correlate with job performance. Managers who show more empathy toward direct reports are viewed by their bosses as better performers in their job.

As further evidence that women are better leaders because of an increased sense of empathy, we need look no further than the already-discussed Zenger Folkman study, in which researchers found that female executives excel at nurturing-oriented competencies such as fostering careers and building relationships.[11] Even more tellingly, in the traditional male bastions of sales, legal, engineering, IT, and R&D

functions, women actually received higher effectiveness ratings than men. The concern that women are unable to perform well in those functional areas is resoundingly refuted by the data.

Women have the ability to productively share emotional experiences with those around them. This sensitivity at the individual level significantly helps women to effectively build and maintain relationships with people whose perceptual screens are different from their own.

My ability to understand what each person sees through their own perceptual screen has made me a very popular boss. Where my male counterparts require team members to fall in line and focus on achieving whatever end result they envision, regardless of their feelings or opinions, I listen to my people and make them feel that they and their contributions are valuable. This talent of reading minds helps me—as it does any good leader—to perceive the worldview and temperament of others and adjust the approach as needed.

Is this strategy somewhat Machiavellian? You bet it is! But it's also immensely effective. Don't buy into the classic misconception that your subordinates are simply there to serve your needs. Your team is not made up of cogs; these are real people with their own talents and experiences who are ready to make important contributions. Use your ability to read minds, and continue to sharpen it, so you can maximize everyone's contributions. *That's* what the best leaders do.

QUALITY #2: PLAYING WELL WITH OTHERS

Women understand that a team functions far more efficiently and finds more joy in their work if their leader:

- influences and inspires them.
- uses empathy and an awareness of the dynamics of the group.
- coaches and mentors.
- is flexible, motivates and applauds the results of teamwork.
- shares credit for the team's achievements.

So many of our male leaders need a remedial trip to kindergarten, where the rest of us learned to cooperate, share our toys, and use our words to get along better. From everything I've seen—and based on a wealth of studies in psychology and management—women do a much better job of keeping these basic lessons in mind.

Remember that the successful production of any type of work really boils down to the people who contribute to the work—and people simply produce more when they do it *together*. When you play well with others, the whole is greater than the sum of its parts.

I can speak to this based on decades of experience. The most important cases of my career have reached a level of complexity that most lawyers never get to touch. In that context, the work and information load is tremendous; you must rely on hordes of people, from senior partners down to first-year associates, plus paralegals, assistants, and interns, to pull everything together. No one person can possibly do it all.

As the lead attorney on cases like these, I know that the work product and the overall performance of the team are exponentially greater when everyone feels a sense of ownership—not of *the* work, but *our* work.

PwC was under attack from multiple fronts. In addition to the civil lawsuit, they had drawn the attention of the SEC, the Arizona Accountancy Board, and the Public Accounting Oversight Board. It was an enormous case, requiring a lot of people, and when I put my team together I was able to handpick colleagues who respected and admired the quality of my work, but also had the commitment to deal with such a complex and politically sensitive case as a *team*.

My primary goal during our first meeting was to lay the groundwork for a cohesive and productive team. After making it clear that striving for excellence was not only expected, but required, I established our rules of engagement.

First, everyone would strive to be a straight talker, myself included. If you had something to say, you needed to say it. I've long known how critical open communication is to the success of any team endeavor, and I would tolerate no harboring of resentments or failing to clarify a source of confusion. We committed to each other that we would always talk through an issue before resentment or a bruised-ego simmered into rage or was blown out of proportion.

Second, every single member of our team mattered. We had regular team meetings where we'd communicate breaking developments. Each person had the opportunity to report on the progress and completion of projects and assignments. Every contributor knew how his or her work fit into the grand design. We embraced the free flow of ideas and sought to learn from spirited but civil disagreements in deciding how the case would move forward. The team knew that I was the ultimate decider and would dictate the final course of action to take, but they also knew that I welcomed their thoughts because we were in it *together*.

Third, we dismissed the traditional corporate hierarchy that limited the effectiveness of many firms and corporations. Email communications were not just circulated to partners. Any associate could politely tell a partner that he was full of shit, provided he could back up that assertion with facts and reasoning. We also tried to inject some levity into our meetings and to the case in general; someone created a dart board plastered with the face of one of the more challenging witnesses for the other side. Once we had developed a sense of camaraderie, it didn't feel awkward to poke fun at each other's mannerisms and pet peeves. It should be noted that we were in no way encouraging bullying or belittling our colleagues; respect is at the heart of any good relationship.

Finally, when people completed excellent work, I'd be sure to reward them with a choice assignment. When there were important depositions and court appearances, for example, I'd make sure to take the team members who knew the most about the issues that would likely come up that day. They were, after all, the folks who helped figure out the deposition questions and exhibits or who wrote the drafts of the briefs, and they deserved to see how their work played out—even when they were the most junior attorneys on the team. Doing that was a signal of real appreciation that they never forgot.

How did our rules of engagement pan out? Each team member became personally invested in the project and took pride in giving it their all. They saw that it wasn't just my case; it was *our* case. And that meant we had a cohesive, loyal, and highly motivated team.

All of this is backed up in the research literature. In a 2011 study published by *Harvard Business Review*, researchers Herminia Ibarra and Morten T. Hansen identified the traits that contribute to successful collaborative leadership, which outperforms the old command and control model—a favorite of the "silverback gorilla" types.[12] Using examples from Salesforce.com, General Electric, and other top companies, Ibarra and Hansen emphasized the demonstrable benefits of communal effort, which include faster innovation and higher overall productivity.

Getting everyone involved—embracing a diversity of skills and view points—is crucial, and women are perfectly poised to do the job. We're primed for openness to other points of view, and we get better results from our focus on building up a team, collaborating, and sharing success instead of succumbing to naked ambition and self-aggrandizement.

Women also understand that it's counterproductive to send the message that collaboration isn't valued. It's always struck me as weak and short-sighted when I've seen male leaders—like my misogynistic, Neanderthal boss—who, for all their posturing, don't have the basic generosity of spirit to give credit to anyone else. Besides motivating your team members to go the extra mile, the collaborative approach demonstrates that you're confident enough in yourself to give others their due. Over and over, the real legends I've worked with, from Babyface to former Secretary of State Warren Christopher, have shown me that if you're really, *really* good, your ego just doesn't need to be an issue at all. You can run the world while remaining participatory and open.

Whether I was the most junior contributor or the head honcho, my commitment to the collaborative approach has been a huge factor in my popularity with colleagues. When you're a junior woman in a man's world, showing that you know how to cooperate, communicate, praise the work of others, and share your success will endear you to men in leadership. Throughout your career, your peers will always appreciate getting the credit that they're due, and they'll tend to think of you favorably when the going gets tough. These benefits are even more pronounced once you're the boss. Celebrating others makes you a joy to work with at any level; when you regularly celebrate the work of your subordinates, they'll lobby for a spot on your team, and once they're on it, they'll go through fire for you.

Some men—the genuinely good leaders—understand this. Legendary football coach Bear Bryant, who won multiple national titles at the University of Alabama, once said, "If anything goes bad, I did it. If anything goes semi-good, we did it. If anything goes really good, then you did it. That's all it takes to get people to win football games for you." From my experience, it's no different in law or the business world. People want to be included and celebrated.

QUALITY #3: UNDERSTANDING HOW EMOTIONS INFLUENCE DECISIONS

Many men believe that they make decisions in a calculating manner, divorced from all emotion. After all, that's what real men do, right?

Wrong.

It's becoming increasingly clear—not just anecdotally, but from brain science—that our mind can't operate independently from our feelings even if we want it to. Nor should we try; rather than exclude emotions, we should try to understand them, both in ourselves and in others.

From extensive research, we now know that excellence in leadership doesn't derive solely from a list of defined strategic or analytical skills. The most important qualities of an effective leader are in fact authenticity and emotional intelligence—a reality that plays directly to a woman's aptitude for being in touch with her own thoughts and feelings, and sensing those of the people around her. Believing the traditional misconception that emotions can be divorced from decision making ignores what is demonstrably true. It reminds me of when my young son would put his hands over his eyes and say, "You can't see me."

Most leaders work hard, and most have good technical skills for analysis, strategy, and the specialized domain of the work at hand—complex litigation, corporate finance, civil engineering, marketing, media, or whatever their field may be. But as I've emphasized, those are table stakes for female leadership; as a woman you had better be ready to continually prove that you're a hard worker and *very* good at your job. What's going to set you apart as a leader, especially as more and more authenticity-seeking millennials enter the workforce and rise through the ranks, is your ability to express your individuality as a real human being.[13]

In a *Bloomberg* article from 2014, Karen Cates of Northwestern's Kellogg School emphasized the need for leaders to cultivate what Daniel

Goleman, the author of *Emotional Intelligence*, has labeled "awareness."[14] As Cates explains, this aspect of emotional intelligence covers both "the ability to read the room (social awareness) and the ability to read your effect on the people in the room (self-awareness)." To be a great leader, she says, you must be able to master awareness and the communication skills connected to it. This applies to leading your team, dealing with your boss (and everyone has a boss—even CEOs have to answer to the Board of Directors), sizing up your competitors, and assessing the effect of strategic actions that you are contemplating. So ask yourself, what role are emotions playing in my decisions and communications? How will my audience—whether within the company, at a public forum, or in the marketplace—react when I institute a new policy, announce an action plan, change up the business model, or hold a motivational session where I want to fire up your team or find investors?

Social awareness also speaks to the earlier challenge of the expectation for people to become inspirational leaders when they reach the top. According to Peter Handal, CEO of Dale Carnegie Training, "Our research indicates that what really matters is that leaders are able to create enthusiasm, empower their people, instill confidence, and be inspiring to the people around them."[15]

Motivating your people is no small matter when it comes to your organization's success. After reviewing many studies, business columnist and coach Carmine Gallo summed up the impact of motivated employees like this: "People who are happy at work feel a sense of ownership in the company's success. They have a sense of purpose. They are acknowledged, praised, encouraged, appreciated, valued, and are inspired by their work and their bosses. These intangibles make the difference between employees who show up to work to collect a paycheck and those who are loyal, eager to help the company achieve its vision, and who offer exceptional customer service as a result of their attitude."[16]

You can't inspire others without being inspired and passionate yourself. But that won't help if you can't read your audience. Before you can use your communication skills to convey that authentic enthusiasm to your team, you need to figure what makes them tick: Are they indifferent or hostile? Or are they gung ho to get started?

Imagine two competent leaders of equal technical ability—one male and one female—and ask yourself the following questions:

- *Which of them is more likely to take the time to make those observations?*
- *Who will be better able to read the emotions expresses through body language and tone of voice?*
- *Who will be more willing—and able—to make an empathetic observation, and then open up a conversation about how people are feeling?*
- *Who will be better able to monitor their own body language to determine what sort of nonverbal signals they are sending to their subordinates?*

I can guess your answers. There are some men who can do this, of course, like the Jack Welches and Bear Bryants of the world. But on the whole, women win this race, hands down.

Every time I start a new case, I begin anew the process of inspiring my team. Part of that inspiration comes in establishing the collaborative atmosphere I described earlier. But it also includes taking into account the personal experience and perspective of each person on my team. I pay attention to nonverbal cues and listen to what each person says and asks questions about. As we work together to hone our short- and long-term strategies for winning the case, I actively solicit each team member's point of view, even if it's a criticism of the team's dynamics.

If you work for me, you know one thing from the start: We are in this together. When we have a victory, I give credit where it's due, and take everyone out to celebrate. When things don't go as planned, I don't play the blame game. We actively figure out how to change course and move forward. We rely on each other.

Years later, former team members will tell me, "The most fun I ever had practicing law was on the case we worked on together" or "I learned the most about how to practice law and deal with a case from working with you." Is it any wonder there's always been a waiting list to get on my cases?

When you put these three aspects of EI together, it's no surprise that women make such great leaders. The advantages we've discussed in this chapter don't just stack up—they multiply.

When you consider how reading minds, playing well with others, and understanding the role of emotions compound each other—and how they can make being on your team everyone's first choice—you realize that women should never strive to suppress their emotions in a fruitless effort to outman the men. We can selectively cultivate traits like tough-mindedness, confidence in our abilities, and an assertive demeanor while using our unique qualities as women to cultivate trust and greater performance. Our intrinsic abilities give us an evolved leadership style that doesn't require us to become a hard-ass, a kiss up, or a Superwoman to achieve success.

It's time to start putting *your* EI to work.

CHAPTER 3

VANQUISHING THE DEMONS WITHIN AND WITHOUT

""If you know the enemy and know yourself, you need not fear the result of a hundred battles. If you know yourself but not the enemy, for every victory gained you will also suffer a defeat. If you know neither the enemy nor yourself, you will succumb in every battle."

—SUN TZU, *The Art of War*

IT IS OUR TIME TO TEAR DOWN THE barriers to women's social equality.

We must go into this battle with eyes wide open—those barriers are protected by ferocious demons. The first are the external demons of traditional gender stereotyping that guard the patriarchal power structure of the business world. But defeating them alone will not allow us to emerge victorious; also lurking inside us are the private demons, who sow the germs of self-sabotage, internalize historical gender stereotypes, and breed self-doubt and fear.

Both types of demons must be conquered, and I'll show you how in this chapter.

First, we'll examine the evolutionary source of gender stereotypes, and look at the broad base of evidence showing how those external demons continue to hold women back in their efforts to reach success.

Second, drawing from my own forty years of professional and personal experiences and from peer-reviewed psychological and sociological research, we'll explore how women frequently allow self-doubt, risk-averse behavior, self-sabotage, and the "impostor syndrome" to keep them from tackling new projects, speaking their minds boldly, and laying claim to leadership roles.

Think of this chapter as the intelligence briefing sent back from the reconnaissance team tasked with spying on the demons. We'll use it as we prepare to make our move.

FACING DOWN THE EXTERNAL DEMON: THE GENDER BIAS AROUND US

- *Do you feel like you have to outman the men to succeed?*
- *Do men call the shots at your company?*
- *Do you compete according to the rules of a male playbook?*
- *Do you believe that stereotypical gender roles are too firmly entrenched to ever change?*

It figures that sex would be the source of the problem.

Not sex as in gender, but as in intercourse. Just one sexual encounter, requiring minimal male investment, can create an obligatory, energy-consuming nine-month investment for a woman. Only a woman can gestate. Only a woman can lactate. As a result, women are left to bear, nurture, protect, and feed their children. While men spread their seed far and wide, we're compelled to make a far greater initial parental investment.

Because the women of our evolutionary past risked this enormous investment as a consequence of having sex, they were as selective as they could be about their sexual partners. Choosing a single partner insured paternal support and locked down access to resources that were otherwise unavailable during her pregnancies. If a woman was promiscuous and failed to form a relationship with a man, it would fall to her alone to provide food, protect her young, and single parent, reducing the likelihood of reproductive success and the survival rate of her offspring. An ancestral woman, therefore, would have a strong preference for a man who shared his resources with her. High up on the selection scale would be a man who provided food, found shelter, defended territory, protected his children, and taught his children survival skills and the ways of the tribe.

Thus, many thousands of years ago, the mandates of reproductive sex resulted in a division of gender roles; women stayed with the children, gathering food closer to home, while men protected them and hunted for game.

Now, even the earliest gender stereotypes have come under fierce attack from certain evolutionary psychologists. They argue that the paradigm for primordial gender roles is far more complicated and depends on, among other things, each group's culture, the stage of its development (hunter-gatherers versus an agrarian society), and the surrounding environment. It is now argued that women sparked the emergence of modern human beings through their development of tools to dig up, gather and store plants.[1] Women may have been the world's first artists and outperformed men on location memory and spatial tasks.[2] Even back in primeval times, women had their special competencies.

The original basis for patrimony disappeared long ago. So why the hell do we continue to act as if male dominance is the natural order of things? Thousands of years of cultural evolution have radically changed humans and the gender roles they play, yet imbalanced gender roles continue to be reinforced through pervasive attitudes about the "proper" role of women, and those attitudes are backed up by laws, social norms, and culturally learned perceptions.

Listen up: We buy our meat and fish at the grocery store. Brute strength and skill with weapons aren't the currency of dominance. Most women have no clue which wild berries are edible, and crops are now tended by farm conglomerates with highly mechanized systems.

What does women's work really look like? In the United States, 57.6 percent of women participate in the labor force, compared to 69.1 percent of men.[3] Some are single. Others are married without kids, or with kids who go to school or are themselves working. And for mothers of young children, we have maternity leave, breast pumps and formula, child care centers, and other child care providers including extended family members.

Yet, like a vestigial appendage, patrimony still reigns. How do men get away with this? Why do we let them?

Does this make you angry enough to fight back—as a woman?

ADVENTURES IN MISOGYNY

I've been dealing with sexism in my professional life since 1977, when I started my legal career as a junior associate with one of the most prestigious law firms in the world. My own prototypical experience of being treated as a lesser person, however, transpired outside the firm. Gender bias has never been limited to the workplace. My experience illustrates not only its pervasiveness, but how ready you must be to fight for yourself.

Imagine me in 1989, a young, big-haired blonde dressed in a sparkly, V-necked T-shirt, tight jeans, and gold sneakers.

Now imagine that ... in rural China.

To the Chinese, I was a curiosity—an exotic delight, or perhaps an unsettling alien. For my part, I simply felt a million miles from the high-stakes, high-pressure arena of Big Law in Los Angeles, where I'd spent the last decade-plus building the foundation of my career.

I drifted along the Jiangnan Canal in a small boat, lazily passing small villages built flush against the water. On the sprawling plantations along the shore, women wearing pink and white conical hats bent at the waist, picking tea and chatting amiably to one another.

I was jolted from my tranquility by a sharp pain in my right side. Was it the pork I had eaten for lunch? Or the "edible" fungi? Was it yesterday's hike through the Classical Gardens of Suzhou? As the pain grew more intense, it was clear it was none of those. Not one to bear anything quietly, I demanded to see a doctor. When we landed at Wuxi, our guide rushed me off to People's Hospital #4 for diagnosis.

This was only a dozen years after the end of the Cultural Revolution, during which Chairman Mao had purged the country of most of its intellectual elite, including its doctors. Plus, I was deep in rural China. As a result, the hospital lacked sufficient medical staff. In fact, People's Hospital #4 lacked sufficient *anything*.

With the tour guide translating, I explained my problem to a nurse. She shrugged, emptied her teacup and sent me to the bathroom to refill it with a urine sample. So began the saga of my emergency appendectomy in rural China, and one of the most important lessons I've learned about being a woman in an often hostile, male-dominated world.

A parade began to form outside the door of my room as staff members and patients' families came to gawk at the young white woman with the big blonde hair.

I asked if I could call the United States for a medical consultation. The surgeon said, "*He* [traditionally there are no female pronouns in Mandarin] can call home."

I felt a surge of relief.

"But," the surgeon continued, "by the time the call goes through, *he dead.*" The doctor then set off on his bicycle for his distant home village while I lay there with an IV pumping God knows what into my veins, caught in a strange limbo of both hoping for and dreading an appendectomy in the middle of nowhere.

When my temperature spiked, the hospital again summoned my surgeon, who began the trek back to Wuxi on his bicycle. Upon arrival, he informed me of two critical (to me) details. First, after surgery, I would have to walk back up to my room—*on the fifth floor*. Second, instead of a general anesthetic, he advised me that he would simply use acupuncture.

That was when the master litigator began negotiating.

I made it clear that I did not intend to climb even one stair after abdominal surgery, let alone the several flights to my room. I also attempted to communicate that I wanted my bikini scar to be as tiny and unnoticeable as possible. He stared at me blankly, glancing over at the tour guide to see if he understood what in the world I wanted. When my wishes finally became clear to the two men, they guffawed with obvious amusement, and completely dismissed me. I was then whisked off to surgery (as well as you can be "whisked" down five flights of stairs with an IV bag), with the issue of anesthetic left unnervingly unresolved.

The surgical facility was nothing like spotless medical centers of home. Its walls were crumbling and water-stained by burst pipes. The surgical bed itself had limb restraints—the kind you'd see in a mental hospital. The surgeon stuck pins into my upper chest and stomach, then asked if I felt pain or numbness. With mounting concern, which began to blossom into a fair amount of panic, I realized that I had lost feeling in my boobs, but not anywhere near my appendix. Only then was he finally convinced to bring on the drugs.

My last thoughts were not ones of optimism.

Four days later, however, sporting a massive scar that no bikini—hell, no *spacesuit*—could ever conceal, I was well enough to depart. After painfully navigating roads clogged with townspeople on makeshift mopeds and trucks laden with enormous hogs, we finally reached the airport. I was still in agonizing pain, exhausted, and desperate to be home.

A large and frustratingly indifferent sign greeted us: "Airport closed due to rain." Apparently, Wuxi's one and only plane did not fly in bad weather. I could understand grounding it in monsoon conditions ... but rain? Fucking *rain*?

That little sign nearly broke me. A primal urge to assume the fetal position squared off against my hardened resolve to get the hell out of there. The latter won out. Even though I was many miles outside my comfort zone, and I found myself surrounded by men who didn't speak my language and eyed me with bemusement at best, I assumed my full stature—all 4'10" of it—and shot them a glare that did justice to the moniker of "The Meanest Woman Alive." I knew that no matter what I did, I might not get what I wanted. But I also knew that if I didn't stand up for myself, I would *certainly* not get what I wanted. It's a lesson that has served me well many times. As hockey great Wayne Gretzky said: "You miss one hundred percent of the shots you don't take." It's a rule worth remembering, even in rural China.

The obsolescent plane wasn't functional in the rain, so I turned to the only other means of escape—the train. Which, of course, was full.

By now, though, I had my own head of steam. (This is a theme I'll come back to again and again throughout this book—when you're operating in a world that resists you at every turn, you have to be ready to use everything you've got.) I stormed into the local political headquarters of the Binhu prefecture, where I mustered my iron resolve, combined with a dash of feminine wiles, to try to get myself on that damn train. The startled railroad officer called his boss, who called his boss, and that continued on up the line until someone contacted the American Embassy.

I wish I knew the words those men in the Chinese bureaucracy used up the chain of command to convey that, "There's a tiny irate blonde American woman here; she insists on securing passage on the next train, and she cannot be appeased." Whatever they said, the point remains: An hour later I was, at long last, once more happily watching the small villages and the sprawling tea plantations pass by, the women chatting among themselves as they picked the tea.

What might have happened had I not demanded the treatment any human deserves? I shudder to think of how long I would have been held back in Wuxi.

THE SLOW EVOLUTION OF EQUALITY

Is a story about misogyny from a Communist country nearly thirty years ago still applicable to professional women today? Sexism, unfortunately, has always been one of the few things that most cultures have in common, and the answer is *yes*.

After four decades of work at the highest levels of law and business, I regard my ordeal in rural China as an object lesson for how capable women are regularly forced to confront rigid, backwards attitudes from men in the chain of command who *still* think they know better by virtue of their phalluses.

There is still an abundance of men like that senior partner at my law firm who confidently told me that no woman would ever become a partner if Darwinian principles applied. Like the men in positions of authority during my Chinese ordeal, these men haven't updated their views about women since they climbed down from the trees.

There still exists a common misconception that men have naturally evolved to go for the jugular, while women lack the inherent aggression and ambition to lead. Cordelia Fine, an Australian professor who studies gender differences, has detailed how science has thoroughly debunked that idea. In many other societies, risk-taking is evenly distributed among men and women. Yet in the United States, Fine found that white men of the type who dominate the business world (affluent, well-educated, conservative) are distinctly more likely to exhibit risk-taking behavior. The research suggests this is because these men think the potential downsides of risks are manageable and, anyway, society won't judge them harshly if they do fail. Sadly, they're right—if you happen to be a rich, straight, white, and conservative American male. But not if you're anybody else.[4]

You might think that plain greed would be enough to overcome men's assumptions about their fitness to dominate. As discussed, it's clear that allowing talented women to advance in the workplace results in greater financial rewards. But, you would be wrong. Ask any professional woman: She'll have several horror stories of mistreatment by men—and rejection of her ambitions—specifically because of her gender. Worse still, those stories generally end with the perpetrators getting away with it. Don't let self-satisfied men tell you that gender bias is a thing of the past. It's alive and well—from rural China to the developed world, from the 1970s when I started my career to now.

Skeptical? Let's take a look back to see how far gender equality has progressed to date. When this book was being written, the United States had just held the presidential election of 2016. Set aside political allegiances for a moment, and look at what happened solely from a gender perspective. As a candidate, Donald Trump wildly objectified women and reinforced their subservient place in American society. He called women "pigs," "dogs," and "disgusting animals." In a widely publicized incident, he boasted about "grabbing [women] by the pussy." He suggested that women should be "punished" for having abortions. He called Fox journalist Megyn Kelley a "bimbo" and said that the tenacity of her questioning was a result of her menstruating: "You could see there was blood coming out of her eyes. Blood coming out of her—wherever."[5] Despite these blatantly chauvinistic comments and many, many others, Trump won the election with 54 percent of the men's vote (a 12 percent margin) and 42 percent of the women's vote. And his actions once he reached the White House didn't do anything to counter his image as an unrepentant misogynist.[6]

By contrast, how are female politicians doing? Let's start by noting that, although women compose a majority of the US population, there have been zero female presidents. Getting to fifty female US Senators, which happened in 2017, sounds like a nice accomplishment until you realize that it's the *total* number of women who have *ever* served in the Senate across its 228-year history. Of those women, twenty-one are serving currently, which is an all-time high. In the hundred years since Jeannette Rankin of Montana joined the US House of Representatives, nearly 300 women have served in that body; the current number is eighty-three out of 435 seats, or 19 percent of the House. A total of thirty-nine women have ever served as state governors in the United States; the current number is six.

At the state level, almost 25 percent of state legislators are women, along with 24 percent of statewide elected executive officials.[7] Only four out of 113 total US Supreme Court justices in history have been women, and roughly a third of all state and federal judges are women.

Legislation in the United States reflects the male dominance of our political system. Just as my doctor in China assumed he would be the one making all the decisions about my body and my health, the same is true of our male lawmakers here. This was underscored on April 8, 2017, when Trump reinstated the global gag rule, withdrawing funding to the United Nations Population Fund (UNFPA), an international program dedicated to delivering preventive care in the form of contraception and childbirth safety assistance to women around the world. The supposed basis for the imposition of the global gag rule was to withdraw support for abortion, despite the fact that no UNFPA money goes to abortion services.

But why quibble? In an Oval Office photo op, a group of men—*only* men—flanked the President as he signed the order. Headlines around the world trumpeted "This photo sums up Trump's assault on women's rights."[8] This prompted an online wave of doctored photos that jokingly envisioned a similar group of female policy makers telling men what they could and couldn't do with their reproductive organs. That fantasy scenario is bitterly funny only because it's absurd to think of it actually happening. While women have very little say in men's health, there has been a backlash from male politicians against institutions, laws, and judicial rulings that allow women control over their bodies. There are constant threats to Planned Parenthood; even though Planned Parenthood cannot use any federal funds to perform abortions, Congress wants to completely defund all of Planned Parenthood's health programs, including screenings for breast cancer, prenatal care, and maternal counseling. New state laws are constantly proposed with the aim of restricting or discouraging women's access to health care services.

Similarly, while there are laws on the books that aim to reduce gender bias and require equal pay, they have been ineffective. Labor Department data from 2016 showed that women earned eighty-two cents on the dollar in comparison to men. The difference adds up quickly: according to a March 2017 report from the National Women's Law Center (NWLC), the pay gap costs women about $10,470 in median annual earnings a year. This gender wage gap occurs in 98 percent of occupations.[9] According to the NWLC figures, a twenty-year-old female entering the workforce full time will lose $430,480 over a forty-year career compared to a male worker. The result? A woman would have to stay in the workforce almost *eleven years longer* than a man to earn as much as he did.[10]

Numerous research studies have demonstrated that women are less likely to be hired, particularly for high-wage jobs, and are likely to be offered lower salaries than men. For example, when presented with identical resumes—with one submitted by "John" and the other by "Jennifer"—a study found that science professors regarded the male applicant as a more competent, significantly better hire than the female applicant. They also offered John a salary more than $4,000 higher, and were ready to provide greater career mentoring to John than to Jennifer.[11]

And that's just the tip of the iceberg. In the business realm, women still find themselves outnumbered and outgunned in just about every industry. Chillingly, women's participation in the workforce has dropped across the twenty-first century as women have been discouraged by sexism in the workplace, lack of access to good child care, and a dearth of good jobs.[12]

For the women who do stay in the work force, lack of advancement is an endemic problem. A major study conducted by McKinsey & Company and LeanIn.org in 2016 presents a discouraging picture. Key findings, based on data from more than 130 companies and over 34,000 men and women, include:

- *Women remain underrepresented at every level in the corporate pipeline. Corporate America promotes men at 30 percent higher rates than women during their early career stages, and entry-level women are significantly more likely than men to have spent five or more years in the same role.*
- *Women negotiate for promotions and raises as often as men but face more pushback when they do. Women also receive informal feedback less frequently than men—despite asking for it as often—and have less access to senior-level sponsors. Not surprisingly, women are almost three times more likely than men to think their gender will make it harder to get a raise, promotion, or chance to get ahead.*
- *Women and men are not having the same experiences at work. Women get less access to the people and opportunities that advance careers and are disadvantaged in many of their daily interactions. Women are also less than half as likely as men to say they see a lot of people like them in senior management, and they're right—only one in five senior executives is a woman.*[13]

Rather than attempt to itemize the nearly inexhaustible list of businesses in which talented women fail to advance, here are a few discouraging highlights:

- While women make up half of graduating classes from law schools, only 17 percent of equity partners are women.[14]
- Thirty-two of the Fortune 500 CEOs were women as of mid-2017. Not *32 percent*, mind you, but *thirty-two individuals out of 500*, or 6.4 percent. After seven straight years of increasing appointments of women directors to corporate boards, in 2016 the number of new female board members actually declined.[15]
- For the top 250 domestic grossing films of 2016, only 17 percent of all executive producers, directors, writers, editors, and cinematographers were women. The number for directors alone: 7 percent.[16]
- Women comprise 34 percent of medical doctors.[17]
- Only 31 percent of college professors with full tenure are women.

- Just 14 percent of engineers in the United States, along with one-quarter of IT professionals, are women.[18] Overall, only about a quarter of those in STEM occupations are women,[19] and that number has slipped in the past generation.[20]
- Among businesses that report payroll, fewer than one in five was female-owned,[21] with access to capital a major barrier to entry for women entrepreneurs.
- In 2016, a mere 7 percent of venture capital recipients were companies owned by women, and when those companies did receive VC funding, the amount they raised averaged 23 percent less than for male-founded companies.[22]

In sum, women remain underrepresented in corporate America. The talent pipeline varies by industry, with some struggling to attract entry-level women while others fail to advance them into a middle management or senior leadership position. Among full-time, year-round workers, *there is no occupation in which women earn more than men*, and only a handful (such as special education teachers) where there is no gender wage gap.

Damn it, women. We need a "shock and awe" attack *now*.

And yet it gets worse. Paradoxically, many men are so threatened by anything that slightly chips away at their exalted status that they now complain that *they*, and not women, are discriminated against. So even though American men earn substantially more than women do in comparable jobs, and even though they dominate the highest echelons of US business and political life, 41 percent of Republican men now say that it's *men* who suffer discrimination.[23]

Consistent with that view point, men continue to act put-upon when a woman dares to challenge their place in the hierarchy. In 2008 when I was working on the biggest case of my life—AMD's antitrust action against Intel—I had to make an argument in the federal court in Austin, Texas, so I flew in from Los Angeles. When my firm's local counsel got up to introduce me, the judge stunned me when he said that *he didn't let female attorneys argue in his court*.

Let that sink in. It was said by a sitting federal judge in a supposedly progressive city during the twenty-first century, on a matter that affected the largest private antitrust lawsuit *ever*. I was running a team of *hundreds* of lawyers—most of them men—but couldn't get a word in, never mind getting any actual respect.

Whether we're talking about statistics or anecdotes, explicitly sexist comments or subconscious bias, the outcome is the same: there are far too many highly successful male professionals who simply refuse to believe—still, today, right now—that women have a place in their professional world. They don't *want* equality for women. What they want is to sustain the hegemony of men.

FACING DOWN THE INTERNAL DEMON: THE GENDER BIAS INSIDE

- *Do you feel like you are your own worst enemy?*
- *Does that critical voice in your head constantly tell you that you've mishandled everything?*
- *Do you suffer from self-doubt, overthink situations, and hold yourself back from speaking up, taking charge, and taking risks?*
- *Do you feel you don't deserve to succeed?*

It's not enough to dismantle the external barrier of gender bias. The ultimate irony of all this is that society has been drilling male supremacy into us since we were little girls, and now this demon attacks us from within, convincing us to buy into the patriarchy by giving away our power. All too often, *we* are our own worst enemy.

You know exactly what I'm talking about. It's that constant critical voice inside, telling you what you should have said or not said, or what you should have done or not done. Harping at you that you're not good enough. Deflating you with whispers that you're going to embarrass yourself. Warning you that you're going to fail, you're a fraud, and you don't deserve your success. Making you doubt yourself. Holding you back. Making you afraid.

As I'll discuss below, even the most powerful women in the world have that incessant, nagging voice—that small but powerful demon sitting on their shoulders and whispering their worst fears into their ears.

Overriding that demon, and telling that voice to shut up, may be the hardest battle you face in the fight against sexism. It's time to dig into this psychology of the internal demon so we can learn to vanquish it.

We've spent our life internalizing the sexism and prejudice that are rampant in our society. It's called *implicit bias*, meaning that certain assumptions about women's roles become foundational for us, even when we might disagree with them on a rational basis. Sexist ideas like "women aren't as competitive as men" or "men are the natural leaders" come to be taken as givens in our society, without needing to be stated in so many words.

We've been immersed in sexism since birth. From childhood, we're told to be good little girls, to behave like a lady, to defer to the boys, to secure approval by pleasing the grownups, and to not be bossy, outspoken, aggressive, or disruptive. Meanwhile, we learn that "boys will be boys," and that behaviors including roughhousing, hitting, yelling, interrupting, or pushing other kids aside are permitted and even approved of.

Sexism is one of the foundations of our society, and its messages are writ large. Everywhere we look—advertisements, TV shows, social media, children's toys, animated films—we see girls and women portrayed as weaker than men, concerned with "girly" things (dolls, ponies, dresses, beauty products), overly emotional, and constantly sexualized. Mixed messages barrage us. Are we fragile princesses in need of rescue? Little mommies and homemakers in training? Or sexy babes aspiring to glamour, thinness, and perfection? Are we to emulate the beleaguered princess trapped in a tower? The mommy trying to feed her baby while fretting about lifting out tough stains with her all-new, improved laundry detergent? Or the perfectly put-together model strutting her stuff?

Researchers agree on the impact of these messages. After an analysis of more than 150 articles, interviews, books, and other social-scientific research, Common Sense reported that gender stereotypes in the media are incredibly effective at teaching kids gender-specific cultural expectations. What makes these messages even more potent is that they are intentionally timed to the precise stages in development when children are most receptive to their influence. Their report finds that decades of research

> *... demonstrate the power of media to shape how children learn about gender, including how boys and girls look, think, and behave. Depictions of gender roles in the media affect kids at all stages of their development, from preschool all the way through high school and beyond. These media messages shape our children's sense of self, of their and others' value, of how relationships should work, and of career aspirations. Tragically, that influence has served to perpetuate notions that boys have more value than girls. Gender stereotypes riddle our movies, TV shows, online videos, games, and more, telling our boys that it's OK to use aggression to solve problems and our girls that their self-worth is tied to their appearance. These images are so deeply ingrained and pervasive that many of us don't even notice the bias, making it more insidious because we don't even realize we're exposing our children to it.*[24]

All of this perpetuates the belief in the core tenet of gender bias—that women are inferior to men—not just in boys, but in *girls*. We lack self-confidence and are afraid to take risks. We let ourselves fall into the same ways of thinking as the men who see us superficially, and view us as underlings or bimbos. In short, we buy into their bullshit, and feed that internal critical voice.

How does this play out in the professional world? Let me break it down for you.

- Women suffer from self-doubt. We question our abilities and downplay our achievements. We aren't comfortable with our own power. We don't own the right to lead.
- Women are afraid to risk and fail. We may only attempt those things we know we can achieve to perfection, believing that competence is enough to put us on top. This is a fundamental misconception. As you'll see, *confidence trumps competence every time.* And if our greatest fears are realized and we do fail or receive negative feedback, our self-confidence and self-esteem plummet.

- Women feel like frauds. We constantly underestimate ourselves. We suffer from imposter syndrome and fear we are about to be found out. Even women who have reached impressive and influential positions cannot shake the feeling that at any moment they will be unmasked as in-competent pretenders.
- Women are unable to rely on past achievements. Far from resting on our laurels—or even allowing ourselves to enjoy them—we ascribe our success to a confluence of luck and the efforts of others, while men credit their own innate skills and abilities.
- Women lack self-confidence. We allow our fears to hold us back—we don't put ourselves forward, challenge ourselves, reach for opportunities, take bold risks, choose growth over comfort, or insist on a seat at the table.

Again, all of these issues have been studied in detail by social scientists, and they've been attested to by countless high-achieving women. Consider, for example, what Supreme Court Justice Sonia Sotomayor told an audience of law students at the University of California, Berkeley:

> *Sotomayor . . . point[ed] out that the articles about her intellect and statements by a Yale law professor who said that she'd never write an important Supreme Court opinion caused her to question her abilities. She called becoming a district court judge earlier in her career "the most terrifying event of my life."*
> *"I was convinced I was going to fail," she said. She said the possibility of failure resulted in her working 12 to 14 hours per day, seven days a week for her first two years on the bench, something she said she repeated when elevated to higher courts.*[25]

Even someone as accomplished as Sotomayor is subject to imposter syndrome. Despite reaching the ultimate professional summit, she sometimes worries that it's only a matter of time until she's found out for who she "really" is—an impostor with limited abilities. It's an easy trap to fall into, and it makes you far less likely to advocate for yourself, take calculated risks, bounce back from failures, celebrate your wins, and *own* your ambitions. You discount your achievements, magnify every little fault, and constantly worry that your career is a house of cards waiting to be flattened by any breeze.

Psychologist Ellen Hendriksen says that impostor syndrome often grows out of what Professor Carol Dweck has called a *fixed mindset*, which makes you believe in some immutable quality about yourself—for instance, that you're "smart."[26] You—and the demon on your shoulder—end up on high alert for any shred of evidence that your mindset is wrong. If someone provides that "evidence," for instance if a Yale law professor questions your acumen, the scales tip the other way. The demon whispers, "Maybe you're not so smart after all," and you start to doubt yourself.

This phenomenon is magnified if you belong to an underrepresented group—such as women, LGBT people, or people of color. As a lonely pioneer in my profession, I can confirm that it's easy to think you don't belong and you will be unmasked as a fraud when you look around and see very few people with whom you can identify. Someone like Justice Sotomayor, not only a woman but also a Latina, faces a double whammy.

Here's the thing to remember about impostor syndrome: *even when you screw up*—and you will—*you are not a fraud*. Don't let your immutable qualities be undermined so easily. You are still smart, and you can't allow someone else's criticism or a mistake (we all make them) destroy everything you are and have accomplished. Nothing and nobody can take away your abilities and achievements. Tell that to the internal demon while you're telling him to shut up. (I only now realized that I just naturally assumed the internal demon is a man.)

Perhaps your internal critic serves as a form of twisted self-preservation, protecting you on a subconscious level from your fears that you don't have the right to issue a masculine command or that the demon won't shut up. If so, try consciously recognizing what your demon is saying and respond with, "Thanks for your concern, but I've got this."

Even when you don't feel like an impostor, you may sometimes find yourself fearful and overwhelmed as you deal with ingrained gender roles. This is what Facebook COO Sheryl Sandberg told Lena Dunham in an interview:

> *You can be the boss and still be terrified, still have the desire to make everyone comfortable.... I do still struggle with my self-con-*

fidence, whereas my male colleagues' self-confidence never seems shaken by people disagreeing with them. And I do always want to be liked, even when I know it is not possible for everyone to agree with me all of the time and I need to make hard decisions.[27]

Many more stories like this are collected in the book *The Confidence Code*, in which news broadcasters Katty Kay and Claire Shipman analyze what confidence is and how women can get more of it. They describe interviewing women leaders at the top of their game—people like German Chancellor Angela Merkel and International Monetary Fund Chief Christine Lagarde—and finding out that these strong women still suffer privately from insecurity. Drawing from that book and other sources, it's clear that many prominent women, including Merkel, Lagarde, Hillary Clinton, and the first four-star woman general in the US Army, Ann E. Dunwoody, address these struggles as Sotomayor does: by working endless hours and over preparing for meetings, projects, and decisions to make sure they are never tripped up by a lack of knowledge about the matters at issue.

But it's not enough to do your homework. You have to understand the ubiquitous power of internalized sexism and be able to diagnose it in yourself. When you are faced with speaking up, taking credit for your accomplishments, asking for a promotion, snagging a chair at the table, or seizing a leadership role, do not allow self-doubt to sabotage your actions.

We'll talk about how to do that in the chapters to come. Whatever else you do, shut down that inner demon and proceed with confidence (even if you fake it at first), but for God's sake ... *proceed.* You *must* challenge the status quo by defeating the demons.

This all seems like a lot to ask. But now that we've thoroughly vetted the two types of demons and are fully armed, we can move on to the lessons on how to vanquish them.

Bring it on!

PART II

THE LESSONS

IMAGINE A WORK ENVIRONMENT WHERE YOUR GENDER IS an asset—a world where you can go as far as you choose, in whatever field you select. To make that a reality, it's time to vanquish the demons, succeed in your chosen career, and help change the world.

Each of the following chapters is focused on a specific lesson. Each lesson addresses aspects of the mindset, interpersonal skills, and strategies that you need to master for the journey ahead. Together, the lessons will help you prevent sabotage by prejudiced men and jealous women, combat pervasive gender bias, and overcome self-doubt and anxiety.

Later chapters will examine the leadership skills that become increasingly important as you rise through the ranks of your profession. Remember, however, that life does not always proceed in a linear way. You may find yourself thrust into a lead role on a career-defining project right out of the gate, or you may have to deal, as Germany's leader Angela Merkel had to, with the most fundamental challenges of self-confidence and self-doubt even as you approach the upper reaches of your field.

Rest assured, the lessons that follow will provide powerful support at any stage in your career; as you amass experience and take on ever-greater challenges, your proficiency with them will only increase.

Let's get started.

CHAPTER 4

DIG DOWN AND SOLDIER ON, SNOWFLAKE

*"Our potential is one thing.
What we do with it is quite another."*

—ANGELA DUCKWORTH, *Grit: The Power of Passion and Perseverance*

- *Were you raised to think you were special?*
- *As a junior employee, do you feel that you are getting only the scut work? Do you think you should be doing more important work?*
- *Do you have true grit? Can you dig deep and soldier on in the face of tough challenges?*
- *Are you brave enough to take risks and seize opportunities?*

AS YOU KNOW, MY FAMILY WAS DECIDEDLY LOWER middle class, and my parents were very careful with money. I didn't buy my first dress in a retail store until senior prom.

Despite our modest means, however, my mother took every opportunity to make us feel special. She came from a background of constant criticism, and overcorrected for her parents' mistakes by lavishing both my sisters and me with praise—something that, as cute little girls craving parental approval, we accepted readily. In my case, I decided early on that receiving love and validation was conditional on my good behavior and accomplishments, a belief that would set up a cycle of people-pleasing and striving to outshine others that I would battle for many years.

Of course, nature left its imprint as well. My mother claims I was born speaking in full sentences and haven't shut up since. I also had the good fortune to escape the trait that leads girls to refrain from speaking up or being bossy, and from an early age I ran my neighborhood with an iron fist. I naturally assumed the role of head honcho of some fifteen local kids, choosing the games we would play and the stories from books or TV shows that we would act out—always assigning myself the best parts, of course. It was my first experience as a benevolent dictator, and one of many seeds that would blossom into a full "snowflake delusion" as I came to see myself as special and entitled to an easy path through life.

Not only had my parents told us unequivocally that we could do whatever we wanted with our lives, there was also no sense that girls couldn't do anything boys could do. In our home, I learned I could use my intellect, talent, and personality to go for whatever I wanted. That attitude, along with my academic aptitude, earned me scholarships to Cornell University and to law school at UCLA.

I aced school. But school is not real life. School is a highly structured environment with clear rules. Your daily schedule is set by the courses you take. You have a read on your professors and your fellow students. Finals are anonymously graded. There are clear milestones, deadlines, and expectations, and your progress can be measured by your grades and your class standing. In short, you know the rules and can play the game.

Then you get to real life. And real life is messy. The conventions are unclear. There aren't consistently defined measures of how well you're doing, whether you're working hard enough or too hard, how your performance compares to that of your colleagues, or whether you have real talent for your chosen career at all. There may be tests, though not on paper, but there are no grades. There are no class rankings. And what you excelled at in the classroom may have very little to do with the skills you need to succeed in your job.

The end result is that no matter what field you choose, you won't fully understand what you've gotten yourself into until you walk in the door on that first day of work—and perhaps not for many months and maybe years thereafter. You begin, as always, as the rookie.

When I joined my law firm in Los Angeles in 1977, I expected to be highly regarded and respected on the basis of my educational achievements. I thought I was still the golden one, ordained by my parents, by my school, and by my innate talents.

The joke was on me. I quickly learned the hard truth that in the professional world, nobody gives a flying fuck how special you think you are.

WERE YOU RAISED TO BELIEVE YOU WERE A SNOWFLAKE?

Thanks to my upbringing, it was a given that I was special, gifted, and destined for success. Fresh out of school, not only was I already a legend in my own mind, but I thought the world would recognize me as such. Worse, despite knowing better, I would eventually raise my son as if the moon and stars revolved around him, too.

I'm not alone. Many women and men, especially millennials, have been raised to believe in their own specialness. We Baby Boomers wanted our kids to feel cherished, confident, and secure. (Why shouldn't everybody on the team get a medal?) We prioritized personal development and self-esteem. The upside is that Millennials now face life with firm confidence in their own abilities. The inevitable downside is that they have loftier expectations—and the potential for sharper disappointments—than prior generations. All that self-esteem is great until it leads you to be disappointed when the world refuses to affirm your snowflake status.

But Millennials are hardly the only ones who feel that they're exceptional,[1] and for those suffering from the "snowflake delusion," the start of your career can be a tremendous shock. You walk in the door absolutely sure you can do your manager's job better than he can, and immediately discover that you're lowest on the totem pole, not entitled to any deference, and expected to do the most menial tasks. Ever hear that lovely expression "shit rolls downhill"? Welcome to Work Realities 101.

Getting over the snowflake delusion is table stakes for making it in the professional world. But while men only have to get over themselves, women carry the extra burden of starting out shackled by gender stereotypes. *We aren't as capable or savvy as the men. We're just working until we find a husband or get pregnant. We don't have the gravitas of a man.*

Add to that the bitter truth that women have to work harder, be better, and show more grit than men to overcome a system stacked against them. As discussed in Chapter 3, gender discrimination in hiring, promotion, and wages, as well as an emphasis on inflexible work schedules rather than skills and capabilities, leads many women to limit their career arcs by deciding early on that "I can't have that role" as they shape their ambitions to climb the professional ladder. A study by the Institute of Leadership & Management found that "73 percent of women managers believe there are barriers preventing them from progressing to top levels—the glass ceiling."[2] And don't be fooled into thinking that things are better as the result of a decline in policies that are explicitly sexist. Contemporary economic research confirms the trend of more subtle "egalitarian gender essentialism," as explained in an article from the Washington Center for Equitable Growth:

> *Despite a decline in explicit sexism, researchers argue that gender discrimination today, whether in the form of stereotypes or social pressures, is perpetuated by a new, "egalitarian" form of gender essentialism—the belief that women and men's social, economic, and familial roles are and should be fundamentally different. While most people now support women's access to all economic opportunities, they simultaneously expect men and women to pursue traditionally "male" and "female" jobs and regard parenting as the primary responsibility of mothers. . .*
>
> *Assuming different roles for men and women at work and at home, male-dominated occupations remain mostly structured to meet the needs of a stereotypical male who is expected to have a spouse at home, a work-schedule issue that not only fails to accommodate*

women but also often actively pushes women out. The idea that women are freely "opting out" of workforce opportunities because they have different career aspirations than men has been thoroughly debunked.[3]

Contemporary economic research may have found a new label for why men are antagonistic to hiring, working with, and promoting female colleagues, but there's nothing new about blatant gender stereotyping and discrimination; as women, we're forced to add it to the list of struggles everyone faces in the workplace.

Snowflakes, here's the bottom line: No matter how inflated your sense of self-worth may be, you can't blame gender bias alone for holding you down if you're not willing to work hard, constantly learn new skills, hone your ambition, and exhibit the mental and emotional toughness required to overcome your failures. Whoever you are and wherever you started in life, you must learn to deal with setbacks and unfair treatment. That's real life. To master it, and leave your snowflake delusion behind, requires a skill that is indispensable for any woman who wishes to live a life on her own terms: true *grit*.

WHAT TOUGH WOMEN DO WHEN THE GOING GETS TOUGH

In one field after another, we see that the highest positions don't always go to the most talented people. Even if they have only limited talent, most high performers are simply hard workers. But beyond the talent and the elbow grease, there is another factor that distinguishes the most successful. That factor is *grit*, and it's a combination of mental toughness, courage, hard work, and sometimes sheer stubbornness to keep going until you reach a goal.

Research is beginning to reveal the science behind the importance of this classic character trait. The concept of "grit" has been popularized in recent years by University of Pennsylvania professor Angela Duckworth and her colleagues. In a seminal article, they addressed this question: Why do some individuals accomplish more than others of equal intelligence?[4] In addition to brainpower, the most successful people tend to be emotionally intelligent, energetic, creative, charismatic, confident, and emotionally stable. Crucially, the authors "suggest that one personal quality is shared by the most prominent leaders in every field: grit." They define grit as:

> *. . . perseverance and passion for long-term goals. Grit entails working strenuously toward challenges, maintaining effort and interest over years despite failure, adversity, and plateaus in progress. The gritty individual approaches achievement as a marathon; his or her advantage is stamina. Whereas disappointment or boredom signals to others that it is time to change trajectory and cut losses, the gritty individual stays the course.*

In response to Duckworth's research (and in the wake of her best-selling book *Grit: The Power of Passion and Perseverance*), other researchers have dug deeper into these concepts and questioned what the exact definition of "grit" should be, and whether it really differs from other concepts in educational psychology such as "conscientiousness."[5] I'm happy to leave those finer points to the researchers, because you and I both know what we're talking about: tenacity, even when the path becomes grueling, and the sustained drive to commit the full panoply of your talents to further your ambitions through hard work.

There's an old quotation, often attributed to US President Calvin Coolidge, that says:

> *Nothing in this world can take the place of persistence. Talent will not; nothing is more common than unsuccessful people with talent. Genius will not; unrewarded genius is almost a proverb. Education will not; the world is full of educated derelicts. Persistence and determination alone are omnipotent. The slogan "press on" has solved and will always solve the problem of the human race.*[6]

If you want to achieve anything meaningful, you have to dig deep and soldier on. That's true grit.

THE MOTHER SUPERIOR TEACHES ME A LESSON SHE DIDN'T INTEND

I first came to understand the need for grit when I lived in a tiny village on the edge of the Andes as a high school exchange student. Through an exchange program run by the American Field Service, I lived for a year with a Peruvian family in the isolated village of Arequipa—4,100 miles from my home, family, and friends. This was long before the days when cell phones and personal computers made communication easy. I was cut off almost entirely.

On the first day at my new school, a Catholic school for girls, the Mother Superior called an assembly to introduce me to the whole student body. In a huge room packed with the teachers and girls from every grade, the Mother Superior had me stand up and face everyone.

She began by asking me questions in Spanish. After an innocuous beginning, the Mother Superior asked me my religion.

"*Soy una judia*," I replied (I am a Jew).

She smiled at me—a sinister smile I can still picture today—then turned to the blackboard behind her, picked up a piece of chalk, and drew an enormous swastika.

Then she turned back to me and said, "I think Hitler was the greatest man who ever lived."

I was astonished. In my head, I translated her Spanish into English several times to make sure I'd understood. I had.

Still smiling, she said, "Do you agree with me?"

"No," I said.

"Why?"

I replied, "Because he killed six million Jews."

The Mother Superior turned back to the blackboard, used the chalk to make the huge swastika even bolder, and then said, "Well I believe Hitler was the greatest man who ever lived."

There was not a sound in the entire assembly.

Inside, I boiled. I was shocked and furious. It was incredibly ignorant and hateful, and even at that age I knew the Mother Superior was supposed to be a leader and an educator molding the minds of the large number of girls in the school. It was a form of rank anti-Semitism that I had never experienced before—or since.

I had no options to combat what had happened—no means to retaliate. The Mother Superior held all the power. Yes, I had spoken up and disagreed, but I had no additional weapons in my arsenal. And I was utterly alone, far from the comfort and safety of my home or any adult help.

I knew I had to attend that school for the entire year, so I summoned all of my strength and went to school every day with my head held high. I behaved respectfully. But I had learned a valuable lesson, in a way that I hope others never have to: it is demoralizing and degrading to be powerless. And I knew I never wanted to be in that position again.

That experience, and my months in Arequipa, helped sow the first seeds of grit in my fertile mind. It helped me cultivate the toughness and bravery I've needed throughout my career. Until I went to Arequipa, I had never seen real poverty. Limbless beggars without hope or prospects lined the downtown area. Assigned to be a teacher's aide for four- and five-year-old children while I was there, I worked in a classroom that was filthy and dark. The children were dirty, with snot-covered faces and open sores on their body. Desperate for attention, they clung to me. My concerns for their well-being were met with utter indifference from the teachers. No one cared for these kids. I was as defenseless as they were, with one key difference: I was blessed to come from the richest country in the world, with comforts and opportunities they couldn't imagine and would never be able to access.

Motivated by these experiences, I made the decision that I would never be left to fight without resources. I needed to become a formidable force to champion what I thought was right and fair. I grasped that I already possessed reserves of deep inner strength to draw on in the face of challenges, but I had learned that I needed more grit than I currently possessed. The Mother Superior may have made my life hell that year, but she did teach me what I was made of, and she began what would become a long process of vanquishing my snowflake delusion.

In addition to grit, my year in Peru gave me a commitment to treat every person with dignity and respect. No one has the right to feel entitled. No one is inherently superior or inferior. Whether you empty trashcans at night or run a Fortune 500 company by day is a function of an infinite number of factors, some of which are completely out of your control—they include where you were born, what value your birthplace accords to women, the resources your family has, and your access to education.

In my career, I've encountered far too many prominent people who couldn't manage a basic level of decency toward others. If you are reading this book, you are among the lucky ones, as I am. We have the option to better ourselves and succeed, and an obligation to treat the less fortunate with respect.

This last lesson has served to advance my career and life in ways I never anticipated. It turns out that when you treat people with the dignity they deserve, not only are they deeply appreciative and loyal, but you receive the gift of a human connection that far too many people undervalue or miss altogether.

GRIT AND THE SOFT WAR ON WOMEN

Interestingly, during my academic life, I usually felt that men and women were treated equally. Yes, there was always one blowhard man in class who wanted to dominate the room by showing off how smart he thought he was, but he usually got his comeuppance fairly quickly. And although men still outnumber women as professors, in many fields outside of STEM the student body is about fifty-fifty. Even when I graduated from UCLA Law School in 1977, six of the top ten graduates in my class were women. It's only once you step into the real world that you find that in virtually every field, men make up the vast majority of senior management.

No surprise here. Whether it's labeled "egalitarian gender essentialism" or plain old sexist discrimination, there is an unspoken assumption, even among the most "enlightened" men, that our male colleagues are better or more committed than we are. Each time you meet a new manager or client, it's as if there's a cartoon bubble over the man's head showing him thinking, "Damn, I ended up with a woman. I'm worried this is not going to work out."

This makes men self-conscious and uncomfortable.[7] We're not one of the "boys" they can connect with by making small talk about sports or cars or women. Facing a deeply embedded unconscious concern that we're not up to snuff, we find ourselves having to prove our worth over and over again each time we meet a new manager or client, immediately working to establish a rapport while impressing them with our competence.

This persistent inability to rely on our prior accomplishments, or even to be given the benefit of the doubt as to our competence, is what is now called the "soft" war on women. In their book *The New Soft War on Women*, researchers Carly Rivers and Rosalind C. Barnett argue, using interviews, statistics, and cultural analysis, that "an insidious war of subtle biases and barriers is being waged to marginalize women."[8] Women must prove themselves over and over again to counter the "descriptive bias" by which men in the workplace continue to assign traditional characteristics to men (decisive, competent, assertive, rational) and to women (caring, warm, emotional, sensitive), which in turn generate negative assessments of women's performance.

In other words, in the years that have passed since I started my career, little has changed. Not only do you have to abandon your "specialness" as a snowflake, but you're going to have to *earn* everything while simultaneously overcoming gender stereotyping. Persistence and endurance are inescapable requirements.

ADVICE FOR SOLDIERING ON

To build and maintain true grit, keep in mind the following principles:

- **Keep things in perspective.** As women, we tend to be people-pleasers and hyper-sensitive to nuance, but that can lead us to waste time and mental energy on minor things. Don't dramatize truly small events or turn them into a source of anxiety. Remember that you are not the center of anyone's world but your own. If the boss frowns, doesn't greet you in the morning, ignores you in the hallway, or is friendlier to someone else, it doesn't mean he doesn't like you or that he thinks your work is bad. He probably isn't thinking about you at all. Your boss has his own life, with deadlines at work and issues at home. Maintaining perspective is the only way to keep your focus on what matters. Take the long view. *You can't stay sane if you sweat the small stuff.*

- **Understand that everyone is out for themselves first and foremost.** While you can and should identify people who are ruthlessly competitive and malicious, do not assume that even your favorite colleagues or friends will put your interests first, especially if it compromises their standing. Self-preservation is everyone's rule number one. Never rely on "the kindness of strangers." Be friendly and collegial to all, but remember: *Only you can take care of your own interests.*
- **Be brave and take risks.** When you are junior, express appropriate deference but stand up for yourself. *If you have an idea or disagree with what's being said for reasons you think are sound, speak up.*
- **Reach for opportunities.** Take the hard job even if it's a stretch for you. If you don't, some guy will, even if it's just as hard a stretch for him. *Put yourself forward.*
- **Learn how to recover from mistakes.** Shake off mistakes and move on. Men do. They also have far better mechanisms for blaming external factors (e.g., "The deadline was ridiculous" or "The other players weren't capable enough") or finding a reassuring personal excuse ("I got hit with another assignment just as I was about to turn to this" or "I could have done it, but I partied too hard last night"). Women obsess about perfection and agonize over mistakes. I know that if I make a presentation to twenty people, and nineteen of them tell me it was terrific, while one tells me he thought it was mediocre, I'll dwell on that one person's comment. Perfection is unachievable. *Learn from your mistakes and move on.*
- **Try another tactic.** Know when to stop or change course. Once something is done, let it be done. There will be a new battle to fight tomorrow. If something isn't serving you well, stop banging your head against the same wall. *Dare to try another way to get to what you want.*
- **Start building your brand now.** We didn't call it a "personal brand" when I was a young lawyer, but I knew that I wanted to carve out a distinctive place for myself in my firm and in my pro-

fession. I embraced my femininity, used my ability to read other people's perceptual lenses, demonstrated that I would be deferential but not be pushed around, spoke up when I thought I had a good idea, and disagreed with others when I though they were wrong. I acted like I belonged, taking credit for my achievements and not backing away from challenges or, occasionally, confrontations. *Start early to distinguish yourself.*

- **Demonstrate the tenacity to prove yourself over and over.** If you want to get ahead in your chosen profession, it's not enough to excel once. Which athletes and entertainers do we praise? The ones who have strung together one great performance after another. There's no resting on your laurels, especially as a woman. *Take on the next challenge and keep achieving.*
- **Remember that if you don't ask, you don't get.** This is huge. How will you ever reach your goals if you quietly perform only those assignments you are handed? *Ask for what you want.*

In my first year of legal practice, my rookie assignment at O'Melveny brought together many of these lessons when I helped to defend computer giant IBM against antitrust litigation brought by a company called Transamerica.

In the late 1970s, IBM was the undisputed dominant force in the computer industry. They made not only the heart of the computer system—the refrigerator-sized model 360 central processing unit—but also peripherals such as tape drives and disk drives. Transamerica, which also made peripherals, contended that IBM had used its dominant market position to engage in predatory pricing to drive Transamerica out of the market.

The stakes were high for two reasons. First, there were hundreds of millions of dollars at risk, and if Transamerica won, the damages would be tripled under the antitrust laws. Second, many other peripheral manufacturers had brought their own lawsuits against IBM, and there was a Department of Justice lawsuit pending, all based on the same charges of predatory pricing. If we lost, IBM faced exposure in all these other cases. As a result, the case was the subject of intense media scrutiny.

When I moved to San Francisco to prepare for and try the case, out of the seventeen lawyers from O'Melveny working on the case, I was seventeenth in seniority. I was as green as they come. We readied ourselves for trial, working our asses off day and night for months on end. As inexperienced as I was, I was still able to distinguish myself by the quality of my work to the point that I was able to ask for, and receive, special assignments unusual for a new lawyer. At trial, when we presented IBM's CEO and an Executive VP, I was the second chair—the second-ranking lawyer for our side standing before the court. I also second-chaired the cross-examination of two of Transamerica's experts, which required me to lead the team of accountants who analyzed the experts' financial data, all of whom were much older.

One day, O'Melveny's antitrust partner Patrick Lynch stuck his head in my office and said that IBM's CEO could see us the next day. We chartered a jet from San Francisco to the CEO's office in Westchester County, New York.

On arrival, I attended strategy meetings where the only other participants were the CEO Frank Carey, IBM's general counsel Nick Katzenbach (a former attorney general of the United States), David Boies (later famous for the antitrust litigation against Microsoft, the "hanging chad" case before the Supreme Court. and the Supreme Court's decision on marriage equality), and my firm's two preeminent antitrust litigators, Lynch and Bill Vaughn.

It was a heady moment for a rookie lawyer to be among some of the greats in the law, and I said little, watching and learning as these powerful lawyers strategized and jousted with each other. What an opportunity! Just having a seat at the table meant I was on my way to building my brand.

During the case, I felt the kind of total immersion and commitment that must be felt by an army engaged in an all-out effort to win a war. We were our own band of brothers and, like soldiers pursuing an objective, we had to show our true grit—a sustained, flat-out commitment to prevail.

Snowflakes and success don't blend well. To succeed in a man's world, you have to use everything you've got—all of your feminine advantages, and all your true grit.

For all its impact, however, grit alone won't be enough. Don't believe for a moment that your internal demon is going to cut you any slack—you'll need to be alert and not succumb to the demon's efforts to sabotage you. In the next chapter, you'll learn how.

CHAPTER 5

GET OVER YOUR OWN BULLSHIT

"I can bring home the bacon, fry it up in a pan, and never let you forget you're a man."

—1980's ENJOLI AD, "The 8-hour perfume for the 24-hour woman."

- *Do you feel that you need to constantly please people?*
- *Are you so afflicted with perfectionism that you won't put yourself forward and take risks?*
- *Do you feel it's only a matter of time before your boss realizes you are unqualified for your job?*
- *Do you feel uncomfortable confronting coworkers and supervisors?*

AS THE SEXY WOMAN FROM THE 1980'S ENJOLI ad suggests, women are supposed to buy into the myth that we can have a great career, maintain the house, raise the kids, be a red-hot lover, and make it all look effortless.

Now, my life has been rich with adventures, and at one time or another I've done all of those things. But the idea that anyone can do it all at the same time without stress and pressure is not only beyond believable, it's one more gender trap for judging ourselves too harshly.

Inexplicably, these outdated societal norms are also firmly entrenched in today's business world. As women, we're constantly at risk of giving in to the nagging critical voice in our head that tells us we're not good enough, we're frauds, we don't deserve our success, and at any moment we'll be unmasked and shown to be incompetent fools. We're *conditioned* to avoid any signs of imperfection. We are afraid to fail, to disappoint, to fuck up, to be found lacking.

What we're really doing is telling ourselves a story. A collective lie that we've come to believe, one that's whispered in our ears by the internal demon who's constantly telling us we're going to fail.

In this chapter, you'll learn how to listen for that harping, critical voice and then *shut it up*. Using my battle-tested approaches, you're going to triumph over caveman-era social nonsense, and kick that demon's ass.

In short, you're going to get over your own bullshit.

IT BEGINS WITH FEAR

First, you need to realize that all of this is rooted in *fear*.

Our fear of disappointing others, of being found lacking, of not being *enough*, goes back to childhood, when boys are encouraged to take charge, and are forgiven when they screw up. And girls? They're expected to go along with the program. The result is a disproportionate fear of failure that leads us to silence ourselves or refrain from taking certain actions. It pushes us to buy into the myth of the Enjoli woman who can do it all, and only adds to the sense of total dominance to which men believe they are entitled.

Men don't put up with the same grief. Not even close. Does society demand that a man have a successful career, maintain the household, nurture and be present for the kids, always be available as a sexy lover, and make it all look easy? Of course not. It's an inconceivable, insane double standard that would be a joke if we didn't face it every day.

And should we choose to "act like men"—by which I mean displaying not testosterone-fueled behavior, but simply aggressive, decisive, and strong-minded conduct as women—then we are penalized. Even as a senior partner in a major law firm, I have been criticized for being too outspoken, opinionated, and aggressive. Do you think *anyone* would criticize a powerful male litigator who leads lawsuits worth billions of dollars? Of course not—he'd be *praised* for those same traits. The fact remains that ambitious, "pushy" women violate unwritten rules about acceptable behavior. Men are judged differently, and judge themselves differently. Men cut other men some slack. They learn to bounce back quickly from criticism, safe in the assumption that no setback is permanent. Women, meanwhile, get slammed for the same behavior, internalize the negative feedback, and torture themselves relentlessly for every shortcoming.

This fear of failure is very personal to me. Growing up, I never failed. I never lost. I always got the best grades in class; I was among the most highly regarded associates in my firm; I became a highly successful partner, winning case after case.

But a 100 percent success rate is an impossible standard to meet. And so, I worried. Constantly. I worried about getting it wrong, about coming up short. I worried that if I failed, a hole would open in the ground and swallow me.

I'm not alone. Women misunderstand failure. Failure is not the opposite of success, or an impediment to it. Failure is *required* for success. My mother used to say she wished I had failed a few times early on so I would understand that there is life after failure. There is no waiting hole in the ground. You can pick yourself up and go on. I've had to learn this late in life the hard way, and now I challenge you to learn it, too.

I dare you to fail.
I dare you to fuck up.

Most of all, I dare you to allow yourself to be exposed for who you really are: *A powerful woman with talents and ideas that deserve to be shared.*

What if you accept the dare? What's the worst that might happen? The world will not end. You won't be scorned or cast out of your job. The earth will not open up and swallow you. You may discover that, quite often, you'll win! And even if you lose—even if you are ridiculed or feel stupid—you can shake it off, figure out how to do better next time, and keep going. Through failure, you acquire the skills to regroup, carry on, and do better. Regardless of the outcome, you do not crawl into a hole and die.

If you want to be successful, you can't undercut yourself, fail to take on challenges, or focus on pleasing others rather than excelling. As women, we will succeed only if we take risks, endure failures, and move forward as advocates for ourselves. And that starts by taking on that voice in our heads that says, *You're not good enough* or *You can't do this.*

CATCHING YOUR INTERNAL DEMON IN THE ACT

Triumphing over self-defeating behavior requires that we recognize and conquer our own demons repeatedly. Listening for the whispers coming from the demon on your shoulder is the first step. The next—and harder—step is to intentionally take action despite them.

One of my women friends is an economics professor at a prestigious college. All of the other faculty members in her department are men. She increasingly noticed that when she spoke up during department meetings, the men weren't paying attention. Her reaction to being ignored was to stop talking. Eventually, she realized why she was disregarded: Every time she made a comment in a faculty meeting, her insecurities kicked in, and, anxious to ensure that she didn't say something stupid, she began her remarks with phrases that undercut her own valuable ideas. Instead of simply stating "I think we should do X," she'd start with, "I'm not sure, but I think ..." or "I'm probably wrong about this, but maybe we should consider ..."

Sound familiar?

This woman is a brilliant, tenured professor. She has as much right as any man in the room to put forward her informed opinion. So do you.

Even female US Supreme Court justices suffer from their use of tentative, non-assertive speech. One study concluded that, "On average, women constituted 22 percent of the court, yet 52 percent of interruptions were directed at them."[1] One explanation proffered is the female justices' use of "women's speech" which "is indirect and polite, while men's speech is more assertive and direct."[2] The direct, assertive male language lacked indicators of hyper-politeness, while the female justices began their questions with phrases such as "I'm not sure I," "I'm sorry," "May I ask," and "Excuse me." While the women were careful not to give offense, the men simply plowed in, speaking over them.

Speaking one-on-one with a friend, or dealing with a delicate situation with a client, you might make the *conscious* choice to couch your words as a way of softening a harsh observation or leaving the lines of communication open. A lot of my own work as a leader and negotiator has relied on this type of diplomacy. But it's madness to go through your life listening to the voice that tells you, "You don't know what you're talking about," "Don't be pushy," "No one likes a know-it-all," and, "Don't be a bitch."

Here's some news for both you and the demon: it doesn't make you a bitch to state your view as clearly as a man would. You only lose ground if you caveat, disclaim, and backpedal every time you express an idea. That's especially true given that you're operating in the world of men, where any sign that you lack confidence makes you an easy target for domination.

The key is to *listen*. Listen to what the voice in your ear is telling you, and pay attention to how it affects the words coming out of your mouth. Be on guard for self-depreciating or qualifying phrases like:

I'm not sure but ...
Can I say something about this ...
Not that it matters, but my opinion on this ...
I'm probably wrong but ...

Take a minute to think about your own "greatest hits" of self-sabotaging language. Jot them down so you won't forget them—and never say them again.

The list of ways women use self-talk to undermine themselves is endless. Take "Bag Lady Syndrome" (BLS), when women, out of fear, tell themselves they will end up homeless and destitute. These aren't just financially marginalized, working women. As Forbes reports, in a study of 2,213 women, a *third* of those with incomes of $200,000 or more, said they "often" or "sometimes" feared losing all their money and becoming homeless.[3] Lance Drucker, a Park Avenue wealth manager who wrote a book about beating BLS, writes that bag lady syndrome is "women's No. 1 financial fear." He adds, "I get women with Ph.Ds., doctors, and attorneys who come to me and say: 'Lance, I'm stupid.'"

In my experience, women have a whole collection of self-talk phrases we use to scare ourselves about money: "I'm not going to have any money because I squandered it all," "I'm going to be unmasked as a fraud and have no job," or "I don't deserve what I earn and it will be taken away." This negative self-talk only serves to reinforce the sense of despair.

When it comes to expressing their career ambitions openly, single women also silence themselves—again, out of fear. A research project led by Leonardo Bursztyn, an economics professor at the University of Chicago, reported that single women put themselves forward less ambitiously if they thought their peers would be able to learn what they said. The women were afraid that they would pay a high social price if they were seen as "too ambitious" by listing a high dollar figure for their desired salary or "too aggressive" in response to the question of how many days in a month they were willing to travel or how many hours in a week they were willing to work. It's a classic case of how external gender bias—in this case, unequal expectations for women and men about what constitutes an acceptable level of ambition—is internalized in a way that causes women to shut themselves off from top-notch opportunities.[4]

Censoring ourselves, succumbing to negative self-talk, downplaying our goals, and framing our ideas with diffident language all cause us to internalize defeatist messages, doubt ourselves, give in to the fear of failure, and avoid situations where we might appear to be—or where we genuinely are—more powerful than men. It's no exaggeration to say that unconscious self-censorship is costing us our power and compromising our career goals.

We have to curb that internal voice by concentrating on what it's whispering. Instead of unconsciously letting it dictate our words and our decisions, we need to bring that voice out into the open, recognize how it affects us, and challenge it. Does the internal demon rule us or do we rule ourselves?

THE ONLY LIMITS IN YOUR LIFE ARE THE ONES YOU MAKE—BEATING SELF-SABOTAGE

We're all familiar with the expression, "it's all in your head." It's formulaically simple: your thoughts create your reality, and since you control your thoughts, all you have to do to control reality is to change the way you think.

If only it were truly that simple. Changing your thoughts might be the toughest challenge you'll ever face.

Self-sabotage is a form of self-defense on the part of your psyche. Your mind carries around deeply ingrained ideas about who you are, formed by external sexism and its internalization, and it aims to protect you from feeling pain or disappointment by keeping you in an emotional comfort zone that reflects your self-image.[5] Often, it does so by making you afraid to do something outside of that comfort zone, or by soothing you with the promise that things will be much easier if you avoid risks and keep doing what you've always done.

To keep you in stasis, your subconscious mind works overtime, using the potent weapons of self-doubt, fear of failure, procrastination, perfectionism, and the need for approval. To effect internal change, you'll need to ruthlessly target your limiting patterns of thought and belief. You'll have to figure out what triggers your self-sabotage, and, when the trigger activates, replace your disparaging, ingrained response with self-affirming thinking.

Upgrading how you talk to yourself is a prerequisite for beating self-sabotage. Just telling yourself not to think belittling thoughts isn't enough—you have to replace your negative script with a positive one. Instead of telling yourself, *I'm going to look stupid* or *Everyone will know that I'm a fraud* or *If I voice my opinion, I'll be seen as bossy,* tell yourself:

I know what I'm talking about.
I've put in the work. I deserve to be here.
I can do this.
I'm the most qualified person for this assignment.
I earned my place at the table.
I am smart and can make a contribution.

I'm not a big believer in repeating affirmations while looking in the mirror. But positive self-talk *is* crucial. The game of success is, at its core, a mental one; it begins and ends in your mind.

Champion athletes know this, and they don't allow themselves to be defined by the fear of playing poorly or even by an actual mistake or loss. When Michael Jordan missed a big shot, he would say "Fuck"—and then immediately move on with the confidence that he would hit the next one. And he often did.

Use your own self-talk to hone the skill of pushing yourself forward, not holding yourself back. Let your enthusiastic, encouraging voice drown out the demon's voice and move you toward success.

Take these steps:

1. **Become conscious of your thoughts.**
2. **Stop and notice what triggers those thoughts.**
3. **Turn off the endless internal script that plays in your head when confronted by a triggering event.** Any event can be a trigger. Your boss asks who would like to take the lead on a new project. You're in a meeting where colleagues are giving their opinion on a proposal or new protocol. You're in a performance review and asked how you think you performed and whether you deserve a bonus, a raise, or a promotion.
4. **Fill your mind with controlled and conscious thought.** If you are the director of your internal script, that means *you get to choose*. Why not choose an inspiring dialogue filled with positive adjectives?

TEN MORE REMEDIES FOR THE BULLSHIT YOU TELL YOURSELF

It is up to you and you alone to conquer your feelings of inadequacy, weakness, fraudulence, and fear. Here are ten more ways, drawn from my own experience, to beat the demon.

1. TAKE PRIDE IN YOURSELF.

You are who you are. That includes all your talents, successes, failures, and drawbacks. Remember that everyone has issues; don't let yours detract from *all* that you are. Embrace them, and yourself.

Step up. Opportunities are rarely handed to you on a plate—you have to reach out and seize them. Take risks and advocate for yourself. When you get your hands on a project, dive into it, take charge, and offer your opinion as freely as any man would. (Tell yourself, *my ideas are as good as anybody's.*) In writing about how to beat BLS, financial advisor Elizabeth Revenko's first piece of advice is to *seize control*—even if that starts with small steps.[6] You'll also discover that it's a lot easier to step up if you never put yourself down. There are already plenty of other people to do that, especially the shortsighted men you threaten. Instead of thinking *I'm stupid* when you're not already an expert on something, tell yourself *Time to bone up on this subject.*

2. GROW.

There's always room for growth. Keep choosing to take on stretch assignments, ask for promotions, and climb higher mountains in your work. If a fixed mindset makes you brittle, the remedy is a *growth mindset*, which keeps you primed for more learning and hard work when you encounter setbacks.[7] So what if you fell on your face this time? Instead of surrendering, get back up and study harder, find allies, or create some new, better way to meet the challenge. Try telling yourself, *there must be a way—I just need to find it.*

3. LEARN TO DEAL WITH CRITICISM—INCLUDING YOUR OWN.

The same emotional sensitivity that gives you a high EQ—the very thing that especially qualifies women for leadership—can also make you wary about displeasing others, risk-averse, and bad at dealing with negative feedback (or even giving it).[8] Accept that you're not going to please everyone all the time. Don't take it as the end of the world when someone's unhappy with you, and definitely don't be too hard on yourself.

Cut yourself the same slack you would cut your friends. And, especially on the days when you *really* feel like your career is going all to hell, remember that *you do not equal your job*. You can, and should, find a more diverse definition of yourself that includes your outside life, your friendships, and all of your good qualities.

4. SHAKE OFF SETBACKS.

They will happen. Sometimes they will be big, and sometimes they will come in waves. One of the best skills I've developed is how to have a very thorough, very private session to rage at the world, or cry (or both)—and then come out refreshed for the fight.

5. DEAL WITH REALITY.

Remember that life isn't fair, and the more success and power you have, the more enemies and detractors you have as well. Live with it. It goes with the territory.

6. FIND WORK YOU LOVE.

It's hard to believe in yourself if you're stuck doing a job that doesn't really matter to you. I think one of the biggest reasons I have enjoyed success in my career is that, even on days packed with drudgery and firefighting, I felt like I was working on big, important things. Find something you love, do it with real gusto, celebrate your wins, and ride that rocket all the way to the top. Tell yourself, *this is the path I have chosen, and I can do this.*

7. LEARN WHAT YOU CAN AND CAN'T CONTROL.

Control is a coping mechanism we use to deal with the randomness of life, and it has its value. But remember that you can't control everything. It's important to keep life in perspective; a crucial part of that is learning when to let go.

8. SEEK FEEDBACK.

If self-sabotage and the other self-defeating behaviors teach us anything, it's that we're often not very good at assessing ourselves. Sometimes we rake ourselves over the coals for some trivial detail, while at the same time we miss a more glaring problem. That's why it's so important to find friends and mentors who will give you candid feedback that you can digest. In particular, look for answers to these questions:

What am I doing that I don't realize?
What am I not doing that I don't see?
How can I do better?

Remember, your professional life isn't like school. Often, finding the answers to these questions won't be as clear-cut as acing an exam. Instead, it's about continuing to improve the way you navigate the much trickier terrain of real life.

9. DISCARD FEAR.

Constantly ask yourself this question: *What would I do if I weren't afraid?* Life is too short to give in to your fears. Once you get rid of your fear of failure, of success, of being imperfect, of not having all the answers, you'll find that many of the internal barriers you face will come tumbling down.

In the next chapter, we'll tackle another internal issue, one that will make or break your career: projecting confidence.

CHAPTER 6

FAKE IT UNTIL YOU MAKE IT

"Power is not given to you. You have to take it."

—BEYONCE KNOWLES

- *Do you suffer from a lack of self-confidence?*
- *Do you see less-qualified men praised, promoted, or paid more than you are?*
- *Do you take the blame when things go badly, and credit luck or the work of others for your successes?*
- *Are you intimidated by new situations, new risks, or cocky, assertive men?*

LET US CALL THIS CHAPTER'S WITNESS TO THE STAND.

"Mr. Smith" is a rival partner at my firm. Arrogant, loud, and condescending, Mr. Smith is completely oblivious to the pride, feelings, or personal circumstances of others—a flaw that hardly matters, because he doesn't care about others anyway. Mr. Smith has driven good lawyers out of the firm because they hated working for him; many of those who remain fear him and live in dread of the call to work on a case together.

Mr. Smith, it's safe to say, is widely acknowledged to be a narcissistic asshole.

He's also not very smart. He relies on subordinates to do the heavy lifting—reading the case law, analyzing the facts, considering the strategies, and breaking it all down for him. Others write the briefs, and he does no more than a quick edit.

So what's your verdict? Is Mr. Smith a liability to the firm?

It may surprise you to learn that the answer is *not at all.* He's untouchable for one reason: he *exudes* confidence.

Mr. Smith *never* falters. He brooks no dissent. Every time he walks into a meeting, he immediately demands, and gets, the attention of the room. He is utterly and supremely secure in the knowledge that he's the best and that his advice is correct.

And for all his narcissism, his clients still love him. He is decisive and tough and strong, and although I've never seen him display any shred of ability to deal well with people, he must establish some sort of bond with them. On he rolls, landing prominent cases and making stacks of money.

This misanthropic, self-absorbed, semi-competent jackass is extraordinarily successful, and it's because he's the poster child for a workplace phenomenon we've all witnessed: the influence of and respect allotted to overconfident people.

THE CONFIDENCE GAP

How many times have you come across a man who's clearly talking out of his ass, yet doing so with the utmost certainty? You're thinking, *Seriously? He doesn't have a clue what he's talking about. I have an idea that's much better*. He, meanwhile, is confidently advancing his ill-considered position without a whisper of doubt. And while you hold yourself back from promoting your worthier position, he's the one who ends up in front of the group waxing eloquent, drawing accolades, and advancing faster up the ranks.

How about when you have a victory? You've worked hard, come up with a new approach, brought in a new client or customer, or made a big sale. You deserve accolades, but do you lay claim to them? Or do you attribute the result to fate or to other people? I bet you do the latter.

Men don't. They fully acknowledge their own achievements, and often take credit for other people's contributions, too. They are always the star of the narrative.

What accounts for this gender gap? It comes down to one word: *confidence.*

A seminal study reported that "men consistently overestimated their abilities and subsequent performance, and ... women routinely underestimated both. The actual performances did not differ in quality."[1] Think about this carefully: same performance, completely different perception. Where men confidently claim the spotlight, women devalue themselves based on preconceived notions about their abilities. We don't believe in ourselves. We are not convinced that we can succeed, and that judgment precludes us from even competing in the first place. When a group of women was asked how confident they considered themselves to be about their performance and their careers, 50 percent of the women described feelings of self-doubt.[2]

This lack of confidence is devastating to our careers. We don't consider ourselves qualified for our current jobs or promotions, we predict we will do poorly when faced with challenges, we hesitate before making key decisions, and we believe we don't deserve job advancement or greater compensation. What begins as self-doubt quickly becomes self-sabotage.

Not so for men. In that same study, less than 30 percent of the men reported feelings of self-doubt. Another study of business students found that men initiate salary negotiations four times more often than women do, and, when women *do* negotiate, they ask for 30 percent less money than the men.[3] Looking at 90,000 entrepreneurial projects on Kickstarter, another study found that men are significantly more overconfident than women. Where self-doubt holds women back, self-confidence drives men forward. When they fail, they pick themselves up and persevere until they succeed—failures are simply stumbling blocks on their way to success—and when they do reach success, they attribute it to their outstanding business skill and acumen. Women, on the other hand, were significantly less likely to try again when confronted *with either failure or success.* If they succeed, they think they've gotten lucky. If they fail, they decide they aren't cut out for entrepreneurship.[4]

In research on the confidence gap between women and men, a study asked 985,000 men and women from forty-eight different countries to rate their own self-esteem. The study found that men of all different cultures have higher self-esteem than women—and that the gap between the genders is most pronounced in the most highly developed countries like the United States.[5]

This confidence chasm between men and women results in gross disparities in behavior and social status. It's a key reason why men in business have more power, money, and influence than women do.

Cameron Anderson conducted a series of studies to determine whether overconfidence enhanced social status and found that "(a) overconfident individuals were perceived by others as more competent and, in turn, afforded higher status, (b) overconfident individuals displayed the behaviors that are used by others to infer competence, and (c) the desire for status ... leads to higher levels of overconfidence." In the conclusion of their analysis, Anderson and his colleagues discussed the dubious wisdom of bestowing confidence-based social status on people like Mr. Smith, noting that:

> *Those individuals among us who are elevated to positions of status wield undue influence, have access to more resources, get better information, and enjoy a variety of benefits. One of the most basic questions for students of human social groups, organizations, and societies, is the question of how we select individuals for positions of status. Although we may seek to choose wisely, we are often forced to rely on proxies for ability, such as individuals' confidence. In so doing, we, as a society, create incentives for those who would seek status to display more confidence than their actual ability merits.*[6]

Regardless of competency, men are accorded the highest social status based on overconfidence. For women, the opposite is true: self-doubt becomes a self-fulfilling prophecy.

It's time we get with the program. Succeeding in the business world requires more than competence. Our efforts to demonstrate that we deserve promotion, compensation, and success based on merit have been misguided because *confidence trumps competence.* As Anderson points out, "When people are confident, when they think they are good at something, regardless of how good they actually are ... They do a lot of things that make them look very confident in the eyes of others, whether they are good or not is kind of irrelevant."[7]

This blows any idea of meritocracy out of the water. What business success truly requires is grit, a large dollop of strategizing and maneuvering, a talent for self-promotion, and, most importantly, self-confidence.

This presents a huge obstacle for women. Exhibiting confidence, never mind overconfidence, runs counter to all of our gender conditioning. Our internal demons—our sensitivity and overreaction to criticism or failure, our need to people-please and to be perceived as likable, our endless brooding and self-recrimination for mistakes—undermine our self-confidence. Add to them the external demons of traditional gender stereotyping and the patriarchal power structure of the business world, and it's a miracle we have any self-assurance at all.

If this sounds bleak, get used to it—it's reality. But the upside is that you have untapped inner resources. Despite what the world may say, you can, in fact, remake yourself to exude confidence.

But how do you it do it without becoming the "Mr. Smith" of your workplace? That answer lies in the old expression "fake it till you make it," or, as the Nike slogan says, "Just do it."

Remarkably, it works.

JUST DO IT—LEARNING CONFIDENCE THROUGH ACTION

Confidence is volitional. It's a skill, and like any other skill, it can be acquired. Better yet, it can be cultivated so that it grows over time.

Step one is to *just do it*. Act confident. Acting is a big part of *any* job. That doesn't mean you need to go through your career pretending. But it is the first step to jump-starting your ability to maneuver with assertiveness and poise.

I can't emphasize enough the importance of taking action. It's a truth I've seen borne out countless times for my clients, my peers, and myself: you need to act decisively. Action breeds confidence. Stop brooding and doubting your abilities. End your self-sabotaging thoughts, and start taking action and taking risks. Once you see that you can do something, it bolsters your ability to take another action or face another risk.

Imagine, for example, a woman who is terrified of public speaking. She is beset with fears about forgetting her talking points, sounding stupid or superficial, or perhaps even stammering or stuttering (even though she normally does neither). Her stage fright is almost incapacitating.

Despite these challenges, however, she forces herself to make a single, short speech. She practices and prepares. And she does it! There's no standing ovation, but she does just fine. None of her fears materialize. What *does* appear, however, are the first blossoming signs of confidence. That single, small step toward mastering her fear of speaking is enough to give her the confidence to speak again. Next time, she may feel comfortable taking on a longer, weightier speech.

Taking action. Risking. *Doing*. These things generate a belief that you can successfully perform a skill, and that directly generates confidence. That, in turn, stimulates further action, and the cycle continues.

Starting now, you have to put yourself out there. Force yourself if you must, begin small if that's what it takes, but *you must act*. Jump in with your opinion. Project positive energy and determination, even when you don't feel it. Stop worrying that you're not 100 percent sure—let loose the Hermione Granger inside of you and raise your hand to offer your answer or volunteer for the assignment. Sell yourself with how you speak, how you dress, and how you behave—even if you're quaking in your boots. Fake it until it becomes comfortable.

Make no mistake, the first time will be horrifying. But it gets easier and feels more natural as you go. The way to expand your confidence is to achieve mastery in something, and that means successfully accomplishing a task or building a skill. Confidence comes from daring to try. Take on a challenge. Perhaps you'll stumble along the way, but so what? Pick yourself up and keep going.

Remember, you don't have to be the best. Learning to play the violin capably will suffice; you need not become the concertmaster of the L.A. Philharmonic. Whenever possible, make the setting safer by doing your homework so you know you're prepared. Thorough preparation is the approach that women like Angela Merkel and Hillary Clinton have used for decades to walk into a meeting knowing that they can hold their own on any topic, especially when they are the only woman in the room. Preparation is fertile ground for early confidence.

Knowing that a substantial part of confidence is a *choice* can free you from the myth that you're stuck at the level of confidence you feel now. As ambitious women, we can choose to expand our confidence—and we must, to unleash our power and change the world.

INTEGRITY IS EVERYTHING

"Fake it until you make it" means acting the part, talking the talk, and presenting yourself as confident even when you don't feel that way. Every time you "just do it," you build your foundation—the belief that you have the skills to accomplish whatever task you want. That foundation, even in the face of fear and uncertainty, is the breeding ground for confidence and provides the groundwork for decisive action.

The purpose of all this confidence-building is to inspire others to believe in you. When your boss, your clients, or your colleagues ask themselves, "Can I rely on her to head up this tough assignment?" or "Is she going to fight staunchly for our position on this?" you want the answer to be a resounding *yes*. You want to inspire confidence that you will tackle every job with tenacity, and move boldly forward to make it a success.

While a large part of their confidence in you is based on your competence and your resolute pursuit of goals, the remaining part has its roots in *trust*. This is another key area where your innate female ability to read people and understand their perceptual lenses is invaluable—those *kick-ass*ets foster trust from the outset. But even that advantage is not enough. The missing essential element is a reputation for integrity and straight talk. And that is something you can *never* fake.

In the first lesson he ever gave me, a male mentor told me, without a hint of cliché: "Your reputation is everything. *Your word is your bond.*" Old-timey or not, it's a winning philosophy. Not only is integrity the moral high ground, it's the most advantageous path to advancing your career. Even if you want to be outright Machiavellian in your tactics, honesty is still the way to go.

There's a not-so-funny joke that *lawyers* should be pronounced *liars*. It's in the same category with, "What do you call a thousand lawyers at the bottom of the ocean? A good start." And while it's true that some of the members of my profession are willing to lie through their teeth, even in depositions or in court proceedings when they are absolutely beholden to tell the truth, this is a principle with no gray area. Yes, spinning or framing things favorably, as discussed earlier, may be a legitimate part of your job. What isn't legitimate is *lying*.

Sticking with the truth in every situation, even when my opponents have been persistently dishonest, has served me well throughout my career. And this applies far beyond the legal profession—you will encounter people in every line of work who are dishonest and will try to advance their position by cheating the system. But even when it appears to work, don't stoop to their level. If they're down in the sewer, don't crawl in after them.

Think of this as playing the long game. Your reputation follows you through your career, whether you change employers or even go into a different field of work. Once it's lost, it cannot be resurrected. Just consider the power of *unfounded* rumors on social media today, which are sometimes hard to dispel even with hard facts; if the claim is true, good luck ever getting rid of that taint.

Maintaining honesty has helped me to develop trust with clients, witnesses, judges, and juries, and it has clearly contributed to winning cases. It's also built up my mental toughness for the fight, a lesson I first learned in *Transamerica v. IBM*, the case discussed in Chapter 4.

Each morning before the jury was brought in, the judge would hear motions on exhibits that would be offered in court that day. If someone had a reason to object, they could argue as to why an exhibit should not be allowed. Even as a baby lawyer, I was permitted to advocate on behalf of IBM about the admissibility of exhibits by Transamerica's lawyers.

There are only two ways to win a legal argument—either by arguing that the facts are on your side or that the law supports your position. The opposing lawyer wasn't picky. He would, with the same confident composure, misrepresent either the facts or the law—or, if necessary, both. It quickly became clear that I was squaring off in court against a *liar*. Worse, the judge would inevitably rule in his favor because I was constrained by the truth and my opponent wasn't.

You can imagine how frustrated I was. It wasn't fair! Why was I obliged to stick to the truth when he was free to use anything he could think of to win? It was as if I was playing basketball with one hand tied behind my back.

I was sorely tempted to join him in the gutter, but the two eminent partners leading the case for IBM, Bill Vaughn and Pat Lynch, were very firm in counseling me to stay above ground. Winning the skirmishes, they told me, isn't worth it when you are fighting a war. If you are reliably trustworthy and do not misrepresent the law or the facts, the judge will come to regard you as a credible source. Even though Bill and Pat understood my frustration, it was ultimately my credibility that meant everything—not just for me, but for the whole team, our client, and the case. They advised me to remain on the up and up, and I did.

Our team's long-term strategy worked. The jury deadlocked, and the case went to the judge for a verdict. He ruled in favor of IBM.

Our victory came in part because the court believed that both we and our witnesses were credible and honorable. In contrast, the corners that opposing counsel cut ultimately undermined their case.

When you lie, I learned, karma has a way of coming back to bite you in the ass.

THE SECRET FORMULA: COMBINING INTEGRITY, COMPETENCE, AND CONFIDENCE

In the business world, the battle between integrity and short-term gain never ends. Years later, I led a case that demanded all the integrity, competence, and confidence I could muster: the defense of PricewaterhouseCoopers US (PwC) against a $2.6 billion lawsuit brought by its client AMERCO, and related investigations by the federal Securities and Exchange Commission (SEC) and state regulators in Arizona. You probably know AMERCO better by the name of its subsidiary, the truck rental company U-Haul.

In the wake of headline-grabbing scandals involving Enron, Tyco, WorldCom, and Adelphia, this high-profile case was on the cutting edge of accounting litigation. It involved the off-balance-sheet items called "special purpose entities" (SPEs) that became notorious because of their misuse by Enron. Before the Enron debacle, standard accounting practice was to leave SPEs out of a company's financial statements. After Enron blew up—and took its auditor, Arthur Andersen, down with it—auditors at PwC told AMERCO that its SPEs needed to be included in its consolidated audit reports, and that PwC would have to redo earlier years' financials. AMERCO was already teetering on the brink of bankruptcy, so PwC's decision hit the company hard. What does an embattled, desperate corporation do in this kind of situation? Sue the auditors, of course.

Once again, one of my opposing counsel played dirty. He never missed an opportunity to "hometown" me, reminding the judge that he was local, and I was brought in from Los Angeles. The attorney made constant references to local events he and the judge had attended together, their mutual acquaintances, and their shared Jewish heritage, even using Yiddish phrases in court. (I'm Jewish too, but there's no way the judge would realize that the blonde lady from L.A. named Linda Jane Smith shared his heritage.)

Then there was the rush to the podium to speak. At hearings, when the judge asked a question and opposing counsel and I both wanted to respond, it became a contest to see who could get to the lectern first. Twice on the way to the lectern, opposing counsel hip-checked me into my counsel table so that he could get there first, leaving me with black and blue marks. Since he was at least twice my size, I knew I couldn't win the shoving matches. I began simply running flat-out to the lectern to try to cut him off.

Perhaps most demoralizing, though, was the long letter we received every single day from that same opposing counsel. It contained a beautifully written narrative cataloging all the alleged offenses my team and I had committed during the prior twenty-four hours. The letters were outright fabrications. They contained baseless claims of wrongdoing, outright character assassinations, and slanderous charges about the performance of one of my partners who had served as a US Attorney.

(My blameless colleague later went on to serve as United States Deputy Secretary of Homeland Security.)

Even though every letter was a complete pack of lies, each one demanded a response "for the record," meaning we had to waste precious time and effort to rebut the allegations, lest we be seen as tacitly accepting the claims as truth.

The unending barrage began to take a toll. Imagine getting a long, literate letter every day accusing you of being a liar, a cheat, and a scum bucket. Though baseless, the letters were a morale killer—day by day, they began to sap the team's confidence.

Finally, I decided that enough was enough, and wrote a response:

> *We are in receipt of your daily letter charging us with all manner of improprieties. Needless to say, we disagree with any and all of your false claims of misrepresentations and misconduct. You are clearly trying to establish a false record, and we no longer intend to waste valuable time and resources responding to your gibberish.*

After sending that response a couple of times, their letters stopped. Meanwhile, our side remained principled, continuing to win the trust of our witnesses and experts, and put forward our case with creativity, integrity, and confidence.

While the lawsuit was pending, the SEC and the Arizona Department of Insurance were simultaneously investigating my client. When tough and powerful government agencies formally challenge your client, the first thing they do is make a series of unreasonable demands. The SEC, in particular, is extremely tough, well aware that they hold the power to severely damage or even ruin a company. Your first instinct in the face of these demands might be to take a staunch defensive posture. The worst thing an attorney representing the target can do in response, however, is to take an entrenched, inflexible position, which immediately sets up a hostile relationship.

I knew the way to win them over wasn't to clash, but to signal a willingness to work together. I exercised diplomacy, willingly prepared whatever special documents they needed to help their investigation, and encouraged the PwC auditors to be forthcoming in interviews and depositions. By being upfront and open with the SEC, while still protecting my client's interest, we developed a relationship of trust and confidence. As with the Transamerica judge, once that relationship was built, it went a long way toward advancing our position.

My team and I worked punishing hours to prepare our case. I played fair. I didn't lie. I stated our position clearly and forcefully. And I cooperated when it made no sense to start a war. In the end, my character and that of my team helped secure favorable outcomes for PwC.

The lesson is clear. You work hard, exercising your true grit to build your skills and a track record of competence. At the same time, you *act* confidently even when you don't *feel* confident. You build momentum over time as confidence comes to feel more natural for you, and as you establish your reputation for getting the job done. And you do it all with rock-solid integrity so that everyone—your bosses, clients, peers, subordinates, and even opponents—knows that your standards won't ever be compromised.

It may sound like a tall order, but women, you are up for it. Fake it until you make it. Walk the walk, and talk the talk. Carry yourself confidently. Act with integrity. The more you do, the more comfortable and confident you'll feel.

Confidence is a belief in yourself that builds through action. Each action, and the sense of mastery it fosters, creates the confidence to take another action, and then another. The more action you take, the more confidence you build. Eventually, you can and will replace the vicious cycle of self-sabotage with the momentum of well-deserved confidence.

And that's how you win.

CHAPTER 7

EXPLOIT THE SILVERBACKS

"A soft woman is simply a wolf caught in meditation."

—PAVANA

- *Do men routinely underestimate you because you're a woman?*
- *Do you feel comfortable with your own femininity?*
- *Do you have advantages in the workplace because you're a woman?*
- *Do you use whatever you've got to advance your career?*

IN A WORLD RUN BY MEN, THERE IS one rule for getting ahead that trumps all others: *You have to use everything you've got.*

The three kick-assets discussed in Chapter 2 are part of that rule. They are powerful tools, and an even more potent combination when you reinforce them with intellect, true grit, and the decisiveness traditionally associated with men.

But that's not all you can use. You have an advantage that is both ironic and unique in a world of chest-pounding, alpha-male silverbacks. There is one thing you are that they can *never* be: a woman.

This chapter explains how to go further, faster, by selectively applying your femininity in key situations where it gives you a distinct advantage over men. You'll learn to deploy your charm, smarts, and womanliness to capitalize on men's biases, insecurities, and preconceived notions of male dominance—and come out ahead.

Let me emphasize: this is *not* about trading on your looks or your sex appeal. I will never suggest you act weak or butter men up with false flattery. This is about exercising the freedom that we have as women to use *all* aspects of our personalities to advance in the business world, while maintaining our professionalism and self-respect.

To put it another way, it's about harnessing your feminine *demeanor* to expertly navigate male culture without being *demeaned*—by yourself, or by men.

THE PSYCHOLOGY OF SILVERBACKS AND HOW TO EXPLOIT IT

Business culture glorifies the male ego. A big ego can translate, as we've seen, into the kind of confidence that people reflexively defer to, which helps to entrench the dominant male's power. Alpha males also enjoy the trappings of corner offices, fancy cars, and trophy wives—all of which serve as signals and deterrents to other would-be alphas.

That same ego, however, is also why men waste time on pissing contests with each other: the silverback has to guard his position as the undisputed alpha. Those in charge must keep their radars finely tuned to detect any potential threat from other men. To put it as bluntly as possible, with men it often comes down to the testosterone-fueled question of who has the bigger dick.

This struggle for power is dangerous enough that humans have developed countless ways to keep it at least somewhat in check. Joe Herbert, a professor of neuroscience at the University of Cambridge, argues that "Much of human society, its laws, inhibitions, customs, and traditions, are really directed towards the social control of testosterone. Males can't behave without restraint, much as they might like to do so."[1] Although researchers agree that hormones don't explain everything—social factors play a major role—numerous studies suggest that, among men jockeying for power, those with higher testosterone are the most likely to dominate. According to psychiatrist Robert Rose, "Hormonal secretions create a propensity for certain behaviors. Testosterone seems most strongly linked to competitiveness and dominance."[2]

For all its destructive potential, however, the male struggle for power also presents an opportunity. Women don't automatically trigger the same hormonal competitive threat to male dominance, and that allows us to fly under the radar. Unburdened by testosterone-induced behavior, we're free to use our emotional intelligence. We can read the perceptual screens of the men in the room, gauge the situation strategically, and choose a nuanced course of action appropriate to the setting.

This doesn't mean acting like "the weaker sex," much less *being* weaker; it means using your whole personality and range of skills to select the best options and to get what you want because men, obsessed with establishing their own dominance over other silverbacks, simply don't see you as a threat.

Alpha male fixation on evaluating potential challenges from other men has paid off throughout my career, providing me with at least three advantages. First, it has been crucial to my ability to give honest feedback and criticism to influential men. Many silverbacks will accept in-your-face feedback from a woman that they would *never* accept from another man. And while beta males reflexively sit back and act as good *yes-men*, taking no action that could anger the silverback, wannabe alpha males challenge the silverback and are crushed. Meanwhile, *you're* the one the boss praises as "having the guts to give it to me straight." If you're the only woman in the room, you are likely to be the only *person* in the room who can get away with straight-talking to the big boss.

Second, women can act as flies on the wall. As I described earlier, being the only woman in the CEO's conference room at IBM headquarters made me privy to all kinds of useful information. Be sure to take any opportunity you have to play that role, even if it means that you only sit to one side and observe. You'll gain a wealth of insider knowledge about strategies, priorities, and plans, while at the same time learning how the key players tick as individuals. You'll find out what their perceptual screens are and what insecurities drive them, which gives you more leverage to deal with them to your own advantage.

Finally, being a woman often means being underestimated. Throughout my career, men have assumed I wasn't a threat—after all, how could a woman *possibly* be blonde, attractive, *and* highly competent and tough at the same time? I've come to relish those moments when a man realizes just how much he underestimated me. In your own career, watch for times when you're underestimated by a rival. When your male colleague doesn't perceive you as a threat because you're a woman, it gives you more time and space to create alliances, compile a track record of success, build your confidence ... and prepare your attack.

Many silverbacks simply cannot regard women as equals. Use their oversight to your advantage.

DON'T TRY TO OUTMAN THE MEN

It's important to be clear that this strategy isn't about trying to become a silverback yourself. There have been women throughout history who have beat men by outmanning them, but they are few and far between, and I would argue that it's not a successful career strategy. Looking to famously tough women leaders like "Iron Lady" Margaret Thatcher and hoping to emulate them by scaring the shit out of any man who would consider crossing you is a risky approach. Thatcher certainly made it work, but that's also *who she was*. It wasn't an act, and it went hand in hand with her extraordinary talent, her fierce will, and her uncompromising political views. It's not the kind of thing you can fake. And if you try it and it doesn't work, you're out of options.

There's no percentage in trying to outman the men for the simple reason that, try as you might, *you aren't a man*. Instead, take all the benefits of being a woman and *work* them.

It's painful to see women try the opposite approach: stiff upper lip, controlled and self-contained, tough as nails. One of the most painful examples was watching Trump stalk Clinton around the stage during the second US presidential debate in 2016, when he left his podium and stood looming behind her. It was creepy and unseemly, but instead of reacting to Trump's bullying and inappropriate behavior as a strong, capable woman might, Clinton opted to maintain the controlled, unaffected demeanor of a man. I think she was terrified that any other reaction would make her look weak and unpresidential. Now, Clinton says she regrets it:

> *This is not OK, I thought. It was the second presidential debate, and Donald Trump was looming behind me. Two days before, the world heard him brag about groping women. Now we were on a small stage and no matter where I walked, he followed me closely, staring at me, making faces. It was incredibly uncomfortable. He was literally breathing down my neck. My skin crawled.*
>
> *It was one of those moments where you wish you could hit pause and ask everyone watching: "Well, what would you do?" Do you stay calm, keep smiling, and carry on as if he weren't repeatedly invading your space? Or do you turn, look him in the eye, and say loudly and clearly: "Back up, you creep, get away from me! I know you love to intimidate women, but you can't intimidate me, so back up."*
>
> *I chose option A. I kept my cool, aided by a lifetime of difficult men trying to throw me off. I did, however, grip the microphone extra hard. I wonder, though, whether I should have chosen option B. It certainly would have been better TV. Maybe I have overlearned the lesson of staying calm, biting my tongue, digging my fingernails into a clenched fist, smiling all the while, determined to present a composed face to the world.*[3]

The funny (or bitterly ironic) thing is that Clinton is incredibly warm and charming in person. I've met her a number of times, and she always comes across as smart, empathetic, and good-humored—*and* tough and decisive. She bought into the wrong brand of toughness during her run for president. She tried to pretend she was an alpha male, and it cost her.

We are not iron ladies or alpha males. We are blessed with a full complement of skills and can gear our responses to any situation—without giving up our identity as women. We can be competent, confident, decisive, and even aggressive, with no tolerance for bullshit. We can analyze, decide and lead, all while still displaying a woman's sensitivity to nuance.

FIGHTING THE DEMON OF OBJECTIFICATION

Unfortunately, the dominance of men also means that you will be evaluated throughout your life for your looks and, to be blunt, your fuckability. Silently or openly, heterosexual men will rate you as a potential sexual partner, and *everyone* will assign value to you based on how attractive you are. In Chapter 12, I cover what to do if it turns into outright sexual harassment; here, I'm talking about the societal norms we put up with and, tragically, adopt for ourselves.

The term "male gaze" was coined in the 1970s to describe how the media—from fashion and advertising to literature and television—portray women as objects for men's pleasure.[4] Nearly a half-century later, the gaze is still going strong, and, as any woman over the age of ten can tell you, we've internalized that gaze, adding it to our demons, reminding us by the hour that we certainly don't look like Cindy Crawford, Gigi Hadid, Miranda Kerr, or Kate Moss.

Do you want to know how pervasive that demon is? In an interview, *Cindy Crawford* said, "I wish I looked like Cindy Crawford."[5] She was admitting what so many of us already recognize: that *no* woman actually looks like the ones we see in our favorite glossy magazines. Yet those unattainable standards of beauty plague us in every phase of our lives, feeding self-doubts about our appearance and playing a disproportionate role in our self-confidence.

The data backing this up is devastating. International studies have shown that 90 percent of all women want to change at least one aspect of their physical appearance, 81 percent of ten-year-old girls are afraid of being fat, and only 2 percent of all women actually think they are beautiful.[6] Even that 2 percent figure sounds like a stretch to me; I have never yet known a woman, even a beautiful one, who was happy with her appearance.

In the same speech where she quoted Cindy Crawford, media critic and filmmaker Jean Kilbourne went on to say:

> *Women's bodies are dismembered in ads, hacked apart—just one part of the body is focused upon, which of course is the most dehumanizing thing you could do to someone. Everywhere we look,*

women's bodies have been turned into things and often just parts of things. And girls are getting the message these days just so young, that they need to be impossibly beautiful. Hot, sexy, extremely thin—they also get the message that they're going to fail, there's no way they're going to really achieve it. Girls tend to feel fine about themselves when they're eight, nine, ten years old, but they hit adolescence and they hit the wall and certainly a part of this wall is this terrible emphasis on physical perfection. So no wonder we have an epidemic of eating disorders in our country and increasingly throughout the world.[7]

The media constantly reinforces the idea that we are trophies or playthings who should rightly spend our time primping and packaging ourselves for men's pleasure—never mind having our own ideas and ambitions. It's hard to grasp just *how much* media warps reality to convey this. I didn't fully appreciate the extent to which a woman can be utterly transformed by media until I watched two videos in the "Infectious Perfection" series.[8] The first one shows the process of photoshopping a full-figured (read: "normal") model wearing a bathing suit. The second video shows the extensive process of digitally retouching a photo of Beyoncé's face.

It's crucial to recognize that media selects high-priced models at the top of their careers because they are extraordinarily beautiful. For a shoot, the very best professional stylists work wonders with their hair, sometimes adding extensions, while world-class makeup artists apply the best cosmetics. Every aspect of the lighting is carefully calibrated by skilled photographers and their assistants, and fashion stylists dress the models in gorgeous outfits with perfectly matching shoes, handbags, and jewelry. *None* of this happens in real life.

Even after having received all these enhancements to her "analog" body, the already gorgeous model is then digitally altered. Her body is completely reconfigured: inches are shaved from the stomach area; her butt is simultaneously made smaller and shapelier; her entire body is elongated, first from her waist to her knees and then from her knees to her toes; her face is digitally reconstructed to be perfectly symmetrical; her neck is lengthened; her breasts are augmented; and all wrinkles, blemishes, and fat bulges disappear.

The result is a perfectly proportioned image that bears, perhaps, a faint resemblance to the real model.

Photoshopping has changed our cultural perception of beauty and created impossibly high standards and expectations. The line between fantasy and reality has blurred. What's natural now appears *unnatural* to us. Simple things that all real bodies do have real effects: smiling leaves lines; real skin has folds, wrinkles, and bulges; teeth are uneven and not flawlessly white; physiques show cellulite, stretch marks, and pores. There is no way a real woman can look like a model in an ad. Yet we've forgotten what real bodies and faces look like and have fixated instead on an airbrushed ideal.

When we're compared to the images in advertising, is it any wonder that women are judged more harshly on our physical appearance than men are? Or that we are much quicker to criticize our own appearance than men are to criticize theirs? We are dealing with terrible confidence wounds, kept unhealed by billions of dollars of media spending.

What should you do about it? First, simply recognize that it happens, and that it happens to *every* woman. If the standards are so unfair that Cindy Crawford feels inferior, it's a clear indicator that the standards themselves are broken, even if we accept hypothetically, just for a moment, that aesthetics are a genuine way to measure a woman's worth or femininity. Second, get past that hypothetical moment right quick: you are *not* your body. It's sad that I even have to say this: you are so much more than some sexual object photoshopped to satisfy a man's fantasies or sell more shampoo. Third, recognize that you can and must own your femininity on your own terms. Whatever you look like, you get to define femininity for yourself. Not men, not Madison Avenue: *you*.

Finally, we all have to do what we can to teach this better way of thinking to our daughters and granddaughters so they're not saddled with the same body-image issues that we've had to deal with. While the objectification of women drives a severe loss of self-esteem for women of all ages, it hits particularly hard in adolescence. The self-esteem of adolescent girls plummets as they compare and catalog their physical imperfections, using the unreal, unnatural photos in the glossy magazines as a guide. Pop culture provides the most damaging and heartbreaking, yet also the most powerful, kind of sex education.

It's time for women to stand up to being objectified, trivialized, and sexualized. And it starts when each of us lays claim to our own definition of femininity.

GETTING COMFORTABLE IN YOUR SKIN

You need to own who *you* are. Whether we're talking about your empathy, your smarts, your hard work, your life experience, or the sense of style you bring to your wardrobe, you do yourself a terrible disservice if you don't call on all of your talents and all aspects of your personality as you define your own brand of womanhood. Be ready to use what you have. And remember that in your career you don't need to be a runway model or a glamor girl to be successful. All you need is to show that you care about your appearance, and make an effort to maximize what you've got.

Let's take gender out of it for a moment. Would you entrust a project to a woman with unkempt hair, clothes that look like they've been slept in, and fingernails chewed down to the quick? Would you entrust an important assignment to a man who looked like that? If you don't care how you present yourself, why would your boss or client want you to represent them?

Nonetheless, the bar is much higher for women. Men can more easily get away with looking "schlumpy" than women can. And when it comes to looks, I can't lie: I know that it has helped me in my career to be attractive. (These days I find myself damned with the faint praise of "You look good *for your age*.") There's no need to apologize if you are good-looking. It doesn't hurt to be easy on the eyes. It is an asset to use, just like any other. Not because you'd ever demean your professionalism by consciously making yourself a sex object, but because sometimes the thoughtful deployment of a pretty smile can make your interactions with colleagues and clients easier. Just make it obvious that your looks are only the icing on a cake of intellect, toughness, and EQ. Be all of you, with the goal that men will want to work with you, not *bed* you.

If you aren't a natural beauty, no worries. Regardless of your level of attractiveness, it's about how you present yourself. Pay attention to your appearance, not through the mirror of the mass media, but simply to make sure that you're sending the right messages to the people around you. We've discussed acting and speaking confidently so that you convey the message that you belong there; this is about grooming yourself and dressing to look the part as well. Appearance can be yet another marker of self-confidence.

In order to telegraph power and stride confidently through the business world, women need to look like they take care of themselves and "dress for success." Whether you are in a corporate environment wearing a silk suit or at Google in jeans and a T-shirt, you need to project self-assurance. You're a professional and a woman, so style yourself as one: no boxy suits to hide your femininity, but no plunging necklines either. Pay attention to how the most successful women in your field dress, then adapt their style so it suits your appearance. Knowing that you consistently dress in a way that flatters your build, your complexion, and even your personality is a great way to build your confidence—which itself will make you more comfortable in your own skin and more appealing to those around you.

Personality can trump or enhance what Mother Nature has given you. Energy, warmth, and a sense of humor are substantial assets that facilitate relationship building, and even silverbacks want to work with those assets. "Easy to work with" is even better than "easy on the eyes."

The fundamental point is to *work it*. We've all known women who, objectively speaking, are never going to win a beauty contest, but who consistently make the strong, positive impression they intend—charismatic, bold, confident—by carrying themselves with that little bit of swagger. They project an attitude of self-assurance ("Damn, that woman thinks she's hot" or "Damn, that woman is so secure about herself") that makes them stand out. Find that attitude inside yourself, and *use* it.

ADAPT AND MANIPULATE YOUR PERSONA

A lot of men have only one mode of operation. They might be the silverback alpha male or the yes-man beta male. They might be the sensitive artistic guy. Women aren't so limited. With our EQ-driven kick-assets, we have many modes to choose from and can gear our personas to situations as needed. We can be sympathetic and nurturing to a colleague who's going through something hard, then turn around and be no-nonsense and tactical when presenting our position in a meeting. We can be fun and inclusive with a group on a project, then become a full-fledged battleax the moment someone on the other side plays dirty in the middle of a tough negotiation.

Women have multiple personalities to draw from, from likable to fearsome, from intimate to remote. And as we develop a shrewd understanding of male culture, we can hone our ability to choose from that arsenal to shape our persona in a way that fits the moment. We can be tough, decisive, strong, and smart "just like a man," while using our emotional intelligence to perceive and relate to people in a human, thoughtful way. Women can—and must—use everything they've got.

Yes, it's Machiavellian. But so what? We face unfair disadvantages everywhere we turn in the professional world; it's fair play for us to combine femininity with ingenuity, savvy, and professionalism to counter those forces and reap the success we deserve.

CHAPTER 8

INFILTRATE THE OLD BOYS' NETWORK

"Leadership is not about men in suits. It is a way of life for those who know who they are and are willing to be their best to create the life they want to live."

—KATHLEEN SCHAFER

- *Do you ever wish you could just be one of the guys?*
- *Are men more comfortable with, and favorably disposed toward, other men?*
- *Are you excluded from male bonding rituals?*
- *Do you feel that you have to be better than the men to prove yourself?*
- *Do you miss out on mentorship opportunities available to your male peers?*

YOU JUSTIFIABLY ASK: WHAT THE HELL IS THE old boys' network? Urban Dictionary sums it up bluntly:

> *An informal system by which money and power are retained by wealthy white men through incestuous business relationships. It is not necessarily purposeful or malicious, but the "Old Boy's Network" [sic] can prevent women and minorities from being truly successful*

in the business world. It entails establishing business relationships on high-priced golf courses, at exclusive country clubs, in the executive sky-boxes at sporting events, through private fraternities or social clubs (such as the Freemasons), et cetera. These are arenas from which women and minorities are traditionally excluded and thus are not privy to the truly "serious" business transactions or conversations. A businessperson who does not travel in these elite circles of influence will miss out on many opportunities.[1]

This brotherhood has been a well-oiled machine for centuries. As fiercely as males compete with one another, they also prefer to do business with, open doors of opportunity for, and pay more money to, members of their own tribe. When men serve on non-profit and corporate boards together, you know it won't be long before they're doing business with one another.

The network exists and perpetuates itself because it works. In elite circles, powerful men make closed-door decisions that favor male candidates who share connections through mentors and sponsors. Men are naturally drawn toward people who are most like themselves, and it's common for high-ranking executives and managers to mentor someone who reminds them of themselves—a "mini-me."

The problem, of course, is that women aren't mini-men.

THE OLD BOYS' NETWORK IS ALIVE AND WELL

Lest you think the old boys' network is a thing of the past, consider England, where the term was first coined to refer to connections among the British elite who, as boys, attended certain male-only public schools. (In England, the term "public school" is applied to elite private schools like Eton and Harrow.) Recently, the Equality and Human Rights Commission (EHRC) studied the fairness, transparency, and diversity of board appointments for FTSE 350 companies—the 350 largest companies on the London Stock Exchange in terms of market capitalization. The study found that the male leaders at almost one-third of the FTSE 350 companies used the network to select and promote white, male associates within their personal networks. None of these posts were advertised—they were all filled by gender-driven favoritism.[2] The old boys' network continues to flourish, now with an infusion of new blood.

Similarly, US studies have found the old boys' network to be very much alive in determining who is part of the "corporate elite"—the inner circle of top executives who are members of multiple boards, exercise real power over corporate policy, are nominated to influential groups like the Business Roundtable, and are in the queue to be named to prominent government advisory boards. Even if women and minorities are invited to join a board, 90 percent of white male directors are unwilling to devote time to counseling or mentoring these first-time members on either the operations or the customs of board participation. That places women at a disadvantage, leaving them unversed in the unwritten rules that can make the difference between being an effective board member with real authority, or a token member included to create the illusion of diversity.[3]

And so, the old boys' network continues to thrive today, renewing itself with an evergreen crop of men to replace those who came before. Even now, the ascent to power of highly qualified, ambitious women can be stymied by this centuries-old network.

Fortunately, there are ways for women to break into this network, and the skills to infiltrate the club can be learned. This chapter discusses how to do it most efficiently.

WHY MEN CLING TO THE OLD BOYS' NETWORK

For elite men, their network is their net worth. The ability to identify and isolate who is part of the corporate elite is the major perpetuator of the old boys' network. But there is another reason for its longevity: the network feeds on the comfort men derive from it. Not only does the old boys' club represent the natural order of the business world ("that's the way it's always been done"), but the exclusive "club" aspect satisfies a deep-seated male need to be connected to other like-minded men.

Men simply feel more at ease with other men. When men get together they talk about three things: sports, sex, and doing business with one another. But interacting with women is another thing entirely. Men feel awkward and less in command around women. Feelings of insecurity and anxiety immediately spring up. In fact, studies have found that men in mixed-sex social interactions exhibit a decline in cognitive function.[4] Or as *Psychology Today* so gloriously put it, "Interacting with Women Makes Men Stupid."[5]

Men like to be in situations that sustain their confidence, and the typical professional man can be confident that he knows what to do around his own tribe. When a male colleague or client asks him to get a drink after work, invites him to play a round of golf, or suggests they grab dinner, they can talk to each other in shorthand while they drink in a bar, play that round, share a meal, or watch a football game—all without ever leaving their comfort zone.

That shorthand spills over into conversations at work. Just think about the times you've sat through meetings led by men where you had to listen to endless sports metaphors: "We need a full-court press," "Aim for the fences," "The ball's in their court," "Down for the count," "We need a Hail Mary," "We're in the home stretch," "It's par for the course." You can be a sports fan yourself and still be overwhelmed by how frequently men use these metaphors; women don't think about issues in these terms. It sounds like something from *Men Are from Mars, Women Are from Venus*,[6] but it's an accurate reflection of the divide between men and women's mindsets right here on planet earth.

There's also a broader issue: many men fear what *others* will say about their interactions with women. When a man and a woman work together, especially if the man is more senior, there can be a sexual undercurrent that is distracting and tricky to handle. I'm not talking about sexual harassment (we'll get to that in Chapter 12), but simply the fear that ulterior motives could enter the picture. For instance, a male boss can ask his male subordinate to grab that drink after work, or to join him and a client for a round of golf, and no one thinks twice about it. No one suspects that the underling wants to sleep his way to the top, or that the boss's wife will feel threatened.

On the other hand—and this happened to me countless times when I was a female associate—men are reluctant to invite women to join them after work because people in the office might speak unfavorably about it. Peers can imply that a woman is getting ahead by using her sexuality, or by actually doling out sexual favors. Wives may be unhappy about husbands developing a close working relationship, especially outside the office, with a younger, attractive woman.

These fears are mostly but not totally unfounded. I know bosses who have left seemingly solid marriages for younger female colleagues. Even if your particular relationship with your male boss remains completely platonic, the broader fear that something untoward *might* happen isn't outside the realm of reason.[7]

This issue was directly raised in March 2017 when the media had a field day with an interview Vice President Mike Pence had given to *The Hill* in 2001. In that interview, he flatly declared that he never eats alone with a woman other than his wife and that he won't attend events involving alcohol without her by his side.[8] *The New York Times* followed up in May 2017 with a poll asking men and women whether it was appropriate or inappropriate to do certain activities alone with a member of the opposite sex who is not your spouse. They found that:

> *Many men and women are wary of a range of one-on-one situations. Around a quarter think private work meetings with colleagues of the opposite sex are inappropriate. Nearly two-thirds say people should take extra caution around members of the opposite sex at work. A majority of women, and nearly half of men, say it's unacceptable to have dinner or drinks alone with someone of the opposite sex other than their spouse. The results show the extent to which sex is an implicit part of our interactions. They also explain in part why women still don't have the same opportunities as men. They are treated differently not just on the golf course or in the boardroom, but in daily episodes large and small, at work and in their social lives.*[9]

The old boys' network continues to thrive because of this male-female professional discomfort and disconnection—the gender division simply *works* for its members on many levels. The professional and personal connections that sustain it have been built up over years, or even *generations*: think of how easy it is for a successful man to give his son a boost in the professional world by calling in a favor from a former fraternity brother, schoolmate, or colleague. And even when there's no family connection in play, research has shown that younger men in business are more likely than their female counterparts to receive the helpful tap on the shoulder from senior men alerting them about upcoming job openings or other opportunities.[10]

And so the cycle continues as another generation of men come to see the old boys' network as standard operating procedure.

CRACKING THE OLD BOYS' NETWORK

After all this, you are no doubt wondering how you'll ever get to "join the club."

First, our mantra: you must *use everything you've got*. You'll need to be tough, strategic, charming, adaptable, and very, *very* good at your job. But that's a given for any woman of ambition who wants to scale the heights of the professional world. You must also be ready to ignore the aghast looks men will give you when they find out that you're in charge of a project.

A good starting point is to consciously adopt the attitude that you're going to *be a good sport* and *a team player* (yes, more sports analogies) in how you get along with men. Read the social and emotional cues of the male culture around you, then situate yourself in a way that eases some of the tension men feel when dealing with women. Help men understand that they are not walking on eggshells around you. Establish that you can take a joke, show that you won't take immediate offense at any critical comment or challenge (you're not overly sensitive or, worse, "hysterical"), and feel free to give as good as you get when it comes to "busting balls."

I knew I was on the right track toward the end of my first year at my law firm when we were deep into *Transamerica v. IBM*. All of the associates were scheduled to receive annual reviews and salary recommendations from the partners working on the case. On a day when the court was not in session, the partners, all of whom were men, gave the reviews one after another in a conference room. In order of seniority—meaning I came last—each associate would go in alone to receive feedback about their performance and find out how much they would be paid the next year.

I waited all afternoon for my turn. When I was finally summoned, I walked into the room to find Bill Vaughn, the head of the case, sitting with Pat Lynch and four other partners in a semi-circle with one solitary chair in the middle for me.

I sat down to complete silence. Everyone looked uncharacteristically solemn. Finally, Bill nodded gravely, and in his deep, authoritative voice said, "I'm sorry Linda, but your work is poor, and you're fired."

"Fine," I responded. Then I stood up, turned, walked out, and closed the door behind me.

From behind the door, I could hear the partners laughing uproariously. They were kidding—giving me shit because they liked me and knew that my work was top-notch. And they loved my calm, unfazed reaction.

That type of rapport wasn't created overnight. It was built during many months in the trenches together—the band of brothers camaraderie I described earlier. During those months, I had many chances to apply my emotional intelligence to understanding the verbal jousting, one-upmanship, and ball-busting that men love so well. Even if you find men's razzing a bit juvenile (which it often is), I strongly encourage you to master those rituals. When they make jokes about you being unprepared or unqualified, laugh it off. Avoid being an asshole, especially to your bosses, but do learn how to play their game.

Do make sure to enforce your own standards for what's appropriate for *them* to say, too, and make it clear that you won't tolerate crossing the line of professionalism—no "jokes," for example, that demean your integrity or commitment, or that insinuate that you're using your sex as an advantage. Above all, show them that you won't be intimidated.

Mastering the communication tactics of the old boys' network puts men at ease by showing that you're not some delicate flower, and that they can communicate comfortably with you, and in front of you. Those easy moments when you can jibe at each other, or talk about something other than work for a moment, help lubricate your social interactions with men, making you "one of the guys" without giving up your own identity. As discussed in the last chapter, it's another way to tailor your work persona appropriately to each situation—while retaining your femininity—so that you can get ahead.

PINPOINTING MENTORS AND SPONSORS

In your long-term quest to infiltrate the old boys' network, you'll need to turn your attention to finding a mentor to guide you and a sponsor to promote you.

The search for either is inherently harder for women than it is for men, in part because, as discussed, men prefer to counsel someone who reminds them of themselves, a mini-me or the son they wish they had—and in part because there are so few women at the top levels of the professional world.

Classical mentoring combines support for personal and professional development with sound career advice and counseling. Ideally, your mentor will provide emotional support to increase your sense of self-worth and competence, feedback on how to improve your performance, and guidance on how to navigate the corporate politics of your company. A great mentor can see and put into words for you what you may not see about yourself or be able to articulate. They can help you determine your strengths—what you do exceptionally well and what sets you apart. Each company has its own culture with unwritten rules, customs, and practices, and its own unique political minefields. Mentors can tutor you in those unspoken ways, provide a map to who really wields power, and help you navigate the corporate terrain.

The mentor relationship is critical, but not the end of your quest. Often the best mentors who provide encouragement and counseling are not the high fliers who have the real influence to pull you up to higher levels in the organization.

Unless your mentor is in your company's senior ranks and has a seat at the table for decisions on hiring, promoting, and assigning key responsibilities, you'll need a sponsor as well. Your sponsor must be highly placed and able to use his clout on your behalf and serve as your advocate for your next promotion. (Note that I said "his," because your sponsor is still most likely to be a man with great connections.) Sponsors, not mentors, give you real career traction and put you on the path to power and influence by affecting three things: salary increases, choice assignments, and promotions.

Your sponsor will teach you how to network, provide you with access to senior leaders and to valuable connections outside the company, and direct the senior leadership's view of your abilities and suitability for promotion to the next level.

Studies have determined that the main stumbling block for high-performing women in reaching high-level positions is their failure to acquire the backing of influential sponsors. Sylvia Hewlett has been examining what she has dubbed "The Sponsor Effect" and, in addition to writing extensively on the subject, has co-authored a report on the findings of a comprehensive study.[11] According to Hewlett, "What's been holding women back, the study found, isn't a male conspiracy but rather a surprising absence of advocacy from men and women in positions of power. Women who are qualified to lead simply don't have the powerful backing necessary to inspire, propel, and protect themselves on their journey through upper management. Women lack, in a word, *sponsorship*."[12]

The study found that women are only half as likely as their male counterparts to have a sponsor, and routinely underestimate the key role a sponsor plays in their climb up the ladder, including:

- *Without a sponsor behind them, 43 percent of men and 36 percent of women will ask their manager for a stretch assignment; with sponsor support, the numbers rise, respectively, to 56 percent and 44 percent.*
- *The majority of unsponsored men (67 percent) and women (70 percent) resist confronting their boss about a raise; with a sponsor in their corner, nearly half of men and 38 percent of women summon the courage to negotiate.*
- *A sponsor confers a statistical career benefit of anything from 22 to 30 percent, depending on what's being requested (assignment or pay raise) and who's asking (men or women).*[13]

Despite this evidence, women continue to believe that hard work by itself will reap rewards for them, and they worry that getting ahead based on connections is somehow cheating and unethical. That concern is reinforced by the appearance that when a powerful executive is boosting his female disciple, it's because she's doling out sexual favors.

Sound familiar? It's the same misguided belief that competence is enough to succeed and that it trumps confidence. The taint of dirty minds believing that the only reason an influential man will help a woman is if he's getting laid simply has to be dismissed as insulting and ignorant. Making the most of mentors and sponsors is not cheating— it's a crucial strategy that both sexes must use to get ahead. Why should men benefit exclusively?

HOW TO FIND MENTORS AND SPONSORS

Let's tackle finding a mentor first. Step one is to figure out what you want. Make a list of your specific expectations and the role you want your mentor to play in your career. Do you want someone who can help you network or someone to provide guidance on how to improve your performance? Do you need counsel on unwritten customs and practices? The skinny on how to best interact with those senior to you? Are you thinking long-term or short-term? Do you want a supportive, weekly mentoring session with someone who will help guide the whole arc of your career or someone who you can go to for counsel whenever you have an issue?

Start your search by looking for potential mentors around you. Is there a professor, a boss, or an executive with whom you have a connection? Look for someone who is willing to help you discover your strengths and talents. Choose men whose work you admire and who possess skills you would like to acquire or improve. Mentors are not one-size fits all—finding the right one can be as important to your career as finding a life partner, and you may want to solicit more than one mentor if you are able to identify and connect with several senior men who excel at different skill sets. For example, one may be adept at network-building, while another has polished skills in sales and presentations. Start forming relationships with your boss and other senior leaders from the beginning, and pay particular attention to cultivating those relationships with the individuals who show support for you.

Next, demonstrate to potential mentors that you are worthy of their investment of time and effort. Most senior leaders receive many requests for mentoring and don't have the bandwidth to say *yes* every time. Mentors select people to invest time and energy in who have the potential to grow, and will help them grow and become more powerful. They select people they want in their army of supporters. It's up to you to show that you have promise. You need to demonstrate commitment and a willingness to work hard, be receptive to feedback, and adjust or change your behavior if necessary. Figure out how to offer potential mentors some help with their workload or some advantage that will both deepen the relationship and provide you with chances to shine. Be specific and make yourself—and your accomplishments—known.

Once you've established your bona fides, it's time to approach your chosen mentor. Successful senior men may be pleased to be asked and willing to advise you, but they are not actively looking for more responsibilities—you'll have to make the first move. The direct approach is usually the best. Reach out and set up a meeting to ask for mentorship. In that meeting, be sure to discuss and share the same level of commitment. Both of you need to be clear on the time required and the availability of your mentor. Remember that the meeting is not a rambling chat. Instead, show up with an agenda that shows you have researched the mentor's background and expertise, admire and respect his accomplishments, and have targeted the topics on which he can counsel you. Bring goals to your first meeting, and have a list of questions ready to determine your compatibility as mentor and protégée. Does this person's expertise coincide with what you need to learn?

Finally, establish ground rules early on. Does he want to schedule a meeting weekly, monthly, or quarterly, or would he prefer to communicate by email and hold meetings only as necessary?

With your mentor firmly in place, it's now time to seek out a sponsor, unless your mentor is highly placed. You'll need to be very strategic in your search. The standard for a sponsor is not someone who is "simpatico" with you and can coach you on personal and political issues in your work. That's what your mentor is for. A sponsor is someone who has the political clout to power your career upwards. You may not want to emulate their style and the way they lead, but you do want their leverage and influence. According to Sylvia Hewlett:

> *As sympathetic confidants, mentors can't be beat. They listen to your issues, offer advice, and review approaches to solving problems. The whole idea of having a mentor is to discuss what you cannot or dare not bring up with your boss or colleagues. But*

> *when it comes to powering your career up the corporate heights, you need a sponsor .... [S]ponsors may advise or steer you but their chief role is to develop you as a leader. Why? Not so much from like-mindedness or altruism, but because furthering your career helps further their career, organization, or vision. Where a mentor might help you envision your next position, a sponsor will advocate for your promotion and lever open the door. Sponsorship doesn't "rig the game"; on the contrary, it ensures you get what you deserve—and will propel your career far more than mentors can.*[14]

Understand that high-level executives will only lend their relationship capital and sway to exceptional performers. They seek people who can shoulder tough assignments, bring in new business, follow through with the legwork to promote their strategic goals, and complement their strengths and weaknesses. In short, they look for people who will make them look good. (Later in this chapter, you'll read how former Secretary of State Warren Christopher showed his awareness that, for all his brilliance, he lacked a warm and outgoing personality, and therefore carefully chose subordinates—including me—to add that dimension to his repertoire.)

The steps to bagging a great sponsor are similar to finding your mentor, but far more politically motivated. You're looking for men who can leverage their power on your behalf—and who see a benefit to themselves for doing so. You need to:

- **Perform at a very high level.** If you're not exceeding expectations, your hunt for a sponsor is a non-starter.
- **Figure out who the stellar sponsors are.** Analyze how your company works and choose someone who can advance your career. Your sponsor should have a seat at the table when decisions are made, and be able to introduce you to and advocate for you with highly placed individuals both inside your company and in the community. They should be able to secure challenging assignments for you to further your career and provide you with critical advice on how to best maneuver through the political minefields of your company. Try to figure out which senior lead-

ers have a history of developing junior employees and are willing to share credit with subordinates. Stay away from men who are known for not supporting junior people in controversial situations, but are instead perfectly happy to put them out on a limb and saw it off.

- **Volunteer for exposure opportunities.** No sponsor is going to squander his political capital or put his reputation on the line unless he understands both your abilities and your value to him. Look for an opportunity to work directly for one of the potential sponsors you identified, or, if he is too senior for that, make an effort to contribute to a project he identifies with, join a committee he serves on, or do a special assignment in his bailiwick.
- **Promote your own accomplishments.** Women who don't hide their accomplishments advance further and have higher wages than women who refuse to blow their own horns. Overcome your reluctance to self-promote—apprise your manager of your noteworthy successes, seek feedback and credit appropriately, and ask for promotions.
- **Establish clear career goals and share them.** After you have shown your talents and value, make sure that your sponsor is fully informed of your game plan for advancement in the company—you need his complete buy-in.
- **Once you have a sponsor relationship, work hard to maintain it.** Never take your sponsor for granted—the relationship must be constantly nurtured. Sustaining your sponsorship requires that you continue to reflect well on your sponsor. You'll need to perform at the highest level, exceed expectations, take initiative, advance your sponsor's interests and legacy, and prove that you will continue to advance the company's interests. Maintain contact and look for opportunities to forge stronger bonds.

Remember that as a woman, you are both smart *and* strategic—now that we've cracked the code, you can level the playing field by finding and attracting a mentor and sponsor to further your career.

BECOME A PROTÉGÉE TO POWER

When I started as an attorney, there were no women role models—just the other young female associates and the standard complement of secretaries and receptionists. I made the tactical decision to show that despite my obvious differences (I could never be their mini-me or the son they wished they had), I otherwise fit the picture of the perfect protégée and that supporting me would increase their standing in the firm.

My mentor and one of my sponsors at the firm was Bill Vaughn. Bill not only had an imposing physical presence, but he was one hell of a lawyer. As head of the firm's litigation practice, he could also be one hell of an ally.

Bill, however, had no clue about women lawyers. His own wife performed the traditional woman's role, raising their many kids and running their household. He had joined the firm in 1955, and his social circle centered on an old boys' club: the all-male California Club, where he would regularly eat meals and network with the senior partners and male up-and-comers from the other Big Law firms in town. There were exclusive poker nights and golf outings, power lunches and cocktails—all the stereotypical old boys' network leisure activities.

At the time, the California Club was WASP men only—no Catholics, Jews, or people of color. The wives of members had to enter by a side door and were not permitted to eat in the main dining room. If women wanted to eat with their husbands or the wives of other members, they could do so only in the ladies' dining room. That room, decorated all in peach, hardly offered the same opportunities for power networking.

I've already described how I won Bill's trust by showing myself to be smart, tough-minded, hard-working, thick-skinned, and fun to be around. But there was more to my success than that; I also deployed my kick-assets as a woman to great advantage—especially to read men and use that knowledge to assess who I was dealing with and how best to handle them. It's a strategy I used time and time again with influential men, from bosses and clients to opposition counsel and judges, and it allowed me to prove myself to Bill. I won his support and clout as a decision-maker and benefitted greatly from his vast knowledge and experience in litigation.

Making myself the perfect protégée to prestigious men in my firm reached its apex years later when I worked hand-in-hand with Warren Christopher, the former US Secretary of State and longtime chairman of my firm. "Chris," as we called him, was a remarkable person—smart, diplomatic, strong-willed, witty, and generous with his time. Among his talents was the ability to make a highly contentious group (including his partners at the firm) think that they had reached a consensus when in fact they had not, then proceed on that basis.

Although he was a brilliant man, Chris also clearly understood his own limitations. He was so impeccably formal that Bill Clinton, for whom he served as Secretary of State, once said that Chris would eat M&Ms with a knife and fork. He had a slight physical build, an understated persona, and was always perfectly groomed and impeccably dressed. When our firm installed a new system designed to turn off the lights when there was no one moving in an office, we had a running joke that Chris must constantly find himself sitting in the dark.

Knowing that he lacked personality traits like spontaneity and warmth, Chris strategically chose to surround himself with complementary players. He brought together people, among them me, who possessed those traits he lacked.

In one instance, we held a meeting with the worldwide managing board of my client PricewaterhouseCoopers to present our views on the state of the world and its current crises as well as an analysis of PwC's most pressing current and potential future legal issues. With his acumen, poise, and diplomatic background, Chris was able to answer their questions about the political and economic situation for virtually any country in the world; I was able to present the latest legal challenges and risks in my more dynamic style. Our complete contrast in temperament and experience meant that we complemented each other perfectly and left the client far better informed—and highly impressed.

Working and socializing with Chris taught me scores of lessons, but one that has been crucial for my success—and will be for yours—is to recognize your strengths and weaknesses and then play to your strong points while compensating for your weak ones.

THE TIMING FOR A SPONSOR IS *NOW*

While you may never have a sponsor who's held a federal cabinet position (I still marvel at how fortunate I was), you need to make it your mission to find and cultivate allies and influencers like Chris among the old boys' network in your own workplace.

The good news is that today, more of the "old boys" are showing his type of enlightenment about the roles women can and should have, and are wise enough to actually *want* more women in leadership. Some of them are true believers in overcoming the unequal treatment that women have undergone. For instance, Canadian Prime Minister Justin Trudeau—who certainly qualifies as an "old boy" given that his father was also Prime Minister—happily calls himself a feminist; his first cabinet was equally split between women and men.[15]

Other leaders are thirsty to identify and promote talent, and they're not hung up on sexist ideals. John Veihmeyer, global chairman of KPMG, was a strong advocate for Lynne Doughtie as she rose through the ranks of the firm and ultimately became the CEO of its US practice in 2015. Growing up with five high-achieving sisters may have influenced his views on diversity.[16] Venture capitalist Jeff Jordan may appear to be a paragon of the old boys' network in Silicon Valley (he runs early-morning pickup basketball games at the Stanford gym, which bring together tech honchos and former college athletes in a more current version of Bill Vaughn's poker games), yet he also met his wife when they were both playing in a pickup game, and was mentored in his own career by Meg Whitman. He has drawn praise from several female entrepreneurs, one of whom he helped with a big career transition when she was six months pregnant.[17]

For still others, mercenary impulses may be the driving force. It might be that they understand the business case laid out earlier—that what's best for their company's financial performance is to have more women in the upper ranks. Others recognize that they risk missing out on opportunities for investment if they ignore women. Silicon Valley titan Marc Andreessen, who heads the VC firm where Jordan is a partner, acknowledged that the firm nearly declined the opportunity to make a hugely successful investment in Pinterest in 2012 because they didn't understand its special appeal to women until a female researcher on his staff convinced him to rethink his position.[18]

Whatever the reason, there are well-connected men who do indeed *get it*. Find them and make yourself their perfect protégée.

DANCING AS FAST AS YOU CAN

If you want the old boys' network to truly accept you, you need to go beyond knowing your stuff and being easy to work with. You have to force the good old boys to see that your abilities will help them succeed far better than they ever thought they could.

When I take on a new client, I often end up working with men who aren't used to regarding women as peers and who certainly don't trust their work, much less their ability to run the show. Remember that most of my cases are "bet the company" cases where, if the client loses, it faces billions of dollars in potential liability, along with potentially devastating damage to its reputation. When I walk in the door on the first day to take charge of whatever high-stakes, staggeringly challenging legal matter brought me there, I can practically see the thought bubbles form over my clients' heads—usually some combination of "We're totally fucked!" and "Seriously, *this* is who they hired to save our asses?"

From the beginning, I have to dazzle them. I need to show that I am completely in command of the law and the facts of their case and have a clever strategic plan for beating the other side. And, as if that wasn't enough, I also have to manifest the authority and confidence that I can lead this group of men and control the room. I privately call this "dancing as fast as I can" to overcome their initial skepticism, if not shock, and gain their confidence and trust.

Is it fair to have to prove yourself this way every single time? Hell, no. At times it's disheartening, depressing, and even enraging to have to do so much extra work that is not required of the men at my professional level. I wish I could tell you that it gets easier, or that at some point, it ends, but I can't. My honest advice is that you should *expect* to have to prove yourself with each new person and challenge.

If your clients don't believe they're in good hands with you, they won't be able to overcome their covert or overt biases. You have to use both your expertise and the force of your personality to show them you're so damn good that you deserve to be in charge and that your presence is crucial. You need to keep dancing as fast as you can; then and only then will they cede to you the leadership that influential men command the moment they walk in the door.

My first experience of this came in a case that should have been a recipe for failure for a young woman associate lawyer: a trucking case, of all things, which threw me into an all-white group of good ol' boys from the South. The senior partner I was assigned to work for, a very bright man and highly capable lawyer, shared that same background with our clients. He was a former Marine and had a framed set of crossed swords on the wall of his office. His favorite joke, which was only sort of a joke, was that women are most useful when they are barefoot and pregnant.

In this case, a small trucking company claimed that the rest of the companies in the industry had worked together to put it out of business. That meant all the other trucking companies in the United States were co-defendants accused of conspiracy to restrain trade. Naturally, those co-defendant trucking companies employed lead counsel who themselves were white, middle-aged, good ol' Southern boys with a lifetime of experience working on trucking industry cases.

While the partner I worked for would have fit seamlessly into this group, he sent me to all the strategy sessions and depositions instead: a young, female associate with absolutely no knowledge of the workings of the US trucking industry.

Before the first deposition, the men of the trucking companies' defense counsel assembled for a strategy session, its members flying in from all over the South. I, the lone woman, flew in from Los Angeles.

We assembled at a solemn Southern law firm in a conference room with a big walnut table, leather chairs, and dark wood paneling. Every good ol' boy was wearing a suit with cowboy boots; some of them had on hats and string ties.

Then I walked into the room. I was twenty-seven years old and buxom, with big blonde hair, in a Beverly Hills tailored outfit.

The good ol' boys were gobsmacked. But not for long. They found it hilarious that "the little lady" was representing one of the leading trucking companies in the country, and soon began to tease me mercilessly. When we went out to eat, they offered me "mountain oysters," AKA bull testicles, and laughed uproariously at my choice of girly drinks as they downed glasses of whiskey.

Tamping down my feelings of anger and nervousness, I quickly showed that I was talented, smart, and strategic. I wrote strong briefs, articulated my points clearly, and outworked all of them put together. I was dancing as fast as I could. Crucially, I never underestimated their savvy or intelligence. Good ol' boys from the South may speak with a slow, heavy drawl and pretend to be country hicks, less sophisticated than us "Northerners," but in my experience, they are shrewd and cagey.

From the beginning, instead of fighting them all, I was a good sport. I laughed when they poked fun at me, but drew a clear line as to what was fair game and what was not. As we developed a strong camaraderie, the teasing largely stopped. Since I wrote well and was willing to do all the work, I prepared the briefs on behalf of all the defendants. Then, with everyone's consent, I started taking the lead in depositions and arguments before the court.

When I returned to L.A., I was able to report to the Marine that all was well. He left the case in my hands, and the barefoot and pregnant jokes for someone else.

PENETRATING ENGLAND'S ANCESTRAL OLD BOY NETWORK

In the early 1990s, I had to infiltrate an even tougher old boys' network, this one full of stiff-upper-lip white Protestant male Brits. I had traveled to London to meet with the senior management of Price-waterhouse UK. The stakes couldn't have been higher. I was the lead in defending PwC UK in a $30 billion case filed in the federal district court in Los Angeles—a case that was brought by more than one million depositors after the collapse of the notorious Bank of Credit and Commerce International (BCCI). By the time its operations were seized by officials in the United Kingdom, Luxembourg, and the Cayman Islands in mid-1991, BCCI was the fifth largest private bank in the world and operated in seventy countries. It was alleged to have committed massive wrongdoing, including financing international terrorism, narcotics, and arms dealing; using bribery and fraud to prevent governments from interfering with its activities; and carrying out a giant Ponzi scheme that defrauded the depositors. The cloak-and-dagger aspects of the case threw the media into a frenzy and landed BCCI on the cover of *TIME* magazine in July 1991. Still notorious today, the case inspired the 2016 Bryan Cranston film *The Infiltrator*.

Among our seventy-five co-defendants were the ruler of Abu Dhabi, Bank of America, Ernst & Young, former US Secretary of Defense Clark Clifford, and former dictator of Panama Manuel Noriega, who was served with all papers at the federal penitentiary where he was incarcerated. My client was involved because it had performed two years' worth of worldwide audits of BCCI.

By then I had made partner and won a string of big decisions, but I still faced the biased impression that I was "just a woman" and entirely unsuitable. During my first meeting at PwC UK's headquarters in London, I arrived to find, WASP conservative Brits and their solicitors, all wearing black suits, white shirts, and club ties. When I joined the meeting, wearing my conservative suit but still looking like me, the executives and their outside solicitors did a double take. They were "bloody horrified" at the woman from California who had been sent to save them.

It was time to start dancing. Once again, I took charge quickly so I could direct our defense, and show them that I was eminently capable of handling all the complex challenges ahead. I was a force to be reckoned with, projecting confidence—some of which I felt, the rest of which I faked—as I set forth our tactical plans for defending the case in the United States. I turned on the charm, used a bit of mild humor, and showed the executives due respect by being ready to listen and learn. I purposefully cultivated an atmosphere of collaboration, but I also made it clear that, while I was more than willing to discuss strategies and ideas, my decisions would ultimately prevail, and my position would be respected. It didn't take long to establish a constructive, collegial working relationship.

There were some stark cultural and legal differences to navigate. Most glaringly, American trial lawyers are accustomed to coaching witnesses to help them put the best face on the facts. Witnesses are most often laypeople, accountants, or technical experts in a given area, not trained public speakers, and they generally have a hard time explaining what they did and why without speculating or getting tripped up by opposing counsel.

During depositions or trials, it's routine to talk to witnesses at lunch, at night, or even in hallway conversations during breaks in the day to clarify points and give them advice on how to tell their story—always supported by the facts and the law, but framed in the way most favorable to our case. We coach our witnesses at every turn to get their points across clearly. This concept is alien to the British judicial system. Once your witness goes into a deposition or testifies at trial, neither the barrister nor any other attorney can speak to them about the case at any time until they have completely finished their testimony. Coaching of witnesses is strictly forbidden.

And when I mentioned "spinning the facts"—meaning, as explained above, presenting the facts truthfully but in the best light possible—there were aghast murmurs in PwC UK's conference room. I'm afraid I did corrupt the British clients and solicitors. By the end of my time in London, they were casually asking, "How can we best spin this?"

The cultural divide came to a head in a meeting some weeks later. While I had already won over the PwC auditors, their executive team, and their outside solicitors, this was the first time I encountered their barrister.

The barrister was the *very* senior attorney who alone could speak for the company in the Crown courts, where an ancillary proceeding was pending. He had "taken silk," meaning that he had been given the esteemed designation of Queen's Counsel, and he acted as if he were entitled to extreme deference.

In my first meeting with him, he sat stiffly and listened to my take on how the case should proceed. When I finished, he took several puffs of his cigarette, looked at me with disdain, and then said in a very posh British accent, "Well, I don't know how they do things in bongo bongo land, but that's not how things are done in the United Kingdom."

There was a sharp intake of breath around the table, followed by a very empty silence.

I was unperturbed. I simply smiled and replied, "Well I'm telling you how it is done in bongo bongo land, and that's where our case is."

Research has shown clearly what women have known for ages: that we are judged more critically than men when we speak up assertively.[19] You need confidence on top of your track record of success to infiltrate the old boys' network and to get away with saying something like I did to the barrister. I dismissed his comment and moved on to the work at hand.

Many months later, all the defendants moved to dismiss the case, with my firm arguing the motion before the court on everyone's behalf. The judge ruled that the entire $30 billion case should be thrown out. My clients were so thrilled that they threw me a party ... at none other than the California Club, now integrated enough to allow women in the front door.

CHAPTER 9

WATCH YOUR BACK

"Dear Karma, I have a list of people you missed."

—UNKNOWN

- *Have you been the victim of unfounded gossip or political sneak attacks in your organization?*
- *Do you experience competition from other women who believe there are very few seats at the table for females? Or worse, that there is only one seat for the "queen bee"?*
- *Do you wish you had an old girls' network to counteract the old boys' network?*

GIVEN THE ENTRENCHED NATURE OF THE OLD BOYS' network, the perks (for men) of gender discrimination, and men's discomfort with women in general, it's easy to understand why a man would try to tear you down. He might be threatened by your current standing, especially if you've surged ahead. He might be wary of your career ambitions if he sees them as competing with his own. He might think that his own predominance ought to go unquestioned, and that you're "too aggressive," "bitchy," or "ballsy" in challenging him. Or, like my previously mentioned law partner, he may just be an asshole who will never regard women as anything other than a lesser form of life.

The sad truth is that women who climb the ladder of success must always be on the lookout for people who will try to take them out. The opposition could come in the form of a direct challenge to your authority or a sneak attack to discredit you with your bosses and peers. Ask any powerful woman, and she'll tell you how simple it is for a carefully planted seed of doubt or a well-placed bit of gossip to jeopardize your position by raising questions about your professional competence, your morals, or your fitness to lead. Watching your back, unfortunately, is an inescapable part of the price of success.

Worse, when it comes to protection from sneak attacks, all too often you'll find you have to go it alone. This chapter will teach you why these attacks happen, and how to protect yourself when they do.

SNIPER ALERT: KING SNAKES AND QUEEN BEES

I once took on a significant, high-stakes case and needed a team with a full complement of associates and at least one junior partner. The case was a big one—a full-time commitment and then some—but all the junior partners I wanted already had case assignments. Arriving to the "rescue," my fellow senior partner volunteered to "help" me. As soon as he signed on, however, he imperiously asserted that he'd be taking over direction of the entire case. I seriously doubt that he even thought of it as trying to push me aside—he just barged ahead in his typical male-chauvinist way. To his thinking, if he was going to be involved, he was going to be *the* boss.

As you might suspect, I didn't take his attempt to usurp me lying down. But dealing with these sniper attacks is tricky business. A well-placed male enemy with deep connections in the old boys' network is no small matter. If you're not careful, one back-room political maneuver by a jealous rival could knock you off the rung you earned with your merit and grit.

For all the attacks that may come from men, however, what is often more unexpected is an attack from another woman. Whether arising from naked ambition or from the perception that there can be only one "queen bee" in the company, a backstab from within your own tribe carries its own unique sting.

While I was running the AMERCO/U-Haul case on behalf of PricewaterhouseCoopers, I recruited several junior partners, including one woman. Within two weeks of her entry onto the case, she tried to poach PwC away from me. I was blindsided by her actions and stunned that she would even consider such a thing. Fortunately, I had spent fifteen years building deep relationships at PwC and serving as their legal gladiator around the world, and she didn't have a chance in hell of succeeding. Still, the betrayal by one of your own is difficult to forget.

The label "queen bee syndrome" is used to describe a woman who has succeeded in her own career but refuses to help other women do the same, or a woman in a position of authority who views or treats subordinates more critically if they are female. I have always believed that this phenomenon is rooted in the perception that there is only room for one female seat at the table, but I was taken aback when I read recent research theorizing that queen bees are simply trying to fit in with their male counterparts by adhering to the gender stigmas in the workplace. Distancing themselves from female subordinates can allow queen bees the opportunity to show more masculine qualities—ones stereotypically seen as more culturally valuable and professional. By showing those qualities, they hope to further legitimize their right to be in important professional positions, and foster job security by showing commitment to their professional roles.

One study argued that queen bees are trapped in a vicious cycle. As a consequence of the gender discrimination these women experience throughout their careers, when they become leaders they assimilate into male-dominated organizations by distancing themselves from junior women and legitimizing that same gender inequality in their companies. Queen bee behavior, it seems, doesn't create that inequality in the first place, but is actually a response to the misogyny and social-identity threats that these women encounter in businesses controlled by men. This kind of response is used consciously or unconsciously by many marginalized groups to overcome damaging views of their cohorts.[1]

There is also, sadly, the problem of "mean girls"—the women who will undercut or bully you out of sheer jealously, a desire for supremacy, or because of some slight, real or imagined. You may well be thinking,

"Didn't that end in high school?" but, no, "mean girls" can be sixteen or fifty-one. A study done in 2010 by the Workplace Bullying Institute found that female bullies directed their hostilities toward other women *80 percent of the time*—an increase of 9 percent since 2007. By contrast, male bullies were equal opportunity bulliers.[2] A 2011 study of 1,000 working women conducted by the American Management Association found that 95 percent felt they had been "undermined by another woman at some point in their careers."[3]

This phenomenon is terribly sad and unhealthy; more importantly for this discussion, mean girls can sabotage your career, and this is especially true if one of the mean girls is your boss or someone further up the ladder. The problem is particularly insidious because it's often subtle. A man may be comfortable with competition, and as a result, will challenge you openly. You can deal with this using direct countermeasures. By contrast, many women will deploy understated putdowns, exclude you from key meetings, or spread gossip or outright lies to try to get what they want—building themselves up while at the same time diminishing you.[4] Dealing with them requires much more savvy.

To be sure, there are women who root for, mentor, and sponsor other women. But they are few in number and outweighed at this point by the women who believe there is only room for a very limited number of us at the table. Going forward, women have the chance to work together and advocate for each other in ways that I never had when I was making my way up the ladder. If we can do that—if we can build our own "old girls' network"—we can improve the lives of the younger women coming up by eliminating, or at least curtailing, sniper attacks against them.

THE FINE ART OF CAREER SELF-DEFENSE

My recipe for protecting yourself against all of these attacks has five elements, most of which you need to put in place starting on day one of your career.

1. **Maintain constant vigilance.** While becoming paranoid by constantly looking for slights or attacks against you isn't helpful, it does make sense to expect that an attack *could* come at any time, and to have your antennae tuned to detect exclusions, putdowns,

and lies before they go too far. This is a balancing act; too much vigilance and you can become oversensitive to honest criticism or ordinary differences of opinion and waste a lot of time on work politics that you'd be better off spending on the work itself.

2. **Build alliances.** Staying ahead of sabotage—overt or subtle—and countering it when it rises up and tries to bite you, is much easier if you've already built genuine working relationships. With no old girls' network to protect you, and an old boys' network that won't come to your rescue, you'll have to build your own. Well-placed allies within your organization, including people senior to you, can give you the early tipoff you need about sabotage, and support you in your hour of need. While you're at it, be sure to leverage your broader social network by building alliances beyond your own organization. Look for networks you have access to that have more senior people involved, including industry groups and not-for-profit boards in your field. An external network of people who know your value is critical. If you ever do lose a battle and need to change jobs, you'll want help to land on your feet someplace else.

3. **Don't let it slide when you are attacked.** Your enemies need to know that you can't be trifled with—you're tough as nails and will staunchly defend your position against their sabotage. This includes calling out your attackers on their actions. Let them understand in no uncertain terms that you see what they are doing and that either they'll stop, or you'll put an end to it yourself. Make it clear that you're not inviting debate; you're simply explaining that you're fully up to speed and that there's a price to be paid if the sabotage continues. You'll be surprised how effective head-to-head, open confrontation can be. This step goes hand in hand with the previous strategy of rallying your internal and external network around you.

4. **Keep it professional.** Don't answer sabotage with counter-sabotage, and don't resort to underhanded tactics. Just as my bosses counseled me not to get down in the gutter with the sleazy opposing counsel in *Transamerica v. IBM*, you can't stoop to the level of your attackers, no matter how tempting it may be. When the truth

comes out, you want to be the one who can hold your head high. Maintaining your integrity will be what distinguishes you from those who have been trying to undermine you. Management—including the leaders you work for—should be able to understand the difference and trust you. Even if they don't, maintaining your integrity will mean that you haven't damaged your reputation in your next job search.

5. **Go above and beyond in proving yourself.** Once again, as a professional woman, you must be ready to prove yourself at a level that most men never have to. Starting on day one, build your standing in your organization using all the tools we've talked about—talent, grit, emotional intelligence, femininity, and strong relationships—so you'll be in as strong a position as possible when someone tries to question your character or suggest that you can't cut it in terms of performance.

Maybe you'll be that rare woman who makes it through her career without being subjected to sniper fire. I hope you are. But it's smarter to work under the assumption that you won't and prepare yourself thoroughly.

THERE IS NO OLD GIRLS' NETWORK ... YET

I've done everything in my power to help create an old girls' network to help women in the same way that the old boys' network has been helping men for centuries. It's a movement that's long overdue.

In my own career, I've had to go it alone. And, as discussed, most women I've encountered not only don't help other women, they see them as rivals. It's hard for sisterhood to thrive when women perceive that there is only one place for us, or perhaps a handful at most, at the table.

As the only woman of my rank, I felt enormous pressure to serve as a mentor, and sometimes a sponsor, to younger women at my firm. While I did not reach my senior position based on any sort of "affirmative action"—quite the opposite—I have nonetheless been treated as a token because I was either the only woman partner in my office or because for many years I was the most senior woman partner in our entire firm. Other women had made partner over the years but ended up leaving the firm before they reached my level. Because of my unique status, I routinely had to take on extra responsibilities. When recruits came through for our summer program, for example, I had to interview every single one of them, male or female, so they would know that there was a powerful woman partner in the office.

In an article discussing stereotypes of powerful women (that, ironically, characterized women in contradictory ways as both ice queens and too emotional, too tough yet too weak), it was pointed out that former US Secretary of State Condoleezza Rice was frequently devalued as a token rather than regarded as someone who had rightfully earned her cabinet appointment: "Rice was often the only woman in the room, but her gender didn't get her there. 'While companies take their diversity goals seriously, they are not going to settle for less than the best person for the job,' said Lynne Sarikas, director of the MBA career center at Northeastern University. 'Women are hired because of their education and experience and what they can do for the company.'"[5]

The main character in Chimamanda Ngozi Adichie's book *Americanah* discusses in her fictional blog how Barack Obama and other black people who are pioneers in different fields feel as if everything they do as an individual is also taken as a referendum on the qualities of their entire race. Although I can't claim to have a clue what it's like to be black in America, I do know that I have felt intense pressure to always behave as a star in order to reflect well on other women lawyers and not give my male partners the opportunity to say, "You see, that's what happens when you bring a woman into the partnership."

My position has allowed me the opportunity to be a genuine mentor to innumerable women as they pursued their legal careers. I was able to offer them what I never had: someone who shared their perspective to whom they could turn. With me, they could speak candidly about their problems, including the external demons of sexism and their internal demons of self-sabotage. I take pride in knowing that there are now women lawyers who are successful in their own right who I was able to support in their career paths.

I should add that I've been a mentor and sometimes a sponsor to many younger men as well. I was easier to approach because my female kick-assets kept me open to other perspectives and gave me the ability to listen and give candid feedback without being dogmatic. I was no Earth Mother figure, but I accepted a range of personalities and viewpoints, showed more sympathy to admissions of doubt or weakness, had a sense of humor, and was respectful of people regardless of seniority. I'd like to think that my work with these men positively influenced their assessment of women in the firm.

Today, I write and speak to spread the lessons I've learned to younger women across all professions by showing them how to harness our natural talents as women to dominate in business. How else will women thrive? While organizations such as Ellevate and Catalyst are doing excellent work to encourage women and promote their careers, individual women—especially those of us who have managed to make it to the top—must continue on our mission to equip other women to forge ahead. If we want women to claim their rightful place in the world, we have to continue to create networks and mentor those women who are leading the charge to be their best.

If we keep at it, women of the future will be less susceptible to sniper attacks and, if those attacks do come, they'll be prepared to handle them.

CHAPTER 10

DO NOT TOLERATE INTERRUPTIONS

"The worst criticism seeks to have the last word and leave the rest of us in silence; the best opens up an exchange that need never end."

—REBECCA SOLNIT, "Men Explain Things to Me"

- *Do men think nothing of interrupting you when you are speaking?*
- *Do men talk over you even though you haven't finished speaking?*
- *When a man interrupts you, do other people in the room discount what you were saying?*
- *Do men hijack your ideas and get credit for them?*
- *Do you hedge what you are saying with words like "I'm not sure, but I think" or "In my opinion"?*
- *Do you struggle to cut off interrupters?*

ON SEPTEMBER 27, 2016, THE DAY AFTER THE first Trump/Clinton debate, author Jessica Bennett wrote in a *New York Times* op-ed that she had counted forty interruptions by Trump, during the debate, versus *one* by Clinton.[1] Bennett quoted the Huffington Post, saying, "This is what manterrupting looks like."

Both "manterrupting" and "mansplaining," which I'll discuss in this chapter, are forms of male interruption that go much deeper, and have far more significant implications, than rude conversation. Both are, in fact, good old-fashioned sexism and a default cultural preference for male domination.

As Bennett notes, "Women are less likely to speak up, and less likely to be heard, in groups that are mostly men—which is why gender equality in places where people are required to speak is so important," and that, "In mixed settings, research has shown, women are less likely to have their own ideas attributed to them—in many cases because male credit is simply inferred."[2]

This infuriating gender discrimination is not isolated to younger women or those in lower positions. It happens to every woman, in every role, and at every point in a career. You *must* take forceful action to stop it.

THE ROOTS OF INTERRUPTION

This pervasive gender bias is born from a fundamental difference in why we speak. While men speak to determine and achieve control, power, and status, women speak to communicate and achieve connection. The stakes are inherently much higher for men than they are for women—men are compelled to display their supremacy by seizing control of groups whenever possible. Women are trying to accomplish something entirely different, and tend to default to different conversational rules.

This paradigm has practical implications as your build your career. Whether it's a one-on-one with the boss, a strategy session with a client, or a presentation to a large audience, you must speak up and get your ideas across clearly, *forcefully*, to get ahead. Even when it's not your meeting, or you're not the first to talk, you won't get very far until you make a habit of sharing your views with the group.

There are two other forces at work when women try to be heard. First, women are less likely to receive credit for their own ideas because men hijack them. Have you ever been in a meeting where you came up with a great plan, which was then summarily disregarded? Later in the same meeting, a man offers *your* great plan claiming it as his own, and that plan is then taken seriously, with the man applauded for coming up with it. I bet that has happened to you more often than you can count.

Second, and worse, under the category of "damned if you do and damned if you don't," studies have shown that when power and gender are considered in the context of volubility, powerful women "incur backlash as a result of talking more than others."[3] Where speaking up more makes men seem knowledgeable and competent, speaking up "too much" as women leads our peers to evaluate us as less so.[4]

The bottom-line assumption is that what men have to offer is far more important than anything a woman has to say. When men assert themselves confidently and competitively, they are rewarded for it with more power. When women do the same, they lose stature.

This needs to stop now. Whatever male power imperatives and hidebound stereotypes are at work here, they are insufficient: women are entitled to be heard and listened to, *without interruption*.

This is more than a parity issue. We have much to contribute. Given our abilities to analyze problems and strategize using a more creative, less-linear process, injecting our EQ into the mix results in more inventive solutions and better overall profitability.

But our contribution only works when we are given an uninterrupted voice to express it.

THE PERVASIVENESS OF MANTERRUPTION

Secretary Clinton is hardly the only one to endure manterruption. Studies have shown that men interrupt women in business settings three times more often than they interrupt each other.[5] A few months after the 2016 election, newly sworn-in US Senator Kamala Harris faced two glaring instances of this when two Republican men—her fellow members of the Senate Intelligence committee—told her, in essence, to pipe down because her questioning of Attorney General Jeff Sessions and Deputy Attorney General Rod Rosenstein was too pointed.[6]

Harris knows something about questioning reluctant witnesses. She prosecuted many crimes as she worked her way up to become San Francisco's District Attorney, and then California's Attorney General. Despite her expertise, however, her older male colleagues John McCain and Richard Burr saw fit to interrupt her in the middle of doing her job. This blatant silencing of a female colleague on the floor of the United States Senate clearly shows that the legislative branch, even at the highest levels, is not immune to the gender inequalities across the rest of society.

Sadly, this is a phenomenon that women litigators know all too well.[7] Even female Supreme Court justices, who have reached the highest pinnacle of the legal profession by virtue of their intelligence, analytical abilities, and grit, face this same injustice. Research demonstrates that the male justices on the Court interrupt the women about three times as often as they interrupt each other, and about *eight* times as often as the women interrupt the men.[8] And, as counter-intuitive as it seems, the more female justices are added to the bench, the more the male justices interrupt them. The study found a consistently gendered pattern: in 1990, with Justice Sandra Day O'Connor as the only female member of the Court, 36 percent of interruptions were directed at her; in 2002, 45 percent were directed at Justices O'Connor and Ruth Bader Ginsburg; and in 2015, 66 percent of all interruptions on the Court were directed at Justices Ginsburg, Sonia Sotomayor, and Elena Kagan. The researchers who have studied these patterns conclude:

> *Our findings that female justices are consistently interrupted more than their male counterparts in this setting show that gender dynamics are robust enough to persist even in the face of high levels of power achieved by women. Furthermore, our findings that there is a gender disparity on our nation's highest Bench adds strength to Zimmerman and West's theory that micro-level interactions between the genders are microcosms for a much larger issue—society's apparent gender-based hierarchy.*[9]

Moreover, even the male advocates before the Court interrupt the women justices. The rules of the Court require that lawyers arguing their cases stop speaking *immediately* when one of the justices begins speaking, and that they *never* interrupt a justice. Yet male advocates unabashedly interrupt the female justices. (Female advocates virtually never interrupt any of the justices.) Beyond being rude, these interruptions actively prevent female justices from having a larger impact on decision-making by wasting their limited time during oral arguments, and depriving them of the critical information they seek to elicit through questioning.

Both kinds of interruptions reduce the power of female justices who sit on the Court. As the researchers who studied these interactions noted, "Oral arguments shape case outcomes." They go on: "This pattern of gender disparity in interruptions could create a marked difference in the relative degree of influence between the male and female justices."[10]

Even female pop stars are not immune. During the 2009 MTV Video Music Awards, as Taylor Swift accepted her award for Best Female Video, Kanye West lunged onto the stage, grabbed the microphone from her, and launched into a monologue. "I'mma let you finish," he said as he interrupted Swift, "But Beyoncé had one of the best videos of all time." It became an iconic moment in pop history, but it started when he flat-out interrupted her. Who invited *him* to publicly challenge the decision of the judges that Swift—instead of Beyoncé, who was nominated for the same award but lost—did not deserve the honor she was literally in the process of accepting?

On February 7, 2017, Mitch McConnell interrupted Senator Elizabeth Warren's speech in a near-empty chamber, as debate on Jeff Sessions' nomination for US Attorney General headed toward an evening vote. McConnell stated that Warren breached Senate rules by reading past statements against Sessions from figures such as the late Senator Edward M. Kennedy and Martin Luther King's deceased widow, Coretta Scott King.

In order to silence Warren, McConnell cited Rule 19, an arcane provision in the Senate rules which had only been invoked in two previous obscure instances, once in 1902 and once in 1979. Warren was taken aback and said she was "surprised that the words of Coretta Scott King are not suitable for debate in the United States Senate." When she asked to continue her remarks, Mr. McConnell objected.

"Objection is heard," said Senator Steve Daines, Republican of Montana, who was presiding over the chamber at the time. "The senator will take her seat." It was if he was disciplining a small child and not a distinguished senator.

Rare is the woman who hasn't experienced similar humiliation, but we don't usually experience it on national television, in the US Supreme Court, or on the floor of the US Senate. While McConnell, West, and the rest of them would surely claim otherwise, their actions illustrate what has been attested by women across a range of professions[11]: *men want us to shut up and take our seats.*

None of these women is the type to cave easily, nor suffer the self-consciousness many women would feel in these situations. Yet despite all of their accomplishments and experience with public confrontation, men were still able to silence them. It can happen to any of us, and it's not going away.

THE SPECIAL CASE OF MANSPLAINING

In her essay "Men Explain Things to Me"—the piece that later inspired others to coin the term "mansplaining"—author Rebecca Solnit concluded that, "Most women fight wars on two fronts, one for whatever the putative topic is and one simply for the right to speak, to have ideas, to be acknowledged to be in possession of facts and truths, to have value, to be a human being."[12]

Males prefer to have their primacy unchallenged. Solnit opens her essay by recalling the night when a silverback ("an imposing man who'd made a lot of money") kept her and a friend waiting at the end of a party he was hosting so he could talk to Solnit. He had heard that she'd written some books, and when she began to tell him about her latest one, the silverback cut her off to talk about the "very important" recent book on that same topic. As he talked about it, Solnit's female friend sitting at the table kept saying, "That's her book."

It took several tries before the man got the gist:

> *[My friend] had to say, "That's her book" three or four times before he finally took it in. And then, as if in a nineteenth-century novel, he went ashen. That I was indeed the author of the very important book it turned out he hadn't read, just read about in* The New York Times *Book Review a few months earlier, so confused the neat*

categories into which his world was sorted that he was stunned speechless—for a moment, before he began holding forth again.

That vignette would be hilarious if it wasn't both true and tragically typical.

It's true that a man *could* mansplain you without technically interrupting you. But the effect is the same: by condescending to explain something to you that you already know—and maybe know far better than he does—the man is reinforcing the idea that he's the knowledgeable one who should be doing the talking. Your role is to listen and, I guess, marvel at his brilliance. In another, equally condescending version of "mansplaining," you get to hear a man explain to a third party what you are "trying to say." In my experience, almost all men in the workplace will mansplain and try to manterrupt you. And some segment of that group—the true assholes—will just tromp right over you if you let them.

This condescension and dismissal is what we're up against with manterruptions and mansplaining. Both undermine our authority and influence, and diminish the impact of our knowledge, our experience, and our EQ-driven kick-assets. Men lose out on our enhanced capacity for analysis and our astute comprehension of interpersonal dynamics because they're too damn busy either trying to take control or patronizingly explaining the world to us.

Get used to seeing the ashen look Solnit describes; because from now on you're going to be seeing a lot more of it as you put the following method into action.

STOPPING INTERRUPTIONS AND ASSERTING YOUR OWN VOICE

Manterruptions are attempts in group settings by male speakers to maximize their power by staking claims to dominance. Researchers have found that in professional settings "males assert an asymmetrical right to control topics and do so without evident repercussions," and that "men deny equal status to women as conversational partners with respect to rights to the full utilization of their turns." As was the case when examining the prevalence of the male justices' dominance at the US Supreme Court, here the researchers considered whether these instances of men interrupting women in business meetings to assert their power are simply mirroring the operation of gender-power relations in our society.[13]

The way to defeat this behavior is to deal assertively with male interruptions using your feminine kick-assets of emotional intelligence so you can artfully navigate situations and establish your strength and confidence in any group. Speaking from long experience, doing so is *crucial* for you to establish and maintain your standing among men.

This is another instance when you may need to act the part for a while—to fake it at first—until you have real confidence about yourself in these situations. But the effort and initial discomfort is well worth it.

Follow these nine techniques to shut down interruptions when you are speaking, and build your professional authority:

1. DO NOT YIELD, AND CALL OUT ANY MAN WHO INTERRUPTS YOU

You must have a zero-tolerance policy for interruption. When you are interrupted, shut the man down politely but firmly. Say, "There are a few more essential points I need to make. Hold on to that thought, and we'll turn to it as soon as I'm done," or "I know I will appreciate your feedback, but please hold off until I'm done." You can also try to make the man feel like he is speaking prematurely, with insufficient information, by saying, "Hold on, I need to give you the full picture before you respond" or "You need to let me finish my thinking on this issue, I may already have a resolution for your concerns."

If all else fails, cut to the chase with any of these approaches:

"You'll have a chance to speak, but wait until I'm finished."

"Stop interrupting me and let me finish."

"I've listened to your views, now listen to mine."

"I'm not done speaking here."

"I'm sure you think your view is very important, but so is mine."

It may feel uncomfortable, but calling out the interrupting man works. Former Google CEO Eric Schmidt will no doubt think twice about manterrupting after he was called out for repeatedly interrupting US Chief Technology Officer Megan Smith, the only woman on a conference panel with him. (Irony of ironies, the panel was discussing how diversity leads to more innovative ideas.[14])

2. DROP THE CAVEATS

Hedging conveys uncertainty and self-doubt; the self-deprecating language discussed in Chapter 5 bears repeating here: women should use empowering language that exudes confidence.

Do not apologize before you speak. The word "sorry" should be banished from your vocabulary. Do men ever say it before speaking? Women sometimes preface their remarks with "In my opinion" or, worse still, "I'm not sure, but I think." Don't provide a caveat to what you are about to say. It's hard enough to get men to listen to women—don't make it harder by giving them a reason to discount what you're about to say.

Don't sabotage your own right to be taken seriously. If you have something to contribute, don't question it, just say it. I am not suggesting that you speak—as men too often do—just to hear yourself talk. But if you have a position or a plan worth sharing (and I know you do), put it out there.

3. REMEMBER THAT BODY LANGUAGE MATTERS

Make your physical presence known. Use the strategies that men already use: lean forward at the table, point to the person you've chosen to acknowledge for a comment. Stand up and walk to the front of the room, put the flat of your hand on the table to make a point as you look someone squarely in the eye—whatever it takes. Not only do these high-power poses make you appear more authoritative, but research suggests they increase your testosterone levels, and thus your confidence. Men tend to interrupt women more often when we lean away, smile, or don't look at the person we are speaking to. Look them in the eye, lean forward, and take yourself seriously if you want to be heard.

4. PAY ATTENTION TO YOUR WORD CHOICE

Because of deep-seated gender differences in the way people speak, men tend to be more assertive, direct, and succinct. This isn't just anecdotal observation—linguists have done careful studies of things like the verb tenses and positive versus negative words used by both genders. Women tend to use more affirmative and engaging speech, and relate experiences and emotions using personal pronouns and intensive adverbs. While this may reflect a greater range of empathy in women, among men this kind of language is often perceived as weak, unassertive, and tentative.

When each of the female justices on the Supreme Court first came on board, she tended to frame her questions politely, starting with phrases such as "May I ask" or "Excuse me," or by specifically addressing the advocate by name. Sadly, this respectful conduct provided an opening for a male justice to jump right in before the female justice could get to the meat of her question. As female justices became more experienced, they altered their speech, refraining from politeness. Now, women justices, and especially Justice Ginsburg, start off with more assertive language and more aggressive, direct speech patterns to prevent male justices from butting in.

When you're among men, as you will be in most professional settings, speak with assurance and force. Don't be wishy-washy or timid—use words with vitality. Furthermore, use shorter sentences so your breaths in between aren't as long, making it harder for men to interrupt you. Be sure to speak with conviction, using words like "know" instead of "believe," and "will" instead of "might."

5. STOP NODDING AND AGREEING

When a woman nods, she simply means, "Go on, I'm listening." But a man will interpret a nod as agreement with whatever point he's making. (It's not hard to convince most men that they're right.)

Similarly, when a man mentions something he knows, it's a bid to establish his status. In response, a woman will acknowledge the man's point, thinking that she will, in turn, be expected to share, and that a connection will be made. Not so. The man takes her agreement as submission to his higher status. Take note of your congenial nature—women's habits of politeness and social facilitation are misconstrued as supporting male dominance. Instead of nodding your head, be ready to challenge and question.

6. SPEAK UP

You don't have to yell, but you do need to be heard. The booming voice of my first mentor, Bill Vaughn, gave him an automatic advantage in meetings and the courtroom, and I would have been lost if I had let that shut me up or torpedo my confidence. If you're too meek, you may be drowned out by loud men, or pitch your idea too tentatively, only to have a man repeat it with authority and then get the credit. Learn to speak up boldly, firmly, and with confidence.

7. LEAD THE MEETING AND SET THE AGENDA

Whenever possible, make a point of being the one who calls and runs the meeting; it's that much harder for a man to talk over you if he's sitting in your office. Draw up an agenda so you can dictate the issues you want to discuss and the order in which the discussion takes place. If someone else calls the meeting—or grabs control of it—and you think they are leading the group astray, step up and point out firmly why that person's approach is not the best way.

If you're delivering harsh feedback to the big boss, as I described in the chapter on using your feminine wiles, the fact that you're a woman may actually help you get your point across. In other cases, it's useful to build consensus ahead of time, discussing the main issues with the other players separately until you have formed a group of supporters. Regardless, you need to have a plan and execute it, or you'll be drowned out by the male egos in the room.

8. AMPLIFY OTHER WOMEN WHEN YOU CAN

In her article on Trump's interruptions of Clinton, Jessica Bennett noted that women working in the Obama administration used a technique of "amplification" to support one another when they were being ignored by the men—the majority—in the meetings they attended. Washington Post correspondent Juliet Eilperin described the practice like this: "When a woman made a key point, other women would repeat it, giving credit to its author. This forced the men in the room to recognize the contribution—and denied them the chance to claim the idea as their own."[15]

My own experience in Big Law, usually with no other women in sight, made me extremely self-reliant—and I want you to be self-reliant too. But if you hear a worthy woman colleague who's making a good point, chime in with your support. Chime in twice as loud if a man tries to derail her, talk over her, or take credit for her idea. While it's inevitable that you have to spend most of your time and effort looking out for yourself, it's good to pay it forward when you can by making it harder for men to pull their bullshit.

9. BE PREPARED TO DEAL WITH PUSHBACK.

Men don't like to be challenged, and they don't like having to revise their thinking—including their idea that women's ideas are worthless. Be prepared for the interruptions to continue, and keep fighting back. You have every right to have your ideas heard and to have your savvy and confidence rewarded just like the men.

We are not going to let men get away with steamrolling us, talking down to us, or stealing our ideas. In meetings, we will eschew social politeness and use only terms that convey strength. We will call out interrupters, use empowering language, speak with conviction, make eye contact, avoid long pauses, and insist that we be heard.

It's up to you to reorient the power dynamic by changing your language and demeanor to make it clear that you will never tolerate condescension. From now on, you're going to stop interruptions cold—every single time.

CHAPTER 11

ISOLATE AND NEUTRALIZE ASSHOLES

"Before you diagnose yourself with depression or low self-esteem, first make sure you are not, in fact, just surrounded by assholes."

—@DEBIHOPE[1]

- *Do you have to deal with assholes at work? Are any of these assholes your boss or someone who can negatively affect your career?*
- *Do you have effective survival techniques for dealing with these assholes?*

THIS CHAPTER IS ABOUT ASSHOLES.

To be clear, I'm not talking about the many men who are tone-deaf, arrogant, insensitive, or sexist. While that description may perfectly fit the hordes of men you have to deal with in business, I'm referring to *bona fide* assholes—that special category reserved for men whose conduct is unrelentingly detestable.

Some of these men are drunk with perceived power and the knowledge that they stand at the top of their company's hierarchy, or at least their little piece of it. Some are born misogynists, who are as drunk on their own gender as they are on their position. Either way, they are men who feel entitled to treat their underlings as morally inferior and disposable. They are unfailingly narcissistic, aggressive, mean, impatient, and oblivious to others.

They are, simply stated, assholes.

Regrettably, assholes are not limited to men above you in the structure of your organization—the bosses, department heads, chairs, team leaders, C-suite executives, managers, and owners that make up the farm teams for the asshole major leagues. You can also find assholes in the ranks of demeaning and disrespectful colleagues, underlings, clients, and customers. And they can just as effectively damage your productivity, undermine your reputation, and destroy your sense of well-being.

The author of the *Asshole Survival Guide*, Bob Sutton, lays out in an interview the three kinds of behavior that assholes use: "The first is when everything you do is constantly challenged, critiqued, or responded to by the asshole,"[2] either by verbal attack or, without using words, by his expression of scorn or incredulity that you could be so stupid. "The second kind is beyond disapproval; it's treating someone as less of a human-being, when an asshole makes clear that you are beneath them" or of such little import as to be completely unnoticed. And "the third is backstabbing," badmouthing, belittling, and undermining you behind your back.

What is going on in the psyche of these assholes that causes them to act this way? It's all about power, influence, and entitlement. (Does this sound like the components of misogyny?) Aaron James, the author of *Assholes: A Theory*, provides three criteria for when someone meets the asshole standard: first, "they help themselves to special advantages in cooperative life" such as showing up late for meetings without apology, failing to yield the floor to other speakers, or deciding they don't need to evacuate during a fire drill or that they are entitled to park in a prohibited zone. Second, "they do these things out of an entrenched sense of entitlement"; only *other* people have to follow the rules, such as not smoking in non-smoking areas or not talking on their cell phones in church, because those other people are of lesser importance, or no importance at all. And third, "they use their sense of entitlement to justify their behavior and deflect any complaints that may arise,"[3] again because they are above the rules, which were made for other, lesser people.

When you are the target of these assholes' behavior, you are left feeling humiliated, demeaned, and disrespected. It sure as hell doesn't motivate you to go the extra mile for the asshole or even to show up for work. Instead, his behavior undermines every aspect of your performance, including your productivity, your sense of camaraderie with your colleagues, your creativity, your motivation, and your sense of well-being. The negative effect on victims of abuse from assholes can even result in physiological symptoms such as high blood pressure, exhaustion, and sleep problems, and psychological manifestations such as anxiety and depression.[4]

ASSHOLES VERSUS SILVERBACKS

Facing down assholes is a far different battle than simply coping with "jerk" behavior from a typical alpha male. Many silverbacks will try to push you around, undercut you, and patronize you, both as a demonstration of their power and as a reflection of their unthinking misogyny. We've already talked about how to deal with that kind of garden-variety alpha male jerkiness: you use your emotional intelligence to read situations, pick your battles, and, when you need to put a jerk in his place, you choose how to do it—sweetly, matter-of-factly, or forcefully. Generally, this leads to an improved working relationship, perhaps even some measure of mutual respect, while making it clear that there are boundaries he cannot cross.

But with *real* assholes? No chance. According to Professor James, an asshole, with his "entrenched sense of entitlement,"[5] needs his ego gratified at every turn, and enjoys lording it over his victims in demeaning, degrading ways. In these cases, you can forget about establishing mutual respect: you have to implement survival strategies. Abusive assholes like my one of my firm's senior partners, or Donald Trump, *simply do not change.*[6]

True assholes call for entirely different rules of engagement.

WINNING IS THE BEST REVENGE

Big Law is a particularly ripe field for world-class assholes. Fortunately, it's also an arena where sometimes you get a truly decisive outcome that puts an asshole in his place—and there are few things in my life more satisfying than besting a true asshole.

Earlier I described the $30 billion BCCI banking corruption case as "contentious," but that doesn't begin to do it justice. The case was *ugly*. Shortly after I took the defense lead, my O'Melveny partner Bob Vanderet introduced me to the lead opposing counsel. It was a moment that offered a pristine example of an alpha asshole in his natural habitat.

The opposing attorney was possibly the most flamboyant and wealthy plaintiffs' class-action lawyer in the United States. Since Bob had opposed this lawyer in many cases and had established a solid relationship with him, he offered to introduce us.

Cases like these can go on for years. It's not unheard of for lawyers from both sides of a case to spend thousands of hours together. And while this lawyer and I would be rivals in the courtroom, this was a routine call to say hello—a common courtesy between professionals. I had never met him before, but I expected some trite professional pleasantries to start off what would likely be a long working relationship.

We met in Bob's office and called my opposing counsel on a speakerphone. Bob said, "I'm calling to introduce you to my partner, Linda Smith, who is going to lead up the defense for Pricewaterhouse UK in the BCCI case."

Without missing a beat, a voice crackled loudly from the speaker and echoed through the room: "Linda I'm going to take this case and shove it up your ass."

Now, I can appreciate *tough*. I *am* tough. But when this lawyer was completely uncouth from his opening salvo, he went straight to *asshole*. From then on, I would never give him the benefit of the doubt.

This class action lawyer, of course, wasn't the first or the last asshole I've tangled with. Clients, opposing counsel, competitors and even jury consultants can all make the grade. But what he didn't know was that I've had some of my most satisfying encounters jousting with the likes of him. I'm competitive by nature, so I enjoy any legal duel. And if that means sticking a lance into an asshole's oversized ego, all the better.

With this man, it was especially satisfying when, many months later, the entire case was thrown out ... and he was paid nothing. I never had to say, "Now who's had this case shoved up their ass?" He knew.

Assholes won't respond to reason, and they are devoid of empathy. Exact your revenge on them by achieving your goal: total victory.

USE ASSHOLES TO FIRE YOURSELF UP

An asshole will provoke you any way he can, and the wrong response can be the reward that encourages him. Give nothing back to the asshole—no spike of anger or grimace of pain. That only provides ammunition for his next attack. Let every abusive remark and every underhanded ploy stimulate you to work even smarter and harder than before.

Years ago, I led the team representing the Hollywood Foreign Press Association (HFPA)—best known as the group that gives out the Golden Globes—in a nasty legal action. In a case that drew worldwide attention, the HFPA was fighting a big production company that was trying to argue that they had *perpetual* rights to the annual Golden Globes award show. Everywhere we turned in that case, my team and I faced one of the sleaziest, most conniving lawyers you can imagine; it was as if one of our opposing counsel and representatives of his client were trying to embody every single negative stereotype about backstabbing Hollywood executives.

There was no tactic too dirty for this particular lawyer. He lied constantly and was personally vicious to everyone he encountered. He always looked to gain any advantage, no matter who he had to run over or what corners he had to cut. His behavior was so foul that when it was time for a deposition or other action, we would actually draw straws; the loser had to deal with him.

I'd be damned if I was going to let him beat me. Each time he attacked, I dug in deeper. When he tried to pull a fast one, I made it my business to outsmart him. When he lied in court, I unflinchingly set the record straight. My favorite instance was when he asked to have the record reflect that I was "towering" over a witness to intimidate him. (Remember, I stand not even five feet tall.) I rebutted him by saying, "Let the record reflect that counsel cannot tower over the witness because she is the same height when standing as he is when sitting."

I met his every attempt to manipulate the situation or the evidence with creative strategies and blunt, unambiguous facts. And you'd better believe I took great relish every time I bested him.

Redirect the anger, frustration, and outrage you feel when you are the victim of an asshole. Use it to energize yourself instead of feeling demeaned and degraded. Channel the emotional heat generated by the interaction to add to your strength.

When an asshole tries to get under your skin, don't get mad, get even.

DON'T LET THE BASTARDS GRIND YOU DOWN

That may be easy to say but hard to live by. Assholes are skilled at getting under your skin; they know exactly what buttons to push to maximize your torment. Armed with powerful weapons, they will wear you down by constantly demeaning and oppressing you until your rage and misery overwhelm you. That's when you need to use all your willpower and self-control not to lash out or fall apart. Your mission is to remain stoic. Either don't respond at all or come back with a measured response that does not trigger retaliation. Do not let the asshole know that he is getting to you.

Keep in mind that this won't make an asshole stop. He cannot help himself. But if you let him know he's getting under your skin, he will up the ante and become even more loathsome and infuriating. He thinks of you as the tuna, and himself as the shark. Smelling blood in the water will only cause him to accelerate his attacks.

Do not give in to hysteria or lash out. (Misogynistic assholes *love* to accuse women of being "hysterical" if they show the slightest hint of emotion.) If an asshole explodes at you, it's going to be tempting to explode right back, and it will feel maddening when you don't. But you have to calmly travel that high road, or you're playing right into his hands.

It's perfectly fine to feel fury, fear, and teeth-grinding frustration—but only on the inside. In fact, feeling like that is a sign of your own humanity: a decent person *should* find it upsetting to deal with a man who lacks basic civility, or, in the case of my opposing counsel in the HFPA case, even the vaguest allegiance to ethical behavior. Feel free to vent those feelings privately, but put up a brave front whenever the asshole is around. If you need to cry or scream with rage, do it in a safe space.

One of the best ways to achieve stoic calm in the moment is to focus on the facts, not the personalities. So what if the asshole just called you a "bitch" and said your plan for the project was stupid? Ignore the "bitch" part—you won't change his mind about that anyway—and calmly marshal the evidence in favor of your plan.

Maintain your emotional detachment. Develop your psychological armor. They are crucial survival mechanisms when dealing with an asshole. Never throw gasoline on his flaming narcissism, entitlement, arrogance, and misogyny by handing him control of your emotions.

PRACTICAL CONSIDERATIONS FOR DEALING WITH ASSHOLES—ESPECIALLY YOUR BOSS

It's easier to deal with an asshole who's openly your opponent, as with my legal adversaries mentioned above. It's harder when the person is inside your organization. Even the men you supervise, if they are socially adept backstabbers, can undermine you by pretending to agree with your ideas and then not implementing them, or implementing them in a way calculated to cause them to fail. They may even do the complete opposite of what you wanted. Hardest of all, however, is when the asshole is your boss. So, what do you do about it?

First, try to limit the frequency and duration of exposure to the asshole's abuse. Do what you can to reduce your facetime by eliminating encounters with the asshole at meetings, in the office, or at work-related social events whenever possible. Change your lunch hour or where you eat, move to an office or cubicle farther away from the asshole, or attend meetings through conference calls. If you must attend the same meeting in person, at least sit as far away as possible, and on the same side of the table as the asshole to eliminate eye contact.

Second, outmaneuver the asshole if possible. If he's shrewd, be even shrewder. Figure out his strengths and weaknesses, along with his place in the power structure, so you'll know where and when to make your move. Go above his head, if you can.

Third, enlist allies for your cause. Most assholes are equal-opportunity abusers, and it's unlikely that you are the only victim. Find the others and band together. A good organization won't let a man like that continue to poison those around him. Professor Sutton puts it this way: "It is far more difficult for management—or a judge—to dismiss a complaint from a group of victims than a single victim." Sutton goes on to cite detailed research that "suggests that people who work in concert with others to battle back experience less distress, are more likely to keep their own jobs, and are more likely to force bullies out."[7]

Fourth, document his asshole behavior. When confronted with a "he said/she said" situation, you need to be able to cite his abuse, chapter and verse. Save your emails, along with any writings and social media exchanges, and keep detailed notes of all your in-person interactions. If the guy is bad enough that he deserves to be fired, you should be prepared to provide evidence that your claims are fully justified.

Fifth, if you choose to confront him, do it in a public setting, not behind closed doors. Ideally, this would come at a moment when you have allies present to back you up. Always keep in mind that assholes can be vindictive and venomous when crossed, and may lash out at you and your allies.

No matter what this despicable man has done to tear down your psyche, follow the rules discussed above: channel your anger, adopt a composed, rational manner, and muster all your facts. You can speak with carefully controlled force, but no yelling, name-calling, or abusive language. You want to be perceived as a fair-minded person simply seeking just treatment and not as vengeful or irrational.

Finally, recognize your own limits. You can't expect an asshole to change his ways. Don't be like Sisyphus, forever pushing the same rock up that hill; if you can't force an asshole boss out of the organization—or at least out of your chain of command—the smartest thing to do for your career progression and your mental health may be to move on to another job. If it comes to that, channel your righteous anger into your work so that you will shine in your next role.

These strategies may not feel quite as satisfying as beating a sleaze ball opposing counsel in open court, but they may well result in dealing the asshole a stunning or, in career terms, lethal blow.

CHAPTER 12

DEALING WITH MEN WHO THINK WITH THEIR DICKS

"The academy ousted the powerful Hollywood producer [Harvey Weinstein] over multiple abuse allegations, prompting social media users around the world to proclaim a simple idea: that sexual abuse is a common experience in women's lives. The tweets [hashtagged #MeToo] and other social media posts—mostly from women, but also other survivors—describe a culture of silence around sexual assault."

—SARAH MCCAMMON, National Public Radio[1]

- *How do you decide whether a behavior is sexual harassment, not just office banter or "boys will be boys"?*
- *Have you been sexually harassed? Did you speak out or report it?*
- *Were you afraid to report it for fear of slut shaming, retaliation, or termination?*
- *Do you have strategies for stopping a sexual harasser without losing your job?*
- *Are you aware of your company's sexual harassment policy and your rights under the law?*

MY WORK ON THE TRUCKING CASE WITH A phalanx of shrewd good ol' boys from the South was more than just my introduction to doing business as a young woman. It was also my introduction to major sexual harassment from a client.

Although the case involved southern companies, there were major depositions held in Washington, D.C. The general counsels of the defendant trucking companies decided to attend and use the occasion to meet with their lawyers to discuss joint defense strategy, and so I found myself headed to the capital.

The general counsel of the company I represented was a dour, stick-in-the-mud man with no sense of humor. He was all business, all the time, and I was unable to establish any rapport with him. *This is what we're doing, and this is what I expect* seemed to be his only mantra. There was no personal level of interaction between us, and in fact, we hadn't spent much time together at all—he hadn't been involved in any of the previous depositions, hearings, or meetings.

Before the first joint defense strategy meeting in the capital, he proposed that I meet him for dinner to discuss our positions. I agreed, but dreaded the evening ahead, imagining the struggle I faced just to keep any conversation going with this straight-laced, disengaged man.

Just before I left my room to head down to the restaurant, however, I received a message that said, "Please meet me in my room at 7 PM."

That's weird, I thought. *Why would I meet him in his room?*

Since then, of course, there have been many instances when clients, associates, or other partners have all gathered in someone's hotel room to discuss strategy or to put together a deposition outline, exhibits, or an emergency filing. In fact, whenever I can, I now try to book a mini-suite with a table area where people can work so we don't all need to sit on the bed.

But this was the first and only time I was asked by a client to meet him in his hotel room alone, and I couldn't think of any reason we needed the space or the privacy to discuss our strategy for the next day's meeting. The whole thing seemed *off*.

Nervous, but unsure of what else to do, I went to his room at 7 PM and knocked on the door. He let me in and then sat on the edge of his bed. He was his typical uptight, unfriendly self. He neither asked me to sit nor offered water or a soda. I just stood there in front of him. Eventually he spoke.

"Here's the deal," he said. "I would like you to be my mistress."

It was if the room had just tilted. I felt like Alice stepping through the looking glass. Had I entered an alternate universe? Until this moment, we'd had no personal exchanges. No flirtation, no warm pleasantries, nothing.

He seemed completely oblivious to my shock, and continued speaking very calmly and without affect, as if he were downstairs in the restaurant as planned, ordering an entrée from the dinner menu. "I will buy you a condo in Los Angeles," he continued, "and I will support you. I'm telling you right now that I do not intend to leave my wife and kids, but I will see you whenever I can. I would like you to be exclusive to me." *I'll have the steak, but hold the mushrooms.*

I was absolutely floored. I just stood there, flabbergasted, as he calmly waited for my response.

My mind raced. I was a young, female associate at my firm—a rare thing at the time. I was already navigating uncharted waters, and this case was a big one for me. The stakes were high. But this ... this was ... what the hell was this?

And what the hell was I going to do?

THE NOT-SO-SECRET, DIRTY LITTLE SECRET

In October of 2017, the *New York Times* published a story revealing allegations of sexual harassment against film producer Harvey Weinstein. The cascade of media coverage and further revelations over the coming months simply illustrated what women have known all along: Weinstein is not alone—either in Hollywood or anywhere else in the business world. And his downfall was not caused by his nearly three decades of sexual harassment and assault. Instead, "Hollywood Producer Harvey Weinstein Wasn't Fired for Being a Pig, He Was Fired for Being Exposed as One."[2]

But Hollywood is a unique world where there is a long-standing tradition of "the casting couch," and starlets trade sex for possible stardom. Weinstein is just a stereotypical example of a powerful director using his ability to make or break a woman's career in order to obtain sexual favors. This doesn't happen in "real life." Right?

Guess again.

Sexual harassment based on the power imbalance between male bosses and female subordinates permeates every industry. And the same factors at work in Tinsel Town serve to cover it up in workplaces everywhere. To make matters worse, other men are often complicit, silent witnesses who know what's going on, yet take no action to stop it. According to sociologist Michael Kimmel, "There is this web of enablers. Bob Weinstein doesn't say to Harvey, 'You better stop or I'll kick you out of the company.' Billy Bush does not say to Donald Trump, 'That's disgusting, not to mention illegal.' In the sexual assault world, we often talk about how we incorrectly interpret women's silence as consent. Well, we also mistake men's silence for assent."[3]

In addition to the male conspiracy of silence, men protect other men, raise doubts about the accusations of female victims, or rationalize each other's behavior in any number of ways, including favorites like "she really wanted it," "look at how she dresses," and "she's constantly flirting and dropping hints." These are more colloquially known as slut-shaming.

In Weinstein's case, as with Fox News founder Roger Ailes, Uber founder Travis Kalanick, and SoFi CEO Michael Cagney, it took a village of women to trigger a reaction from powerful men in an industry. Multiple women have to speak out to embolden others to come forward until the accusations finally reach a critical mass. Then and only then do the men in power take the sexual harassment allegations seriously and address the culprit.

Just as Weinstein's conduct was an "open secret" in Hollywood, here's the dirty little secret of the business world: It's inevitable that at some point, no matter what career path you follow, you'll be faced with sexual harassment from a colleague, superior, or customer. That harassment will come in many flavors, from commentary about your physical appearance to demeaning sexual remarks about women in general, from unwanted fondling to threats that your career will be trashed unless you put out. It's awful and unjust, but it's also part of life for women who work.

This was graphically demonstrated after the previously sacrosanct ban on disclosure of men's unwanted sexual behavior was lifted by the slew of celebrity actresses who came forward to accuse Weinstein. Facebook, Instagram, and Twitter were flooded with messages from women who used the hashtag #MeToo to acknowledge that they had dealt with sexual harassment or assault. A tweet posted by the actress Alyssa Milano inspired the online campaign: "If you've been sexually harassed or assaulted write 'me too' as a reply to this tweet." In its first twenty-four hours, that hashtag was used over half a million times by women from all lines of work.[4]

Time Magazine designated the "Silence Breakers" as the 2017 person of the year.[5] The victims of sexual harassment who have used the hashtag to speak out span all races, all income classes, and all occupations. They range from movie stars to Uber engineers to hospital workers to associate professors to aspiring lawyers, doctors, accountants, business women, office workers, and scientists. All of them have lived with shame (*Could I have caused this*?) and other psychological reactions, fear of retaliation, the threat of losing their jobs or seeing their reputations ruined, and, in some cases, actual physical threats against themselves or their children. Men from mighty CEOs to petty bureaucrats have used their power and influence to take sexual advantage of these women.

We need to face and address these stark realities. We live in a society where men still dominate and control the workplace, and where women, for fear of repercussions, are systematically discouraged from coming forward with bona fide accusations of sexual harassment and even rape.

I could kill countless trees writing and raging about the downright unfairness of it all, but we already know how unjust it is. What needs to happen now is *change*, and that begins with you. As a badass woman committed to gender equality, no longer will you go through your career freighted with the baggage of sexual harassment. Working hard and ably is enough pressure. An additional layer of stress and anxiety that men do not share—and which they, in fact, *create*—is unacceptable.

You are bright, accomplished, and hardworking. You also happen to be a woman and do not hide your womanhood. You are entitled to be who you are, and your achievements entitle you to a career. You should, and *must*, be judged impartially on the merits of your performance alone. Full stop.

Be scandalized by Harvey Weinstein—but don't just react to *him*. Be outraged that countless pigs like him continue to debase women sexually. And then step forward to expose the ones you've suffered through or to support the women who have. Only then will we begin to turn the tide of sexual harassment.

Tragically, that tide is a powerful one. We have a long way to go. As of 2017, one of every two women has reported experiencing some form of sexual harassment at work. Even that ratio is a gross understatement, because a significant share of victims of sexual harassment remain silent out of fear of retaliation, worries that their co-workers will make them feel ashamed, and concern that they will be blamed.[6]

It turns out that women's fears of retaliation, slut-shaming, and being blamed for instigating a sexual dynamic are well grounded. An article in the Harvard Business Review confirmed this when it asked the excellent question: "If 98 percent of organizations in the United States have a sexual harassment policy, why does sexual harassment continue to be such a persistent and devastating problem in the American workplace?"[7]

The findings in the article are as dramatic as they are depressing. The researchers found that sexual harassment is deeply embedded within organizations—even serving an important cultural function for some. Those organizational cultures, in turn, are part of a larger national culture that has typically elevated men over women. This, in turn, can lead women to accept male domination as the norm. As the HBR article puts it, "The male-centric nature of our national culture is so pervasive that even many women are male-centered, aligning themselves with men and masculinity to tap into male privilege while attempting (usually unsuccessfully) to avoid the disadvantaged space that women occupy in the workplace." It's just one more example of women trying to blend in by outmanning the men.

Within that cultural framework, sexual harassment becomes inverted so that it's women who create the problem by being "irrational and highly emotional." Sexual harassment policies were written to regulate *behaviors*, most often perpetrated by men against women, such as inappropriate touching or telling lewd jokes. In practice, however, men's power—and the cultural expectation that men's views will prevail—twists this around so that the focus is not on men's bad behavior, but on men's *perception* that they are being unfairly targeted. Thus, simply touching a female anywhere (like on the arm or the back) or making comments about her appearance could subject an "innocent" man to senseless persecution. The result? Women who have suffered harassment are seen as the perpetrators, while the men who have done the harassing become the victims. With that attitude, it's no wonder harassment policies are ineffective.

The lesson? Policy isn't going to save you. *You* are going to have to make decisions and take action.

Which is exactly the position I found myself in, standing in shock in the hotel room that evening in Washington, D.C.

A DIFFICULT CHOICE

I was obviously not going to sleep with him; that wasn't even in the realm of possibility. But as I stood there, for what seemed like an eternity, but was just seconds, I imagined having to go back to the partner—my boss—in Los Angeles and tell him that I had been propositioned by the client's general counsel and that, when I said no, had gotten the firm fired.

That partner, of course, was also the "barefoot and pregnant" joke telling, ex-Marine. He had crossed swords hung on the wall of his office, and a reputation for misogyny. Getting fired would have demonstrated to a fare-thee-well why there shouldn't be any women lawyers in the firm in the first place.

So, there I stood, faced with two unacceptable outcomes.

When I look back on what I decided, I have mixed feelings. I am proud of myself for my creativity in handling the situation. But I'm also ashamed, because I think what I should have said was simply, "Fuck you."

Unfortunately, women are screwed—hopefully not in the literal sense—in that kind of power relationship. The man who's doing the harassing is in a position of influence—influence over your employment, your advancement, and your psychological well-being. In that moment,

I stood to lose a great deal—my reputation, my career, my income. They all seemed to hang in the balance.

Looking back, however, I think it was my pride that was most at risk. After stalling as long as I could, I finally said, "That is an incredible offer. But I can't accept. I don't think I could live with not having all of you, all of the time. If you're going to stay with your wife and kids, that's just not going to work for me."

Unbelievably, that worked. Although he was rejected, he felt incredibly flattered. He assumed that he was such a stud that I wanted him full-time or not at all, and that his proposed arrangement just wasn't enough for me.

He said, "I understand." And that was the last we spoke of it. He stayed on as our client until the case was over.

As for me, I struggled to process not just what he'd done, but how I'd responded. After the depositions and meetings wrapped up, I went back home and told the partner what had happened.

I wondered whether that was wise, given that we hadn't lost the client, and whether I would be reinforcing the partner's sexist prejudice. But I felt that he should know. His reaction was unexpected and very heartening: He was angry that the general counsel had propositioned me and thought that the firm should fire the client. Sometimes we find allies in unexpected places. I told him no, that I thought it was all under control, and we could proceed with the case.

And that's what we did. Score one for the women.

DEALING WITH HARASSMENT

You can see the challenges here. Harassment is beyond difficult, and when it happens, which it will, often there will be no one to help you. The key is to be ready for it when it comes. From the casual crude comment, to the guy with the wandering hands; from the unfunny jokes, to the demand that you have sex or be fired, demoted, or shamed, you need to be prepared. I'm going to give you the tools for the job.

First, some general guidelines. You have to decide how much time and effort you want to devote to fighting sexual harassment. If you rise to the bait every time someone talks about how your sweater clings to your breasts or how you're wearing your "come fuck me" heels, you will do little else at work besides deal with this nonsense. There are easy techniques, explained below, to make it appear that you are completely untroubled by these kinds of comments, that the harasser is a jerk, and that you're cool with your colleagues.

The trickier part comes when casual sexual remarks shift to something more threatening or persistent. Then the question becomes how you evaluate the severity of the harassment and what you ultimately decide to do about it.

Sadly, there is no distinct line, in a legal or practical sense, between office banter and sexual harassment. It's like what Justice Potter Stewart of the US Supreme Court said about pornography: "I know it when I see it." But here's the general definition: Sexual harassment exists when there are unwelcome sexual advances or conduct of a sexual nature (innuendos, flirting, touching) which interfere with the performance of your job duties or create an intimidating, hostile, or offensive work environment.

Let me emphasize this in no uncertain terms: In pursuit of your career goals, you should never have to give up or compromise your principles. No matter what organizational culture you work in, it's not part of the job description to endure harassment or feel like you have no choice but to allow unwanted fondling or to have sex. And, while it is probably ridiculous to even mention this, you should never agree to sleep with your boss or your client to get ahead. You may hear apocryphal stories of starlets launching their careers on the casting couch, but I can assure you that this approach will never help you get ahead in a business career. No matter how smart and talented you are, if you go down that road everyone will attribute any advancement you receive to your sexual charms, not your abilities. Make no mistake: you will never be taken seriously again.

Granting sexual favors will always come back to bite you. Either the man you slept with decides to dump you, his wife finds out and there's hell to pay, he changes jobs or gets fired, or someone above him puts a stop to it and punishes both of you—or just you. No matter what the outcome, you'll be stuck with the "slut" label and end up alone, without your sexual partner/protector. I have yet to know a woman who slept her way to the top—or anywhere near the top. I do know women who have tried. They are long gone.

To combat malicious sniping and avoid fighting a war every time it happens, use your feminine wiles to outmaneuver men (see Chapter 7). Rely on your ability to read the man's intent, and use your instincts to maintain the right balance with each individual man you deal with. No two men are the same: Some men think that if you look directly at them while talking, you are indicating you want to sleep with them, but most men are more balanced than that. React to the signals the man is putting out and pull way back if you think he's being sexually aggressive. Work to distinguish simple teasing, offhand comments, and minor isolated incidents from bullying, sexual coercion, unwelcome advances, outright requests for sexual favors, and other verbal and physical harassment that affects your work performance or creates an offensive work environment. Follow Justice Stewarts' advice—you'll know it when you see it.

In instances where the aggression is minimal, the best approach I've found is to act like a good sport, perhaps with a "Fuck off" or "You should be so lucky" thrown in for good measure. Try to get a laugh out of those around you while making the guy look foolish or crass. A roll of the eyes, a smile, and comments like "What a loser" can often shut down that kind of behavior right there and then. It's how I've handled any number of jokes or innuendoes that crossed the line.

Infrequently, even a "casual" approach to equally "casual" sexism can result in pushback. You may be labeled a bad sport, a prude, or a bitch. Tough. He will back off, if he wants to keep his job.

When sexual bullying or overtures go beyond the minimal, and especially when they come from a boss or client with the power to damage your career, it's time to take serious action. In the rest of this chapter, I'll give you a range of options and show you how to confront a serious harasser head-on when it's time to unleash your inner badass.

Let's start with the direct "fuck off" approach, or as I like to call it, "The Mick Jagger," then move on to strategies for dealing with more direct harassment.

MICK JAGGER CAN'T ALWAYS GET WHAT HE WANTS

When we were both first-year associates, my fiancé worked at a different firm, one specializing in music law. The Rolling Stones were his boss's premier client. When you're an attorney to an artist or a band, you not only serve their legal needs but also end up acting as their shrink, their minder, and sometimes their errand runner. The partner who had the Rolling Stones as his client would do anything to please the band.

This was almost forty years ago, when Mick Jagger was still a very sexy man. The Stones were in town, and my fiancé and I were invited to a party in their honor at the law partner's house in Bel Air. We pulled up to find a mansion with a big circular drive and a front yard the size of a football field. We walked in through the house's giant foyer, which was large enough to hold an entire party on its own, and featured a staircase designed to showcase whatever VIP was sweeping down it.

It was a typical party—a lot of drinking, talking, and hanging around, but with the added thrill of knowing that we were partying with the Rolling Stones. Everyone was flush with drink, joking and laughing, as the music played. *We were partying with rock royalty!* We knew that for years to come we'd casually find a way to tell stories that started with "When I was hanging out with the Rolling Stones ..."

My fiancé and I were in the foyer with fifty of what I was sure were my new closest friends, when Mick himself decided to take his leave. He strode through the foyer, bodyguards flanking him. Everyone stopped talking, as he knew they would, and simply *gawked.*

Mick glanced around, a lion looking for his next prey. Then he approached me and said, bluntly, "You're with me tonight." At that, he spun on his heel and walked on, never looking back, as if there was no doubt that I would obediently follow close behind.

My good feeling vanished.

What an insufferable, entitled asshole, I thought. I wasn't some babe he could just grab for a one-night stand. *Who did he think he was?*

Maybe he expected to hear the clack of my high heels on the marble behind him. Or maybe when he reached the door he was actually going to wait for me to join him rather than leaving me to trail behind him like a trained dog. All I know is that when Mick stepped outside, he turned around.

I hadn't moved. And judging from the look on his face, he was genuinely shocked.

The crowd grew even more quiet, watching this drama unfold. Was I actually presuming to deny Mick Jagger his booty call? Mick stared at me and said very forcefully, as if perhaps I hadn't heard him the first time, "I said you're with me tonight!"

I looked at him and just shook my head. "No, I'm not."

He was staggered, and the other people in the entryway gaped, open-mouthed. Mick continued to stare at me for another moment, clearly trying to come to grips with being turned down (for the first time ever?), and in front of so many people. With no other choice, he turned abruptly on his heel once more, and headed for his limo.

Now, there was no doubt I wanted my fiancé to succeed at his law firm. He was a new, young associate like me. Yet I had just shut down *Mick Jagger*, the firm's preeminent client, in front of his boss. Even my fiancé was shocked—he would clearly have been okay with me leaving with Jagger! No doubt his boss would have, too. But should I have followed Mick out the door and slept with him to further my fiancé's career? Hell, no.

WHEN IT'S TIME TO CONFRONT HARASSMENT

I wish I could tell you that these run-ins were the only times I was propositioned in such a blatant and degrading way, but they weren't. I was sexually harassed on the job many times, in ways that ran the gamut from a federal appellate judge putting his hand on my thigh under the table at a trial association dinner to a drunk senior partner pounding on my hotel room door to let him in during a business trip.

In these instances, the "Mick Jagger" approach is often called for, as are more creative approaches like my response to the general counsel of the trucking company's request that I become his mistress. But don't be surprised if, at some point, you have to confront a harasser head-on.

Mild flirting, minor innuendoes, and the like—that's the stuff you can choose to let slide. But if it goes further than that, you have to be ready to draw the line and fight back. There are things you should have zero tolerance for. No obscene jokes or lewd comments. No touching. No implications that you have doled out sexual favors; no tolerance for flirtations that allow a man to think he's making progress toward bedding you; no allowing a man to imply or state that he has slept with you. And no sleeping with a man to appease him. If a man touches you inappropriately, flirts with you when you've told him to stop, or implies that you've doled out sexual favors (to him or anyone else) as part of your career—it's time to unleash your inner badass.

Here are my strategies to stop a harasser without putting your job in jeopardy. A disclaimer: I'm a great lawyer, but I'm not *your* lawyer. Employment law is not my field of practice, and I don't know your specific situation. My strategies are supported by the law and by labor attorneys, but as I'll discuss below, if this escalates, you may need an expert in the field.

Our first stop is Plan A. If it works, an attorney won't be necessary—you'll be done with the harassment and be free to concentrate on what you were hired to do: your job.

There are two parts to the plan. *First, be sure to document everything.* Documenting the harassment is important for use in your company's internal process, or as evidence in a case or complaint. If applicable, photograph or keep copies of any offensive material you encounter in the workplace. Keep a journal detailing instances of sexual harassment. Note the dates, the nature of relevant conversations, and the frequency of offensive encounters.

Tell other people, if possible, including personal friends and co-workers. If the man is a serial harasser, enlisting the support of other victims lends credibility to your accusations. There are instances where this is effective, as it was with Harvey Weinstein, but it usually takes a village of women to trigger a reaction from powerful men—multiple women have to speak out to embolden others to come forward until the accusations finally reach a critical mass. Then, and only then, will the men in power take the sexual harassment allegations seriously and address the harasser.

If you don't have a village of women to help you take down your harasser, *your next step is to confront him.* He may not be a media mogul like Weinstein, but taking him on can loom just as large in your mind, whether he's your direct boss or the guy who works down the hall. Hang tough. This may sound counter-intuitive, but you'd be surprised how often confronting the harasser works—if you do it right. When you face off with your harasser, you'll be the one setting the agenda. You'll be the one reinforcing everything you say with a strong, confident, no-bullshit demeanor.

Let's discuss this demeanor. Confronting a sexual harasser is hard, especially if that person is your boss or your client. Because you are scared, there could be a tendency to be sweet and coy about the harassment, maybe even a little jokey. You could even inadvertently exhibit behavior that falsely allows the man to believe that what he was doing was okay. (Remember, some men will see encouragement to sexual overtures *everywhere.*) Resist those temptations. In order for this to work, you must be serious and firm.

Start by getting right to the point: Tell the harasser that his actions are offensive, and tell him to stop. While it may be hard to believe, telling a harasser to stop what he's been doing is usually the most effective method of ending the behavior. Even when the harassment is obvious to *you*, the harasser may not be aware that his behavior is offensive. Or (and this is far more likely) he might try to pretend to be oblivious to what he's done when he's been confronted. Let him act as shocked as he wants; *don't buy in.*

Here's the way to confront your harasser and nail him:

- Set the location, preferably in your workplace. If there is a conference room with glass windows or if your office has glass windows, that will work. It should be where you can be seen if not overheard—not in a windowless office with the door closed.
- Do the unexpected: Name the behavior. Whatever he's done, say it, and be specific.
- Hold the harasser accountable for his actions. Don't make excuses for him; don't pretend it didn't happen. Take charge of the encounter and let him and other people know what he did. Privacy protects harassers, but visibility undermines them.

- Make honest, direct statements. Speak the truth, with no threats, no insults, no obscenities, and no appeasing verbal fluff and padding. Be serious, straightforward, and blunt.
- Demand that the harassment stop.
- Stick to your own agenda. Don't respond to the harasser's excuses or diversionary tactics.
- Say what you have to say, and repeat it if he persists. Remember that his behavior is the issue.
- Reinforce your statements with strong, self-respecting body language: full eye contact, head up, shoulders back, chin up, a strong, serious stance. Don't smile. Timid, submissive body language will undermine your message.
- End the interaction on your own terms, with a strong closing statement: "You heard me. Stop the harassment now."

If you are uncomfortable facing the harasser or you want to put an additional scare into him, you can write him a short letter or email clearly stating what he has done and letting him know you want the behavior to stop. Again, no mincing words or trying to be either diplomatic or regretful. Writing is powerful. Words create a record. Hold on to copies of everything.

This should be "Game Over." Problem solved. And bravo to you!

But if the initial meeting or message doesn't work, then move to Plan B and escalate your complaint to the next level of management.

First, take a look at your employer's sexual harassment policy, and the procedure for making complaints. You should use this procedure to promptly report any incidents. If the company's policy says to report it to your supervisor, do that—unless he's the problem. It's not going to help if the policy has you lodging a complaint for sexual harassment with your harasser himself, or with a superior who just happens to be his close buddy.

If that's the case, report the complaint to someone else. Frequently there is an ombudsman or human resources person specifically designated to deal with sexual harassment. Usually, company policies will tell you to go to whomever you're most comfortable speaking with about your situation, as long as they are someone designated as responsible for taking immediate action.

Increasingly, sexual harassment policies include "bystander interventions" as a required response to predatory sexual behavior. This is in contrast to most traditional policies, which place responsibility for reporting harassment exclusively on the target—putting you in a vulnerable position. If you report the behavior, then you are likely to be viewed with suspicion by your colleagues, often becoming socially isolated from your coworkers. Mandating bystander interventions, meaning that *anyone* who witnesses sexual harassment is required to report it, can relieve you of your sole responsibility for reporting and stopping predatory sexual behavior. It rightly places the responsibility for creating a healthier organizational culture on *all* members of the organization.

Then there is employment law. Hopefully it's some comfort that it's not just your job on the line here. Under law, employers are responsible for the conduct of supervisors and managers. They also have a responsibility to protect their employees from harassment by non-employees (customers, clients, vendors, suppliers). Moreover, managers are liable for sexual harassment between co-workers if they knew or should have known about it, and took no steps to stop it.

You can expect your employer to promptly investigate your claim. And under the law, your employer is in deep shit if he retaliates against you for bringing harassment to his attention or for filing a complaint.

Cooperate with any investigation. The investigator will need to know all the details of the harassment, however hard or embarrassing they may be to reveal.

If, based on the investigation, your employer determines that sexual harassment did occur, you should expect your employer to take action to address the harassment. Disciplinary action for the harasser might include oral or written warnings, deferral of a raise or promotion, demotion or reassignment, suspension, or discharge. After any of these, the harassment should stop. You're done, and (again) bravo to you!

If the harassment doesn't end (is the harasser a complete ignoramus, an asshole, or both?), or the employer retaliates against you (big mistake), you have the option of taking legal action. I know that, by this point, it may well seem to you like the male-dominated business world has won. There's no shame in quitting. But staying and fighting—showing your true grit and standing up for yourself and your rights—is a brave act, a self-esteem booster, and a statement of support for all women who simply ask to be able to do their work free from sexual bullshit.

Your first stop is the EEOC (the US Equal Employment Opportunity Commission), otherwise known as Plan C. Before you file a claim, I suggest you consult with an attorney. (If you are unsure about how to find a qualified attorney referral or how to judge the attorneys you interview, just contact me on my website and I'll walk you through it.) You have to file your claim within 180 days of the last incident of harassment. You can't skip the EEOC and go directly to the courthouse. If the EEOC doesn't resolve it (which it generally does), you can file a lawsuit.

Women, you are on your own. It's unfair but true: In cases of sexual harassment, the onus falls totally on the woman. But you can summon your arsenal of resources to defend yourself. Anytime a man harasses you, gauge the situation and choose how you react. If the situation becomes uncomfortable or affects your work, try to defuse the threat. Confront your harasser, and tell him to stop. If he doesn't, summon whoever you can to jump in or go through the company's procedures. Above all else, do not succumb to any bullshit.

It is your right to be as pretty and feminine as you please and to exercise all of your talent and skill without having to put up with disrespectful or degrading behavior. You are entitled to be confident, competent, and willing to draw the line at unwanted behavior by anyone, regardless of their supposed seniority or power over you. That is both the right thing to do and your only path to career success.

CHAPTER 13

SPEAK TRUTH TO POWER

"The truth is always something that is told, not something that is known."

—SUSAN SONTAG

- *Are you intimidated by very powerful, successful men?*
- *If everyone is sucking up to a powerful man by agreeing with him and you have a different viewpoint, do you give your real opinion?*
- *Do you know how to speak up so that you are not abruptly shot down, ignored, excluded from the discussion, or punished for your honesty?*

IF YOU WANT TO ADVANCE IN YOUR CAREER, you'll have to learn how to play with power. The further you go, the more you must to be prepared to take on powerful, egotistical men when the circumstances call for it.

In your work, it may be the self-important, entitled big cheese you'll need to face, but it could be whoever is calling the shots, from your direct boss or team leader, to your department head or the CEO of the company. And that doesn't rule out the powerful egotistical men you deal with outside the company—the head honcho of an important client, vendor, or customer. For now, let's call all these men with the power to affect your career trajectory the "VIPs."

To be clear, VIPs don't have to be assholes intent on degrading and disrespecting you. (See Chapter 11.) They are, however, alpha-male "kings of their world," and have the ego that comes with it, whether that world is impressively large, like a multi-billion dollar company, or the narrower domain of a business with a small number of employees. No matter the size of your ocean, you're going to have to face and navigate your way through currents of ego.

The advice that follows isn't meant to help you simply make waves as a rebel or naysayer. In this chapter, I'm talking about situations which will inevitably come up as you progress in your career—ones where you have to interact with the VIP, and you strongly disagree with his position or approach. Perhaps you're helping prepare him for a presentation or offering comments on a new policy or decision. For his benefit and the good of the company, someone should "speak truth to power" and tell him he's wrong. You need to be prepared for that someone to be you.

The challenge is that VIPs don't expect pushback from anyone, much less from subordinates, and *especially* not from women. VIPs are inevitably surrounded by yes-men who try to please them so they can reap bigger compensation, promotions, and other career rewards.

In our current system, executives are selected for their most competitive qualities (decisiveness and toughness), rather than teamwork and respect for candor and honest feedback. Moreover, VIPs consciously or unconsciously use their position, personality, and sense of entitlement to intimidate those around them and cut off any contrary input. They assume that employees will not question them or company policy. Unaccustomed to even highly constructive criticism, these VIPs take umbrage when contradicted.

As a result, it may feel easier to just go along with the program. But don't buy into it. While being a "yes-woman" might work as a short-term strategy for currying favor with powerful men, in the long run, it labels you as just another lackey. And being a lackey is a death knell for your reputation. If you want to be regarded by VIPs as a high achiever who contributes to the company and deserves to be regarded as a peer of men in power, you cannot be a toady. Devaluing your brand is the last thing you want when you're trying to climb the ladder. Instead, you must demonstrate that you bring valuable insight to the company and that your voice deserves to be heard and respected.

I've had to tackle this challenge head-on time and again in my dealings with top executives, clients, judges, politicians, studio heads, and movie stars who are inevitably surrounded by sycophants trying to ingratiate themselves. These VIPs expect people to agree with them, praise them, and defer to them.

Those are difficult expectations to knowingly challenge. It can be tough to stare down a VIP, but you can do it. Using examples from my career, I'll show you why it works best to give your real opinion and be willing to stand behind it—and how to make that happen without self-destructing.

GIVING THE BRUTAL TRUTH TO JERRY SANDERS

In my experience, there's no better example of a powerful, highly successful man with the ego to match. A legend in the technology industry, Jerry co-founded the semiconductor company AMD and served as its CEO for decades. He was famously flamboyant—he drove gorgeous cars and wore exquisitely tailored suits that set off his silver-white hair and beard. He looked like a modern version of a riverboat gambler, except with a private jet and multiple palatial homes.

During AMD's antitrust case against its archrival Intel, it was my job to set the strategy, manage hundreds of lawyers, and personally coach top executives on how best to give their testimony. It was a job that took all of my grit, smarts, legal experience, and feminine wiles every day, and nowhere more so than with Jerry. He did *not* like to be contradicted, much less told when he was full of shit, but it was my job to tell him so—often using those exact words.

Penetrating the defenses of a serious VIP like Jerry requires a strategic approach. You never pander to him like the sycophants surrounding him. You don't adopt a kittenish tone and say, "Oh, Mr. Sanders, you're so smart and successful." He wouldn't respect you, and you wouldn't respect yourself for trying this approach.

Instead, you use your feminine wiles in exactly the ways we've discussed. You use your EQ-driven kick-assets to find diplomatic ways of telling him what he needs to hear rather than what he *wants* to.

My approach was to frame the issues, show him all the key evidence, no matter whether it supported or hurt our case, and discuss the trouble spots with him. I was respectful, but also blunt: "Jerry, you know how to form and run a microprocessor company. I know I couldn't do your job. But I know how to prepare for and conduct a deposition, and if you take the approach you're suggesting, our case is fucked." With a serious player like Jerry, you can't dance around the truth. You give him legitimate strokes that acknowledge his standing and capabilities in the world, but you also make it clear that when it comes to your expertise, you respect both yourself and him too much to tell him anything other than the unvarnished truth.

This doesn't, of course, mean that things will go as smooth as silk. Jerry gave me plenty of counterarguments about the positions he wanted to take, and at times reacted angrily to my criticism. Our preparatory sessions were demanding and confrontational. But ultimately Jerry did an excellent job—and asked me to defend him when he had to testify again.

As discussed in Chapter 7, as a woman you have an advantage in situations like this. First, alpha males will allow women to confront them in a way no man ever could. The same objections from a man would be seen as testosterone-fueled challenges. Even more importantly, women can employ their EQ to decode a VIP's perceptual screen, evaluate where he is coming from, and then select the best approach to interact with him.

Keep in mind that at some level, speaking truth to power is about showing *courage*. It is often shocking just how deferential everyone else is to a VIP. It takes guts to break that trend, give your real opinion, and then stick to your guns. More often than not, your courage will reap rewards. You'll be perceived as an "honest broker" who tells it straight, is not intimidated by VIP status, and is motivated by the desire to better serve the VIP and the company.

CALLING OUT MICHAEL DELL

Carrying yourself with that kind of confidence will help you command the attention of VIPs. Combining strength of will and extreme preparation with a personal touch will keep you from being browbeaten and help you break new ground in your career. It certainly did for me.

During the AMD case, I had to conduct dozens of depositions, each with a goal of eliciting testimony to support our claims. The most prominent subject of those depositions was Michael Dell, whose company, we believed, had been Intel's main collaborator in illegal practices that prevented AMD from selling its microprocessors.

Dell flat out refused to testify. When the Delaware court that had jurisdiction over the case ruled that he had no choice, he tried to pull an end-run by going into a court where he had home-field advantage. (Thus, sparking my run-in with the federal district judge in Austin who did not allow women to speak in his courtroom.) Fortunately for us, the Delaware federal judge's ruling was upheld, and that left Michael Dell stuck with me for two long days of deposition.

I feel this world is sufficiently hard that you need a sense of humor to survive. From what I can tell, Dell somehow manages to proceed without one. He was joyless and gruff, and those two days were endless. The stakes were high. The conventional wisdom was that we would win or lose based on the actions and documents of Michael Dell's company and Dell himself. Dell, whose fortune at the time made Jerry's look like chump change, was the author of numerous smoking-gun emails that gave crucial support to our claims. Dell needed some way to distance himself from his own damning memos, so he took the position that all of his writings, rather than reflecting the truth, were simply "posturing" to help him negotiate for what he wanted.

To test his commitment to this viewpoint, I began to show him—politely, but unapologetically—one email after another from him to his own senior executives about the company's strategies. He held fast to his position that all of his words in those messages were merely his posturing. When I asked him why he would "posture" (lie) to his own top people when important decisions were being made, he stuck to his story. He even claimed, farcically, to be posturing in his emails to his second-in-command, Kevin Rollins. In a book Dell wrote called *Direct from Dell*, he described his relationship with Rollins like this: "It's a myth that one person can run a company. It wasn't true when I was CEO and it's not true now that Kevin is the CEO. It's essential that leaders share the same vision for what a company can be and the same belief in the best way to get there."[1]

In his book—which I made him read out loud for the record during the deposition—Dell went on and on about how he and Rollins were so aligned that they could substitute for each other in any meeting and finish each other's thoughts. Yet he clung to his position that he was posturing even to Rollins when he wrote a long memo that was very damaging to Dell and Intel.

Where I come from, bullshit is bullshit, and I wasn't afraid to say so. I said it in politer terms than that, given that my words were going on the record, but I confronted Dell's power with the cold truth. It's all recorded on video.

To cap it off, I showed him a memo to the file that he had written to *himself* that was detrimental to Dell and Intel. I then asked him, "Were you just posturing here?" There was a long silence. Finally, he said, "No, that would be like lying to myself." Nailed him.

It wasn't surprising to me that someone like Dell would try to get away with brazen lies to avoid liabilities. Nor was it surprising that the Securities and Exchange Commission later charged Dell with failing to disclose to investors that, to meet its earnings targets, it received payments from Intel in exchange for not buying AMD's microprocessors. When those payments ceased, it used fraudulent accounting to make it look as if the company was meeting Wall Street's expectations. The company paid a $100 million penalty to settle the SEC's charges, and Dell and Rollins each agreed to pay $4 million in penalties.[2]

Michael Dell was no stranger to depositions. Legal matters come with the territory when you run a company that large. What was most striking to me, however, was a conversation I had with one of Dell's general counsel after the deposition. The lawyer pulled me aside and said with some measure of awe, "No one has ever talked to Michael that way."

"That way" wasn't inappropriate, or rude. There were certainly no screaming matches during the deposition. I was unfailingly polite and professional. But I did speak truth to power. I think what the lawyer meant was that Dell was shocked that he was pinned in his lies and actually had to pay the price for his wrongdoing.

This is a stark example of the entitlement VIPs feel and how they expect the world to cater to them. And the outcome of our case—an enormous win for AMD—demonstrates that it's not in your best interest to join the parade of those who play their game.

PUNCTURING THE EGO OF SUMNER REDSTONE

Among other marquee clients, I also represented Warner Bros. for more than fifteen years. I have to admit that working in the inner circles of showbiz added a patina of glamour to the grueling legal work I did for them. The walls of the general counsel's office were decorated with cartoons of Bugs Bunny, Daffy Duck, Porky Pig, Yosemite Sam, and the rest of the gang, all hand-drawn by their original creators. Meetings with the studio heads, Bob Daly and Terry Semel, took place in a private conference room lined with shelf after shelf of Oscar statuettes. Lunch in the studio cafeteria inevitably meant running into movie stars and directors who had come to pay tribute to Bob and Terry.

The VIPs who ascend to become studio heads—and I've met them all—have some of the biggest egos I've encountered (surprisingly, Bob and Terry are exceptions). If I hadn't known that already, it would have been driven home when I represented Warner Bros. in antitrust litigation brought by independent video retailers across the United States. The class-action suit was filed against Blockbuster, its parent company Viacom, Viacom's CEO Sumner Redstone, and all the major US movie studios.

The specifics of the case were complex, and they seem like ancient history now that video stores have become extinct, but the short version is that when the home-video industry sagged in the late 1990s, Blockbuster and other video chains struck big new revenue-sharing deals with the movie studios that were too risky for the independent mom-and-pop stores to match. The mom-and-pop stores claimed that the new pricing arrangements were part of a conspiracy orchestrated by Blockbuster,

Viacom, and Paramount—and their chairman, Redstone—to put the independents out of business.

The first witness called to deposition was a man more powerful than any of the studio heads; his stature in the business world made both Jerry Sanders' and Michael Dell's domains look puny. Sumner Redstone was a self-made man who had built a $400 billion empire. His original theater company, National Amusements, acquired Viacom, which in turn bought or created assets in the form of broadcast networks (CBS and UPN), cable television networks (MTV, VH1, Nickelodeon, Comedy Central, BET, TV Land, CMT, and Spike TV, among others), pay television (Showtime and The Movie Channel), radio (Infinity Broadcasting, which produced the immensely popular Howard Stern Show), outdoor advertising, motion pictures (Paramount Pictures and DreamWorks SKG), television production (Spelling Entertainment, Paramount Television, CBS Productions, and others), and King World Productions (a syndication unit that distributed shows including *The Oprah Winfrey Show, Dr. Phil, Wheel of Fortune, and Jeopardy*!).

For decades, he had evoked awe and fear from the many business leaders who were exposed to his breathtaking pride and force of will. Even among the executives in the case, legendary Hollywood CEOs like Terry Semel, or Michael Eisner of Disney, Sumner was a standout.

Astonishingly, in the days right before his deposition, Redstone had published a book called *A Passion to Win* that contained endless details about his life and work, including his heroic efforts to save Blockbuster through the revenue-sharing arrangements with the studios. In doing so, Redstone had cataloged every aspect of the "alleged" conspiracy in chapter and verse. I knew the plaintiffs would use Sumner's book to do great, perhaps even irreversible, damage to our case.

When the time came to prepare Redstone for his deposition, I sat down with him and his counsel, looked him squarely in the eyes, and said, "What the hell did you do?" He was shocked to be addressed that way, and his counsel sat open-mouthed. Sumner acted mildly sheepish—which was enough to give you whiplash if you had any idea of his typical demeanor. My next question was, "How the hell are we going to explain this—or do you want to just write the independents a check right now?" We went to work.

Once the deposition began, the lead counsel for the mom-and-pop retailers took out Redstone's book and marked it as Exhibit 1. Much as I had done with Michael Dell, the lawyer had Redstone read selected excerpts of his own words, agree that he wrote them, and state that they were true. The whole experience was painful to observe. Redstone was a powerful, enormously wealthy man who always got his way. Yet he wrote in the book that, "As far as the Street was concerned, Blockbuster was worth less than zero. It was a liability and so was I. And the sad fact was that, to the extent there was failure on the part of Blockbuster, it was my failure."

Case closed? No way. I was able to capitalize on Sumner's enormous ego in two ways. First, I suggested that he wrote the book because he had to portray himself as a hero—not a failure—who saved the day by coming up with the revenue-sharing plan. Second, I framed the whole story as being not about the facts or the law but about Redstone and only Redstone. I was able to show that he thought he had engineered the whole so-called conspiracy through his own brilliance, and that he had forced the studio heads of some of the world's most powerful corporations to bend to his will. He lost credibility by looking like a bragging, arrogant master of the universe trying to redeem his image by spinning a good yarn.

It helped that none of the studio executives was going to buy into Sumner's ego trip. These were the same executives that the actors and filmmakers in the studio cafeteria had fawned over—the same men who could make or break Hollywood careers, even for the biggest stars. *They* certainly would not be intimidated by Redstone, any more than I would.

I helped prepare the studio heads for their testimony. As always, the point was to get them to tell the truth while also presenting their testimony in a way that favored our case. Along the way, I came up with a speech that embodied the advice I have been giving you throughout this chapter. While being very direct and ensuring that I could take charge of their depositions, it also allowed me to be deferential to these studio heads, so accustomed to controlling everything and everyone around them.

Here is what I told them—the same thing I say to this day whenever I'm coaching a client from the C-suite:

Before we go over your testimony, I want to discuss a fundamental truth. Business executives and high-net-worth individuals like you are used to being in charge, and in control. They do not want to appear to be anything less than fully in command.

That's why the best way for an attorney to get what he wants out of you is to make you feel out of the loop, like you're unaware of key events, or like you are not in command of the facts or your people. The attorney will say things like, "You may think you are so powerful, but now you're telling me you were not aware that your company had set its prices below cost to drive out the competition." Or they may say, "You're telling me that you didn't know that two of your key executives were committing fraud?" Or they might challenge you even on small things like, "You can't remember the conversation you had with so-and-so two years ago?" or, "You don't remember the month when the board decided to take this action?" The idea is to make you feel marginalized, not in control, or just plain stupid.

Do not fall into their trap. You have accomplished much, and you are in charge. But that does not mean that you have complete recall of all events and timeframes, or that you were part of every executive conversation, or that you always remember exactly who said what to whom and when. There is no shame in saying, "I don't recall" or, "I don't remember" when you don't.

It is far worse—and it will come back to haunt you—if you speculate or guess at the right answer to appear all-knowing. If I asked you to tell me what you had for lunch on Tuesday three weeks ago, how could you possibly remember that off the top of your head? No one could. By the same token, it would not make sense for you or anyone to know or to remember every single thing that happened in your company, even at the highest levels.

If you follow the rules we will discuss, you will be much more in control of your deposition. You can dictate the pace and cut off any frolics and detours by opposing counsel.

One last thing: nobody wins a deposition. This is not your chance to show the other side how right your case is. They will not be persuaded to throw in the towel. We're in a war, and this is just one skirmish.

This speech works like a dream because it gives the VIP the accolades he needs—reminding him that he's rich, powerful, and in control—but keeps him from trying to egotistically take control in a setting where control is impossible and will only lead to failure. It also works because the VIP understands that I'm not trying to best him or put him in his place, but instead trying to steer him in the right direction. I'm there to save him from grief and help him get what he wants: a win. Egotists love winning—in fact, they often believe they're *entitled* to beat everyone they encounter. Using this same approach, you can make egotists *teachable*, at least some of the time, and ensure that they don't waste energy—or endanger your goals—by trying to beat *you*.

I've had much success in speaking truth to power because, as a woman, I've been able to back up my hard work and talent with the emotional savvy to maneuver artfully through the minefields of the biggest egos. Finding a graceful way to craft your message, even for something as extreme as confronting a billionaire with his lies, allows you to face off against even the most powerful VIPs and get them to do things they otherwise wouldn't.

Speaking truth to power in your career may not involve VIPs who command $400 billion business empires, but there are few men in the world who fit that category. Your VIP will likely be someone above you in the power structure of your company, or a significant third party you have to deal with as part of your job. The size of the VIP doesn't matter—the same principles apply. As women, we can speak candidly because we don't trigger the knee-jerk testosterone threat that men do. And as women, we are free to deploy the kick-assets, the range of emotional intelligence, and the interpersonal tools that men lack, and tell the emperor he has no clothes.

CHAPTER 14

ESTABLISH DOMINANCE AND TAKE NO PRISONERS

"Build a house?" exclaimed John.

"For the Wendy," said Curly.

"For Wendy?" John said, aghast. "Why, she is only a girl!"

"That," explained Curly, "is why we are her servants."

—J.M. BARRIE, *Peter Pan*

- *Do you always end up in a supporting role, not the lead?*
- *Do men simply assume they will lead—and you will follow?*
- *When you are the leader, do men still elbow you aside and take over? Do you have difficulty persuading the men to follow your lead?*

SEIZING CONTROL OF PROJECTS, MAINTAINING THAT CONTROL, and convincing the men on your team to follow you is a mandatory part of female leadership. Without that skill set, you are doomed to be forever a team player—a good foot soldier, but never the commander. That dynamic only reinforces male dominance, with women playing a useful but always secondary role. Fail to take and keep control, and you will be left in the dust.

Nobody aspires to eat dust.

Instead, you need to stay on the alert for opportunities to grab leadership roles and hang on to them. Sometimes your shot will come from a promotion, or from a plum assignment where you can prove yourself. At other times, your chance will only come through your own actions: you grab the position and stake out your claim to be in charge. Regardless of how you find yourself holding the leadership reins, however, keeping them requires that you cultivate both your team-building skills and your mental toughness for dealing with competitors and opponents. Don't miss your moment to show what you've got.

This chapter shows you how to establish and defend your dominance as you take control of the vital projects that will define your career trajectory.

WHEN SHOULD YOU ESTABLISH YOUR DOMINANCE?

You're now playing a tricky game in which timing is everything. If a particular assignment doesn't play to your strengths or give you an advantage, don't pounce on it just to be seen as the one in charge. Similarly, if your boss is spearheading the project, it's ill-advised to usurp his role as team leader, even if you are more qualified and have the means to maneuver him aside. Hold off and align yourself with the goals of your boss to help him succeed, sharing your ideas whenever they're relevant for the benefit of the team. Demonstrating that you can be a good soldier and contribute to the group's success won't be your permanent role, but it is part of the drill when you're a junior sister to a band of brothers.

When the time is right, jump at the chance to establish your dominance. Choose the opportunities that will best show your full complement of leadership abilities. While your chance may come in all sorts of different contexts, here are some of the most opportune times I've found for showing off your leadership chops:

- When you're one of a pack in which each person thinks they should run things, but you know that you are the best qualified of the group to secure a favorable result.

- When everyone is bent on advancing agendas that won't maximize the outcome for your company (or client or customer). If yours will, it's time for you to dictate the strategy.
- When you see the team leader taking the project down a path destined to fail, and you know how to prevent that train wreck.
- When, diabolically, the company has set up a head-to-head competition, a "survival of the fittest" test, to see who has the guts and the ability to seize control and run a project.

I've found myself in these kinds of scenarios time and again, particularly at the beginning of any new case where a company has sued multiple defendant corporations, including my client. In those cases, although the co-defendants are aligned against the plaintiff, the issues are complex, and each defendant's role and potential exposure to damages may be very different, so each corporation hires its own high-priced lead attorney. That leads to combustible dynamics.

Co-defendants may want to lay the blame on each other, each one claiming, "It wasn't me, it was so-and-so who masterminded the scheme." That creates a situation any plaintiff would delight in, where co-defendants splinter into factions angrily pointing fingers at each other. Other co-defendants may claim they were not involved at all, or that their involvement was only peripheral. Layer on top of that the outsized ego of each co-defendant's counsel, who invariably thinks that he is a master of the legal universe, smarter than the rest of us put together, and entitled to be the lead counsel. Put it all together, and you have the perfect recipe for a clusterfuck.

Time and again in these situations, I would assess the case, each co-defendant's position, and the qualities of the other attorneys on my side and determine that certainly my own client, but also the co-defendants as a whole, would be better off with me running the show instead of one of those guys.

Yes, I have a super-sized ego just like the men. Guilty as charged. But time after time I had good reason to believe that out of all the lawyers in the room, I had the best grasp of the critical issues in the case and the most comprehensive strategies for how we could *all* win. When you find yourself in a situation like that, it's irresponsible *not* to assert your talent and leadership, no matter how much the alpha males in the room are used to pounding their chests and doing things their way.

As sensible and logical as it may be, however, these powerful men were not just going to roll over and hand me the lead. I had to use all my intelligence, talent, and feminine kick-assets to convince these groups of hypercompetitive men that not only was I the peer of every one of them, but that I deserved to lead the defense and call the shots. You're going to have to do the same.

HOW TO ASSERT CONTROL

When it's time to step up, you need to act decisively, set and run the agenda, and make it clear by word and deed that you are the one in charge. Even if you don't fully feel that way inside, you have to project authority to the other members of the group.

Remember the previous lessons we've gone over about confidence, competence, and how to effectively assert authority. You cannot gain influence over a group merely by behaving assertively, intimidating the men in the room, or pronouncing yourself to be in charge. In order to lead, you need to behave in ways that make you appear to have special abilities for the task at hand and a high level of social skills.

The group must be convinced that putting you in charge gives them the best chance of achieving their collective goals. You do that in three ways. First, you must demonstrate that you have the skills to effectively lead the group, convey the group's vision and strategy, resolve conflicts, read the perceptual screens of the group's members to understand where they are coming from, and inspire others. Second, you must persuade the group that the quality of your ideas supports your superior competence to tackle the task at hand. And finally, you need to make it clear that you are not motivated by personal ambition but rather by your overriding desire to serve the needs of your client and the group.

To pull this off, you have to act with a high level of self-confidence, using the techniques discussed earlier: be a straight-talker, use clear, assertive language with no caveats (never anything like "I'm not sure, but"); speak calmly and authoritatively while maintaining a relaxed posture; make eye contact; and proactively offer opinions and suggestions while cutting off interrupters. These hallmarks of self-confidence will significantly increase the group's perception of your competence to lead the collective mission.

Controlling group dynamics from the outset will also better position you to take the lead. If you can host the first group meeting in your company's conference room, do it. That draws contenders onto your turf, where they don't know the lay of the land and where it seems more natural for them to look to you for guidance.

Regardless of where it is held, take whatever steps you can to run the first meeting. Everyone in the room will have their own ideas about how the project should go; make sure you are the one who backs up her ideas with a detailed agenda that you distribute as the meeting starts. Dictating what the terms of the agenda are —and then leading the discussion through that agenda—goes a long way to putting you in charge. You may want to provide the agenda on paper (remember paper?) because it gives meeting participants something to keep in front of them and write notes on—a physical, official-seeming reminder of your ideas. You can do the same thing less forcefully by projecting slides, or by emailing the agenda to everyone's mobile phone just before or at the very start of the meeting.

Now, your real competitors will be forced to contend with what's on the page or screen. When you put your words in front of everyone, you've outpaced the other contenders and taken presumptive control. Yes, it could be that every player in the room walked in knowing that there were ten important strategic decisions to be made, but you were the one to put them on paper in the order that demonstrated your forethought, creativity, and preparation. That initiative makes it harder for an egotistical competitor to steer people in his own direction (although he will certainly try).

From the moment you say, "Okay, let's dive into the first item," *you have the floor*. You can guide the discussion, size up the people in the group, neutralize any antagonists, and organize everyone around your vision so that your leadership is established.

ASSESSING AND NEUTRALIZING YOUR CONTENDERS

A classic example of this scenario occurred during the *Cleveland v. Viacom case*, where Viacom, Blockbuster, and all the movie studios had to defend themselves against mom-and-pop video stores nationwide. Before I ever got to the point of preparing Viacom CEO Sumner Redstone for his testimony, I had to corral a diverse and competitive group of preeminent senior attorneys on our side, each of whom was convinced that he was God's gift to the practice of litigation.

I decided that I had to take charge of this unruly and unmanageable group to best look after the interests of my client, Warner Bros. The problem was that every other lawyer in the room wanted to be in charge for the same reason. As the only woman there, I had to walk a tightrope, playing nicely with others while making sure that I was actually running the show.

The first meeting of counsel was held in my office (the territorial grab) where I passed out an agenda (the content grab). By taking charge of that first meeting, I guided the group in the direction I wanted them to go and established myself as the de facto leader—for that meeting. From the outset, I paid close attention to the personalities in the room so I could figure out who's who. You'll have to do the same in similar circumstances, asking yourself questions like:

- Who stands to gain the most career benefit by taking the lead?
- Who is the most publicity-seeking showoff?
- Who takes it as a given that he's entitled to rule the roost based on his reputation, his seniority, and his ego?
- How many others in the group will fight you openly for it?
- Who will go behind your back to lobby men in the group for their support?
- Who is especially dismissive of you because you're a woman?
- Who, by contrast, is there to genuinely solve problems and get work done?

- Who is sympathetic to your bid for taking the lead and will support you and perhaps even lobby others on your behalf?
- Who's passive and will fall in line with whoever wins the leadership spot?
- Who's inflexible, and who's open to compromise?
- Who will yield if you treat him as an equal and allow him to assert his own authority at appropriate moments?

You must educate yourself on these issues and other power dynamics within the group to establish your authority and prepare yourself for any coup attempts.

As with creating the agenda for the first group meeting, take it upon yourself to create the first draft of the opening piece of your project, whether it's a legal brief, a marketing campaign, or the conceptual sketch for a skyscraper. I've maneuvered many times in those first meetings, parrying with other lawyers who volunteer their own firms to do the first draft. A favorite response of mine was, "We are already finalizing the first draft for distribution to the group." Remember: the goal is to maintain control.

Even as you keep a firm grip on the reins, you can also create allies by being cordial and inclusive, rewarding people for strong contributions, and emphasizing collaboration. When someone has a really good idea, make sure to give them kudos for it. Even making simple, diplomatic statements like, "I look forward to your comments" or, "As soon as I'm done sharing my ideas on this, I really want to hear your input on it" shows people that you're receptive to input and committed to leading in a collaborative way, not simply by fiat.

Make sure you keep the faith with your allies by fulfilling your promises, honoring your commitments, and exhibiting a strong and determined work ethic. Always be the person who is willing to do the extra work. Show that you're able—and eager—to strengthen the collaboration and improve the end result for the whole group. Those behaviors go a long way toward fostering trust and demonstrating your qualifications to lead, and that in turn reinforces their choice of you as the team leader.

Never condescend to your allies. Instead, treat them as equals—especially if you are dealing with big egos who regard themselves as leaders in their own right. Maintain open lines of communication with the group, and don't hoard information. The group needs to feel included to keep the dialogue, opinions, and support flowing. Choose your battles wisely, letting your allies prevail on certain issues in order to gain their solid support for the important decisions you will face.

Accept that you aren't going to win every time. When you face one of those moments, there are other approaches you can turn to that will still allow you to have influence. You can seek to be part of a governing coalition. Or you can encourage collaborators—and sometimes neutralize potential competitors—simply by throwing them a bone. If I realized that it would help our case, or at least wouldn't hurt our case, for another firm to take the lead on some specific aspect of it, I might answer a rival's assertion of "Our team will do the first draft" with "That's great—I know you will have real insights on that." That way, you disarm your opposition while maintaining your leadership position. That strategy can be used more broadly: divvying up parts of the project and assigning them to different firms (or people) allows everyone to contribute, reduces your own workload, and still leaves you in the driver's seat. Sizing up the parameters of the project, the power dynamics in the group, and the individual personalities in play will dictate when to parcel out pieces of the work, and to whom.

WHEN YOU HAVE TO HIT, HIT HARD

Sometimes none of these approaches will dissuade a competitor who is gunning for your spot. While it's very tempting to go head-to-head in direct confrontation with a hostile challenger, it's best, as the British would say, to "Keep calm and carry on." Getting into a pissing contest is exactly what your challenger wants. If you succumb, you show weakness and a lack of nuanced leadership skills. Far better to pretend that your challenger is simply taking a position that is contrary to yours on an action item. Given your working assumption that the group is comprised of collaborative, smart people, simply treat the challenge as a matter for the group to thrash out and decide. After strenuous debate, if it's clear that your proposal is winning on the merits, accept the endorsement gracefully. Equally, if it's clear that the challenger's proposal is winning, don't hesitate to say, "I hadn't thought of that, but it works great. We'll run with that one." Whenever you manage projects, you want to be forceful enough to make it clear that you're in charge, while allowing everyone a voice and going with the group's consensus about the best way forward. There's nothing to be gained by playing the tyrant.

Striking that balance will convince the group that you have a firm commitment to furthering everyone's best interests—you're looking for the most advantageous solution, not an opportunity to lord it over anybody or to get into a testosterone-fueled fight for supremacy. If you've been actively including others and rewarding them for their contributions, your thoughtful rebuttal of a rival's idea, saying something diplomatic like "I hear what you're saying, but I've seen that kind of argument fail too many times in cases like these" sounds like the voice of reason, not a slam—while also neatly setting your rival off to the side.

If you must oppose a rival head-to-head, do it with full preparation and, whenever possible, with your allies backing you up. If you can deflect the rival with some verbal judo, do it. Using an example from the litigation playing field, instead of saying, "You're not good at making these arguments in court," you could say, "Here's why I think I'm better for *this* one." Instead of "That's a bad idea," you could say, "I think that approach is interesting, but it just won't fly with this particular judge."

If you play it right, head-on collisions will be rare. If it does come down to that, a bit of brute force—"I'm going to do this argument"—works if you've already solidified your position with the group. Rely on your ability to read the group's emotional temperature to tell you whether you have the latitude to gut-punch your competitor. If you've done your homework, set the agenda from the beginning, been inclusive, and demonstrated how capable you are, your leadership will in all likelihood be accepted as a *fait accompli.*

Business is not always a zero-sum game, but over the long haul, there *are* winners and losers. If you want to be one of the winners, your work to establish your dominance will be ongoing: it's never over. There will always be a new project or a new rival to take on. Be ready to do the necessary work every single time.

Keep in mind that people will treat you how you let them treat you. If you respond to intimidation with meekness, you'll always get pushed around. That's why you have to be appropriately tough—and establish your reputation for it—right off the bat. Most bosses and colleagues, and even your competitors, will respect you more if you stand up for yourself when it really matters. You can still use your EQ to connect with people, understand where they're coming from, and win them over to your side. That skill set is invaluable in convincing the group to make you the leader and continue to endorse you. Just keep in mind that when it comes to head-to-head confrontation, *being loved is overrated.*

BUILDING ALLIANCES TO SUPPORT YOUR GOALS

Often, the best way to crush your rivals and make sure people follow your lead is to form coalitions with other power players, all the while biding your time before you make your move. This can unfold in several different ways.

Sometimes a coalition is created in advance by a powerful ally, especially someone more senior who's in a position to command respect, or even fire or demote resisters. Having a very senior ally worked brilliantly for me in AMD's antitrust case against Intel. The top sales and marketing people across AMD were leery about sharing what they knew about Intel's business practices. Intel was the acknowledged 800-pound gorilla in the microprocessor market, and people were terrified of retaliation. Fortunately, I got the kind of introduction we all dream of at AMD's big quarterly meeting, when the company's heavy hitters from sales, marketing, and manufacturing gathered to review results, discuss strategies, and set new targets.

It was my job to interview all of them about their work and gather instances of Intel's misconduct—including bribes, threats, cash payments for exclusive deals, and retaliation against AMD partners. The company's general counsel, Tom McCoy, introduced me to the group as The Meanest Woman Alive and gave the audience members a stark choice: "If you cooperate with her and tell her everything that's happened, when it comes to your deposition or at trial, she'll rip the heart out of the person on the other side. If you fail to cooperate... she'll let the other side rip yours out."

That is some air cover! Even the most senior executives in the room were intimidated. And I played the role of intimidator very consistently at the beginning, walking into every meeting with an aura that I was in charge and *would* be getting every answer I needed. After that, I could soften my stance as appropriate without losing authority. Ultimately, I spent a huge amount of time with those people and ran into no resistance over testimony, even from those who had previously been recalcitrant. As long as you are prepared to execute the authority given, there's no substitute for having the backing of the top brass.

It's much harder to recruit allies on your own, but it still must be done. It starts by being ready to outwork everyone so that you walk into the room as the most prepared person there *every time*—not just on the technical specifics of the project at hand, but in figuring out who the key players are and how best to approach them.

Most often, forming coalitions means building your base person by person. The key is to figure out what appeals to each person's vanity, strengths, values, or shared interests and put that to use. Depending on your assessment of the person, you have a host of tools in your arsenal. You can pitch joining together to reach a common goal. You might use facts, data, and logic to show him that the benefits of working together will enhance his ability to reach his objectives. You can appeal to his emotions, ideals, or values, or flatter him by making him feel recognized or important. Or you can use the classic offer of reciprocity—the old "I'll scratch your back if you scratch mine."

Finally, remember the ancient saying t*he enemy of my enemy is my friend.* Nothing coalesces a group faster than a common enemy. The enemy could be an unsound proposal or policy, or it could be an obnoxious person.

Chances are, there's one guy in the group who loves the sound of his own voice and thinks he's the sharpest tool in the shed—let's call him the Jerk. The Jerk insists on challenging you at every turn with ill-considered or even harmful ideas. He takes you on no matter what you say simply because he's a blowhard who feels the need to dominate. But don't worry about him; give the Jerk a bit of rope, and he'll hang himself. He is a perfect foil. You'll start to notice that he's getting on other people's nerves, too. You'll be able to tell from another man's body language when he's irritated and impatient with the Jerk's grandstanding. During the next break, pull that man aside in the hall and say, "What was *he* going on about in there?" He may start cooperating with you for the simple satisfaction of getting the Jerk to shut up.

If the Jerk is a misogynist, immediately recruit the other women in the group to your cause. If the Jerk's knowledge is limited, find the sharpest man opposed to him and recruit him to your side by telling him that you thought the plans he set forth were well-reasoned and the best approach, and that you and he should work together to make sure those plans are not rejected in favor of the Jerk's ideas. Keep targeting individuals in the group until you have a sufficient number of supporters, and then make your move. Your strategic alliance-building will bolster your bid to lead the group.

Establishing dominance and neutralizing competitors is not for the faint of heart. It's a lot of work, especially on top of mastering the technical specifics of the job itself. Fear not: you can and you will strategically deploy your EQ, your true grit, and your whole range of talents to gain and retain the leadership roles you deserve.

CHAPTER 15

THE HARDER THE CHALLENGE...

"Hardships make or break people."

—MARGARET MITCHELL, *Gone with the Wind*

- *Do you shy away from the hardest professional tests of your leadership skills?*
- *How big do you dream your career might go? Are you willing to tackle the projects that will get you there?*
- *Can you put it all on the line, conquering your inner demons, triumphing over misogyny, and taking on major, risky opportunities?*
- *Once you take on a tough challenge, can you use your true grit, talent, and kick-assets to triumph over that challenge?*
- *Are you ready to reach for the brass ring?*

IT'S GOOD TO BE LEADING THE PACK!

It's very gratifying to be the boss, the powerful one who others look to for leadership. Savor it, because you used your true grit, kick-assets, and sheer willpower to achieve this influence and dominance. You earned it.

Here's the kicker. After basking in your remarkable accomplishments, you can't rest on your laurels. There's always a higher, thicker glass ceiling to shatter. And you can use all of your hard-earned expertise and the confidence you have developed to reach for the next, even more formidable brass ring.

After you finish celebrating a well-deserved accomplishment, whether it's becoming a manager, having your own sales portfolio, making partner, earning tenure, gaining a client, running a corporate division, or ascending to the C-suite, move right on to the next test. Tackle the hardest challenges as you keep rising. Always go for it. Enhance your reputation, prove your worth, vanquish the doubters, and smash through every barrier of male supremacy. Make yourself a force to be reckoned with.

And have *fun* doing it. It's exhilarating to lead the team, overcome all the obstacles, and blow everyone away as you bring home a seemingly impossible victory. It's a sensational feeling to say, "Yes I can. Watch me."—and then deliver.

Here's the best part: after you prevail over arduous challenges and understand that you have the ability to handle them, you realize that you've also developed the self-confidence that you may have been faking in the past. In Chapter 6 we took a long, hard look at the role confidence plays in workplace success, and learned that women have a misguided faith in the myth that if we work hard and demonstrate superior competence, we'll be judged on our merits and receive success accordingly.

Not a chance. A vast amount of research shows that, time after time, *confidence trumps competence.*

But we also learned that confidence is volitional. It's a skill and, like any other skill, it can be acquired and cultivated so that it grows over time when you act decisively and boldly. Women need to stop doubting their abilities, ignore their fears and inferiority complexes, and start taking action and risks. Once you see that you can do something, that bolsters your ability to take another action or face another risk. Action breeds confidence.

And that's exactly what has happened by the time you've become a leader. You've exercised your skills by decisive action and gained mastery. Confidence comes to feel more natural for you until there is no need to fake it—it's just a part of who you are.

That means that when the next difficult challenge comes along, you know deep inside that you can do it. When you say, "I've got this," you *know* that you can back it up—not just with bravado, but with the experience of countless large and small victories over time.

Once you've exercised real power, once you've experienced that feeling, you'll never want to go back to playing second fiddle.

More than that, *you have no choice* but to keep taking ownership and solving the hardest problems if you want to keep on improving your skills and building your professional standing. In order to continue to show that you have "the right stuff," you must take on the next big challenge.

I'm going to pause here to say that, if you've read this far, you know what women are capable of with our kick-assets, and you've learned valuable lessons to help you navigate your way up the ladder of success. You are empowered!

Perhaps you don't want to go all the way to the absolute top, or think that my personal stories from bet-the-company Big Law cases don't apply to you. Neither of those things should stop you. These lessons will help you unleash your power in whatever field you are in and to go as far as *you* choose to go.

In this chapter and the next, I'm going to discuss the two most complex cases of my career. These are the ones that inspired me to dig deeper than ever before to master the thorniest legal issues, the most complex technical subjects, and the most taxing interpersonal skills. These are the cases that drew together everything I've learned—everything I've been teaching you throughout this book—and forced me to become better than I had ever been. I'll highlight a few specific lessons along the way, but above all I want to show you how, when you get to the top of your game, you can muster all your talents, experiences, and kick-assets to tackle whatever project is thrown at you next.

It starts with the wreck of the *Exxon Valdez.*

BIG OIL MEETS BIG LAW IN ANCHORAGE

A few minutes after midnight on Good Friday of 1989, the supertanker *Exxon Valdez* struck Bligh Reef off the southern coast of Alaska.

With its hull breached, the ship spilled eleven million gallons of crude oil into the waters of Prince William Sound—the largest oil spill and the worst man-made environmental disaster the United States had ever seen. It seemed like the end of a world.

Throughout the Sound and down the coast of the Gulf of Alaska, the damage to the state's pristine shores, fish, and wildlife was staggering. Oil drenched or spattered at least 1,200 miles of shoreline. Experts believed that as many as 100,000 birds died, including 150 bald eagles. At least 1,000 sea otters also perished, despite an $8 million rescue and rehabilitation program. Many more species were also harmed, and the economic costs were dire. Among other impacts, the state canceled the opening of its herring fisheries and restricted the annual salmon take, together worth more than $100 million a year.

Exxon, the owner of the ship and the oil that spilled from it, ultimately spent more than $2.5 billion on a cleanup campaign. The company erected booms in the area and worked to siphon off as much oil as it could. Efforts to clean the beaches included hiring 11,000 workers to scour the sand and rocks with everything from high-pressure hot water jets to rakes, shovels, and even paper towels.

Several years after the spill, the native corporations—business entities formed by each of Alaska's native tribes—along with some of Alaska's islands and cities, sued Exxon in state court, alleging that the oil giant had destroyed their way of life by spoiling the land from the shoreline to the mountaintops, killing off fish and other wildlife, and contaminating archaeological burial sites. The plaintiffs in the state action sought a quarter of a billion dollars in damages. This lawsuit was in addition to the federal class action brought by more than 32,000 plaintiffs, in which the jury initially awarded $5 billion in punitive damages against Exxon.

The oil company had already admitted liability for the spill after it had been established that the captain of the *Exxon Valdez*, Joseph Hazelwood, had not supervised the ship's passage through Prince William Sound, but instead had been asleep in his bunk after drinking alcohol. The third mate piloting the ship steered it onto the reef. The question for the jury in the state case was whether the native corporations and other plaintiffs had been damaged by the spill and, if so, by how much.

This case was tailor-made for a specialist in "bathtub law" like me. You won't find Bathtub Law listed alongside Torts, Contracts, Civil Procedure, and the other courses in a law school syllabus; it's the term I use to describe the unique spectrum of my litigation career. In an age when most professionals specialize, I've been fortunate enough to take on complex cases across diverse practice areas. I was one of a very small number of litigators at my firm who were members of multiple practice groups—antitrust, securities fraud, class actions, entertainment, and commercial litigation, to name a few. Ultimately, we decided to form our own group, called the Business Trial Litigators, so we could take on all kinds of high-risk, cutting-edge cases. It's why I'm able to share war stories from complex bet-the-company cases across wildly differing industries, ranging from accounting and high tech, to trucking and show business.

Why bathtub law? When I start a new case, I don't know the law or the facts walking in the door. I need to learn all about the industry, the facts of the case, and the applicable statutes and precedents. I fill the bathtub to the brim with that information and immerse myself, calling on colleagues and clients with specialized knowledge to share their expertise as needed. When the case is done—often years later—I pull the plug and let the bathtub drain until it's completely empty. Then I take on a new case and start filling it again.

Given my diverse work, you can see why "fake it until you make it" has been one of my guiding principles. I worked hard and learned a lot in law school, but my very first big case had me working with the chairman and CEO of IBM and leading a team of forensic accountants on its behalf. I knew nothing about computer technology, antitrust monopoly, or fair and unfair business competition. But I mustered my grit, applied the research skills and people skills that I did have, and channeled it all into months of hard, collaborative work. That cycle has repeated over and over in my career; along the way, my fearlessness has grown in tandem with my legal knowledge and leadership skills.

For Exxon, filling the bathtub meant learning about the oil business and tanker shipping, and getting my head around complex topics in aquatic and fishing sciences, geology, toxicology, intertidal ecology, and the properties of oil. Then I had to position it all against an understanding of Alaska's geography, politics, and native cultures. At first, it was fake it until you make it. But I was able to grasp all of these issues and their implications by using my smarts and tapping into the knowledge of a host of scientists and other experts.

Then the real fun began.

MAKING THE MOST OF A HOSTILE ENVIRONMENT BY USING EVERYTHING YOU'VE GOT

For the state case brought by the native corporations, I was asked to lead Exxon's defense alongside my then-husband Chuck Diamond and my close friend Randy Oppenheimer. When the native corporations filed suit, Chuck and I decided to try the case together not only because we were both skilled in complex bet-the-company litigation, but also because the location and complexity of the case meant that at least one of us would have to move to Alaska for perhaps as long as a year. Our son was still a toddler, and neither of us wanted to be away from him for so long.

It was a pivotal moment. I could have capitulated, pressured by the external demon of gender bias accusing me of being a bad mother unless I put my son ahead of my career and the internal demon of self-doubt telling me I couldn't balance parenting with an all-in approach to my work. Instead, I silenced the demons, decided I could do both, and we made it happen. Chuck and I, our son, and his nanny packed up and moved to a rented house on a cul-de-sac in Anchorage, where my son had all sorts of adventures—playing outside at midnight in bright sunlight, watching a bull moose in our backyard, panning for gold, and whitewater rafting. Throughout the trial, Chuck and I were around each other more or less 24/7. It was stressful but worth it. (Our marriage did outlive the trial, and ultimately lasted twenty-seven years.)

The oil spill triggered high emotions. The entire city of Anchorage—hell, the entire state—despised Exxon. Our case was on the front page of the local paper in Anchorage every day, and national and international media covered the proceedings closely. Faced with death threats, we were escorted by armed guards to and from the courthouse; everyone entering the courtroom passed through a metal detector. Exxon advised us to not tell people we met in Anchorage who we represented out of concern for our safety.

To say that we were at a disadvantage representing Exxon in an Anchorage court is a major understatement. Even picking an impartial jury was a questionable proposition besides being residents of the area, many of the potential jurors were of native descent and might find it challenging to hear all the evidence in an unbiased way.

And what a body of evidence it was! Chuck, Randy, and I found ourselves trying an extraordinarily complicated case that employed many of our own attorneys alongside a virtual army of experts—scores of engineers and scientists from Exxon, as well as outside specialists who were analyzing the environmental effects of the oil spill and the cleanup in painstaking detail. There were many times it felt like I was taking a graduate-level crash course in environmental science. Among the experts I called at the trial were a toxicologist who spoke of how the water was clean, pure, and oil-free; a biologist who talked about the "critters," his word for the organisms of the intertidal zone, who were alive and well; a geologist who covered the properties of oil, including how it degrades and dissipates so that it could no longer affect the land; and a salmon expert who explained that the fish were back to spawn after their 2,000-mile ocean journey, and were perfectly safe to eat.

The whole case was intellectually, physically, and emotionally grueling. Every day we faced new questions: How could we best demonstrate the extent of Exxon's cleanup efforts? Would cameras installed on the shorelines be able to convey the force of the brutal winter storms? Could helicopters be used to take a camera crew and scientists to the most heavily oiled coastlines to collect soil and water samples? How could we strategically deal with the phalanx of NOAA (the US government's National Oceanic and Atmospheric Administration) scientists enlisted to testify for the plaintiffs?

Despite the daunting challenges of the case, I had a blast. I learned about a new ecosystem, and the methodologies and fierce differences among scientists and other experts. We formed a well-oiled (no pun intended), cohesive team. More critically, I once again proved to myself that I could do it.

THE POWER OF CREATIVITY AND COLLABORATION

During the trial, I was entrusted with proving to the jury that the ecology of Prince William Sound had healed thanks to a combination of Exxon's cleanup effort and the natural weather conditions of Alaska. Mother Nature helped considerably. Throughout the Alaskan winters, fierce storms pound the shores and scour the beaches. Huge tree trunks and rocks the size of Volkswagens are hurled by the sea into the coastline. To survive the brutal winters, the intertidal creatures that live near the coast go deep and stay deep. As a result, by the time of the trial, the coast was by and large clean, the intertidal critters were healthy, and any oil that remained was in a form and location where it could not damage the flora and fauna. The challenge, however, was to demonstrate that to the judge and jury.

If any project in my career cemented the importance of creative thinking, it was this case. We had planned to fly the judge and jury to some of the most heavily oiled and remote locations so they could evaluate the state of Prince William Sound themselves, but the court denied our motion. Now, unable to bring the courtroom to the Sound, I knew I had to bring the Sound to the courtroom. And that was a job perfectly suited for women's EQ.

I knew that reading the perceptual screens of the judge and the jurors and finding a way to connect with them would enable me to tell them a story that was not only true, but also intellectually and emotionally compelling. Like a novelist or filmmaker, I needed to appeal to all of the senses of the jury to demonstrate that the natural processes of the Alaskan winter plus the concerted efforts of thousands of people during the cleanup had truly renewed the intertidal areas. I had to show the jurors that, by that time, if you walked the shores that had been most heavily oiled, you would smell fresh seaweed on unspoiled pebble beaches, see and feel and taste the clarity of the water, find the intertidal creatures alive and well under oil-free rocks, and see salmon spawning in streams that had once been choked with oil. We needed those vivid sensations—backed by hard facts—to counter the other side's case.

Our opponents, however, had vivid sensations of their own. Each day, Native Chiefs came into the courtroom to watch and to testify for the plaintiffs. They looked like they had come from central casting, with weathered, wrinkled faces. One particular chief, who seemed to radiate wisdom, testified movingly about how the native people's way of life and their burial grounds had been destroyed by the oil spill. It was very effective and emotionally compelling—until we were able to show that the chief bought his fish at the local grocery store before the spill and that it had been a long time since his tribe's way of life had included hunting and fishing for survival.

As in my other cases, fostering collaboration across the whole team was critical. The bigger and more diverse the team, the more you need to leverage your EQ and communication skills to create an environment where the best ideas can thrive and each member of the team feels a sense of ownership—you need to create the sentiment that the challenge at hand isn't yours, it's *ours*.

Someone on our team had the "wacky" idea of sending our geologist, David Page, to the most heavily affected islands with a pair of white gloves and a Nerf ball. David traveled to five or six of the islands in the Sound that had been heavily oiled. On each island, to show that any randomly chosen site was clean, we filmed David while he went from place to place throwing a Nerf ball over his head as hard and as far as he could, letting it bounce inland. Wherever it landed, he picked the ball up and, while wearing white gloves, laboriously removed the stones and small boulders covering the area to show the critters living and flourishing underneath. On camera, David would then hold up his hands to show that, after all that digging and heaving, there was no oil on his white gloves. He did this fifty to sixty times on each island, and the result was always the same.

With the court's permission, we showed the video during David's testimony at trial and then passed around his actual gloves so that members of the jury could see for themselves that they were oil-free. It was an unconventional but effective way to make our point that the oil was gone and the wildlife was thriving.

The point is that you can succeed by thinking creatively, maximizing the talents and hard work of the whole team, and conveying information to any audience—bosses, peers, customers, students, investors—so that their eyes don't glaze over from yet another dry presentation of boring facts. The jurors in our case no doubt expected us to argue that the oil spill had been adequately cleaned up, but they never expected that evil Exxon would send its expert to don white gloves and heave a Nerf ball around the most heavily-oiled islands.

The jury and the judge also couldn't have guessed that Exxon's lawyers would be real people with real lives. Through the course of the trial, we revealed by our actions that the company hadn't hired the typical "suits," but rather real people with real personalities to whom the jurors could relate as human beings. At the outset of the trial, we announced that Chuck and I were married. Anchorage isn't such a big place, and we reasoned that if we were seen together outside of court, people might think we were cheating on our spouses. Far from being a hardship, I think that the fact we were married helped immeasurably because it made Exxon seem much more relatable.

During the trial, Chuck and I would take verbal jabs at each other, which the jury found highly amusing. One day, for instance, I went to dim the lights in the courtroom so that Chuck could show a video, and by mistake, I plunged the courtroom into darkness. Everyone in the courtroom sat silently in the pitch dark; after a moment Chuck deadpanned, "She can't work the VCR either."

To show that the intertidal critters were alive and well, our biologist had taken pictures of many of the different species, and we had them blown up on huge poster boards and mounted on easels. There must have been twenty of these big boards, and when I presented this witness, Chuck moved the easels and boards around so that the judge and jury could see them better. One of the legal issues in the case was whether the oil spill had destroyed what's called "the highest and best use" of the land. I turned to the jury as Chuck was moving the boards, and said, "This is Chuck's highest and best use." The jury members cracked up.

They also learned that we were parents of a young child. One Friday during the trial, I was cross-examining a witness on the stand, and the door to the courtroom slammed open. My secretary ran in and whispered in my ear. I told the judge that our little son had been in an accident at his preschool and asked if we could take a break to make sure he was okay. The jurors gasped. The judge granted a recess, and we tried to locate my son and his nanny. We couldn't find them right away, but were able to learn that a bee had stung him below his eye and he'd had a bad, but not life-threatening, reaction. I returned to the courtroom and said I thought I could continue, but I soon realized I wasn't listening to the witness's answers. My mind was on our son. When I told the judge, he adjourned for the weekend.

When we returned on Monday, the jurors passed a note to the judge and asked if they could know how our son was. Chuck asked opposing counsel if he could answer, and they agreed. Chuck said, "I understand the jury wants to know about our son. He had an adverse reaction to a bee sting and his eye closed shut. We took him to a trauma center, and he's going to be fine. While he's recovered, I can't say the same thing about his mother, who is still traumatized."

MAKING THE MOST OF EVERY CHALLENGE

My son healed up nicely—and we won a complete victory with a unanimous verdict. Although we won based on the evidence, it certainly didn't hurt that Chuck and I were married and had a young son, an unexpected wrinkle that showed the jury a human side to the world's third-largest corporation.

Let your humanity show through in your work. You don't have to be everyone's best friend and confidante, but it doesn't hurt to remember that the people you interact with during your career are *people*. You can flex your EQ, have outside interests and a genuine sense of humor, and still be a kickass professional in your field.

In the bigger picture, the Exxon case was a perfect example of *using everything you've got* to succeed. Walking into that case, I knew virtually nothing about oil spills or toxicity in ocean water or the properties of oil and its ability to decompose or the lifecycle of a salmon. I had also never cross-examined expert witnesses from NOAA; in the past, my experts had mostly been accounting or forensic specialists, not scientists.

I didn't let any of that stop me. Drawing on the lessons I had been accruing for decades, I channeled every ounce of my true grit, EQ, mental toughness, and creativity into mastering the new challenge and winning the case. And to this day, I believe that, for all my smarts and talent, it was my feminine EQ that made the difference to me. I used my understanding of the perceptual screens of the judge, the jury, the witnesses, the experts, the client, and our team to figure out how to best deal with them. I knew how to lead and get along with all of them.

Finally, I used my aptitude for being in touch with my own thoughts and feelings and sensing the thoughts and feelings of others. I knew by then that excellence in leadership doesn't rely solely on a list of defined strategic or analytical skills. To be an effective leader, you need authenticity, the ability to cultivate people's trust, and the confidence to inspire them to bring their A game.

You have what it takes to do this. Find the next big mountain ahead of you in your own career and climb it with purpose. Tap into all the resources you have inside you, and every resource you can find around you. Tell yourself *I've done it before* and take the next action that moves you forward, each time honing your skills and gaining more confidence. This is the path to follow to grab the next brass ring.

CHAPTER 16

THE SWEETER THE SUCCESS

"The best revenge is massive success."

—FRANK SINATRA

- *Do you choose to keep climbing the mountain of success to ever-higher peaks, or do you want to "make camp" somewhere lower on the mountain?*
- *Can you be an effective leader who inspires people to bring their A game to your project?*
- *Are you secure enough in your self-confidence that you can risk taking on a new challenge without knowing whether you have all the necessary skills?*
- *Are you willing to tap into all your resources, and self-assuredly ask for help from people who have greater expertise?*
- *Can you muster all your experience, smarts, and kick-assets to take it up another notch and keep rising?*

THIS CHAPTER ASKS A CHALLENGING QUESTION: *DO YOU have the right stuff to take on an even greater challenge, or are you growing weary at facing ever-higher mountains to climb?*

There is no doubt you can muster all your talents, experiences, and kick-assets to tackle whatever project is thrown at you next—everything you've learned equips you to keep climbing those higher mountains to greater success. But the ascent can be grueling and arduous. The choice before you is whether to continue to ascend or to stop climbing. The key is to remember that *how far up you climb and when you stop is your prerogative, not one dictated by the male power structure.*

To make your choice, you'll need to continue to look inward as you climb higher. *Is this fulfilling? Am I basking in my accomplishments? Am I having fun? Do I enjoy leading and being the head honcho?*

I elected to keep rising. Each successive peak energized and fulfilled me—each one represented a victory for me, and, at least in my mind, for the women in my firm, in my profession, and across the globe. When I climbed the peaks, I felt I was leading a summit bid for something bigger than myself.

AMD v. Intel was my Mt. Everest. I was called upon to represent David against Goliath in a case that was—and still is—the largest private antitrust case in history. Was I privately feeling overwhelmed and insecure? Of course. Did I know that, based on my experience, kick-assets, and the self-confidence I had developed over the years, that I could take this on? Yes.

In addition to standing as the greatest case I could ever work on, *AMD v. Intel* serves as the ultimate illustration of what it takes to smash glass and kick ass in a man's world. I had to dig deeper than ever before when I tackled AMD. It was the hardest thing I've ever done, but—not at all coincidentally—the sweetest success I've ever tasted.

Everything in the last chapter about the Exxon case went double for AMD. Every aspect of the case held an unprecedented level of complexity, from the underlying legal issues to the logistics of deposing hundreds of witnesses, many of them CEOs, from different companies all over the world. The team I managed was much larger and more diverse, with hundreds of lawyers and other experts spread across multiple continents. The legal challenges alone, including the formulation of a highly creative theory of liability for anticompetitive exclusionary conduct, were much thornier. The technologies and the commercial dealings at the heart of the case were so knotty that they boggled the mind.

Just the sheer volume of information alone was overwhelming. I had to get a handle on a collection of documents, which, if printed on paper and stacked, *would stretch to the moon and back three times.*

And then there were the players. Our opponent—microprocessor titan Intel—was vastly larger, better funded, and more competitive than the native corporations of Alaska in the Exxon case or any of my previous opponents. The ancillary parties to the case weren't NOAA and a battalion of ecology experts, as formidable as they were. Instead the alleged, but not sued, co-conspirators included every major computer company in the world, including behemoths like Toshiba, IBM, Sony, Lenovo, Hewlett-Packard, and Dell.

Based on carefully developed and negotiated search terms, millions of emails belonging to the most senior executives had to be gone over with a fine-toothed comb, and powerful, combative CEOs and chairmen like Michael Dell had to be deposed at length. There were multiple lawsuits, all of which required AMD's intense participation. In the United States there was a civil case brought by AMD, as well as cases by the Federal Trade Commission and the Attorney General of New York. Regulatory bodies operating under completely different legal frameworks brought actions against Intel in the European Union, Taiwan, Canada, and Japan.

On top of all that, my personal life went through deep turmoil during the ten years that the case ran. My then-husband Chuck Diamond and I, who were co-heads of the AMD worldwide litigation team, separated and divorced partway through leading this unbelievable monster of a case, but kept working alongside each other until it was finished.

AMD was the kind of case that litigators dream of just being part of, much less managing, and it took everything I had to make it work. It reinforced all the lessons I had learned through decades of high-stakes litigation, and it forced me to apply those lessons more creatively, more deeply, and with more insight and flexibility than I ever had.

TAKING ON THE 800-POUND GORILLA OF MICROPROCESSORS

You've probably seen Intel stickers on new computers, indicating that the central processing unit (CPU), or microprocessor, was made by Intel, and you may recall Intel's Blue Man Group advertisements and that distinctive five-note theme signifying "Intel Inside." What you may not know is just how big Intel was. By the end of the twentieth century, Intel's dominance in microprocessors for PCs and servers meant that it commanded up to 90 percent of the market.

Against all odds, AMD finally developed a technically superior microprocessor, making a huge breakthrough when it introduced 64-bit (rather than 32-bit) chips designed to run Windows-based computers. Those chips performed better and cost less than Intel's chips, and for the first time, Intel had to chase AMD to develop equivalent technology.

To succeed—hell, to *survive*—against such an indomitable competitor, AMD had to quickly capitalize on its breakthrough in order grow its market share and be profitable. That interlude of technological superiority gave AMD a time-limited opportunity to forever change its status and reputation in the industry.

But not if Intel had anything to say about it. The company moved into high gear to maintain its monopoly, engaging in a relentless worldwide campaign to coerce customers to refrain from dealing with AMD by, among other methods, forcing major customers into exclusive or near-exclusive deals, leaning on PC makers and technology partners to boycott AMD products, and paying computer manufacturers huge rebates for using Intel.

AMD filed an antitrust complaint against Intel in the US Federal District Court in Delaware, alleging that Intel had systematically used secret rebates, special discounts, private threats, and other means to lock AMD processors out of the global market.

This drama played out all over the world.

MANAGING A GLOBAL OFFENSIVE

Chuck and I knew that antitrust actions involving global corporations like AMD, Intel, and the computer makers were increasingly being played out on a global chessboard. Antitrust regulators in one jurisdiction pay attention to decisions by the regulators in other areas—that meant that actions in other parts of the world could directly impact our case.

Our team put heads together with AMD's general counsel Tom McCoy, who you'll remember as the man who introduced me as The

Meanest Woman Alive to AMD's employees, to launch a strategy of using regulatory investigations from around the world to bolster AMD's litigation in the United States, and in turn to use the AMD case to encourage and assist the regulators. By establishing solid relationships with the regulatory authorities, we gained access to documents that we otherwise couldn't have compelled Intel or the computer companies to produce. In return, we extended every cooperation to the regulators—when someone called from, say, the European Commission, to tell us we needed to make a certain AMD executive available for discussion, or that the regulators needed a detailed timeline on a certain commercial issue, we were quick to comply. It was a larger and much more complex version of the same approach of cooperating with enforcement agencies that I had used to protect PricewaterhouseCoopers in the AMERCO case.

We also had to be savvy about which documents and executives we went after, because the US Code of Civil Procedure, which governs how much discovery can be conducted in a case, had never been applied to a case of this magnitude. We worked laboriously with the Court and Intel to choose specific individuals to be deposed, and to formulate sensible search terms that would allow the most relevant documents to surface.

Many a company's downfall is found in the emails its highest executives write. People are very quick to write and respond to emails and texts, without ever considering that those messages could someday be used against them in litigation. While it took *years* to thoroughly analyze the terabytes of documents Intel and the other players produced, there were great days when we sifted jewels out of that mountain of raw digital ore.

One of the jewels we mined turned out to be a smoking gun for our case. In essence, it was Michael Dell angrily complaining to one of Intel's chiefs that he was tired of losing his clients and their money to AMD's technologically superior product. To which the Intel executive responded to the effect that the massive rebates that Intel was paying to Dell should more than make up for any deficiencies in Intel's products.

Boom!

In the Michael Dell story I told in Chapter 13, I gave you a taste of the process of deposing senior executives. Defended by their high-priced, Big Law attorneys, those execs very much do not want to go on the record about the role they play in anticompetitive practices. It took all the experience I had earned over the years of my practice—every bit of my EQ, true grit, and smarts—to assert dominance at each deposition in rooms full of egotistical, alpha-male senior executives and their equally egomaniacal lawyers. Sometimes I wondered during the depositions how there was enough space in the room for all the gigantic egos.

The process was exhausting. I took five days of deposition of the Intel executive in charge of the Dell account. During those intense days, my team and I labored over our plan of questioning. But no matter how strategically armed you are to question any witness, inevitably the witness will surprise you—by denying all knowledge of something they were deeply involved in, by giving you juicy details of a conversation you knew nothing about, or by explaining their involvement in an event you had no idea they were part of. With each new piece of information, you're forced to constantly recalibrate and re-strategize.

Every evening during the deposition, my team would frantically revise the outline of our questions based on the witness's testimony and the documents emailed to us by the team back at our main office. We would work until 1:00 or 2:00 a.m., at which point I would go to bed for a couple of hours of sleep while the team kept working on the outline. They had a key to my hotel room, and during the night they would unlock my door and leave the revised outline on my desk. As soon as my alarm went off, I'd start reviewing the outline.

One night, I got up in the wee hours, fetched some ice from the machine down the hall, and then went back to sleep. When I woke up there was blood all over me and the bed. Without realizing it, I had cut my finger on the metal edge of the ice machine; the trail of blood led straight from the ice machine, down the hall, through my door, and into my bed.

On the way to the deposition, we stopped at a drugstore for butterfly bandages to try to staunch the bleeding. After the lunch break, however, I was so tired and woozy that I took the deposition standing up to keep myself energized. It wasn't enough. About halfway through the afternoon, I passed out in the middle of a question and sank to the floor from a combination of exhaustion and blood loss. We took a short break, I walked around the building to revive myself, and then I came back in to continue the questioning. It's a reminder that sometimes true grit boils down to simple physical and mental toughness.

Those depositions were a trial by fire of my ability to use my EQ to build rapport, even with hostile witnesses. One Dell executive had a scary, stone-cold reputation as a calculating liar. Over the course of days, I eroded his confidence and his ability to lie by forcing him into a rhythm: my question, his denial, then my presentation of a document showing he lied. I repeatedly impeached him with his documents until he began to testify truthfully. Ultimately, I was able to get what we needed from him.

MANAGING AS A BENEVOLENT DICTATOR

The sheer magnitude of the electronic documents that had to be reviewed was mind-blowing. To accomplish the review, my firm hired 250 contract lawyers, employed for only this case and housed in a different building. Their thankless job was to review and code documents using a sophisticated computer program. My firm's lawyers and the contract lawyers had to be in constant communication so that the contractors would know what to search for in the documents, and we would know what they were finding.

This arrangement was a new level of leadership challenge for me. How could I integrate these two groups into a collaborative team? My firm's lawyers were the best and the brightest, but what about these other folks who did a modern form of piecework? Could we rely on them to both choose the most significant documents in the case and find the documents we needed to tell the story of what happened?

My worries were groundless. Based on the leadership lessons I have already talked about, we developed a seamless relationship between the 100-plus law firm lawyers and the contractors. I quickly discovered that the contract attorneys who focused on Dell—the linchpin of our case—were so dedicated and hard-working that I began to think that they might know more about the case than our own attorneys. It was a real eye-opener for me.

No large case remains static from beginning to end, and I continued to adapt our team's methods to deal with new developments and make the most of everyone's talent. As the case progressed, we split the law firm and contract lawyers into separate teams—one for AMD, one for Intel, and one for each of the computer manufacturers involved. I led the Dell team. As in previous cases, I made sure we had an all-hands team meeting once a week, and that emails with key developments were circulated to everyone. Frequently, our Dell working group would gather in a conference room that we called the War Room to review the hottest documents and formulate our deposition outlines. Everyone's ideas were welcomed, and we combined our collective knowledge in real time. We put up pictures in the War Room with the faces of the Dell and Intel witnesses we would have to depose, and after we finished with a witness, we inked a black diagonal line through the picture. We also instituted a tradition that if we worked past midnight, we would crack open a bottle of good Scotch, or whatever else the team wanted, and each have a drink before heading home.

Hashing out the cascade of facts and the twists and turns of the law could have been dull and lonely, but I made it a creative, collaborative process with a fun atmosphere. It was hard and important work on a highly serious matter, but even as I demanded excellence in the work performed, I brought a lighthearted edge to it so that people would want to come back in the morning. I was dedicated to building rapport, intent on achieving transparent communication, and generous about praising each person's contributions. In the end, my commitment to our mission and to the many contributors pursuing it made the entire team resilient in the face of the many complexities, uncertainties, and inevitable crises. Because they were respected and included, each team member felt a sense of ownership in the case.

I came to believe more than ever that management works best when the boss can demand the highest caliber of performance without eliciting terror or resentment. In some ways, that idea goes all the way back to what I learned as a teenager in Peru: people in subordinate roles are often surprised, even thrilled, to be recognized as human beings with their own ideas, talents, and personalities.

Unlike what many alpha-male bosses assume, team members are not replaceable cogs in a machine designed to serve. If you treat them right, they'll repay you with loyal, unflinching service. This is a philosophy of basic human decency that you must extend to everyone. I can't tell you how many times a staff person at my law firm has told me that I am the only partner who has ever treated them like a real person, when all I've done is give them the most basic respect. It's why the guy who delivers the mail will, as a personal favor, hand-deliver a brief to an opposing law firm down the street at a moment's notice. It's why the receptionist will give me a heads-up when opposing counsel and his client are screaming at each other in a conference room. It's why I've always had a waiting list of associates wanting to work on my cases.

It's also why I can sleep well at night; I know that women can smash glass, and kick ass, and continue to be decent human beings through it all.

KEEPING THE PLATES SPINNING

When I was a little girl growing up in Vermont, I used to watch a TV show called *Captain Kangaroo*. Occasionally, the Captain featured a man who would come in and set up fifty or so long poles on stage and then start spinning china plates on them one by one until he had all fifty going at the same time. When one plate would slow down, he would hurry back to it and give it a spin to keep it from crashing to the floor. Anytime a plate started to wobble, my sisters and I would hold our breath until he was able to reach the pole and give the plate a careful spin. I marveled at his dexterity in running around frantically, keeping all those plates going.

I grew up to do the same thing during the AMD case. Between the civil litigation and all the regulatory actions, there was at least one full-blown crisis a day somewhere in the world. If it had been physically possible, I could have stayed up 24/7 and always had something urgent to respond to as we tried to balance so many different developments at the same time.

I forced myself to embody my lessons: *stay flexible* and *use everything you've got*. You can remain steadfast in certain rules of engagement, such as never tolerating a lie from an opponent, yet still be open-minded and creative in the way you read situations and solve problems. You have to calibrate your actions to each conflict that arises: one size does not fit all.

I must admit that solving the daily crisis was also exhilarating. It redefines the phrase "never a dull moment." And bending my efforts to these constant emergencies in collaboration with a cadre of talented professionals made it even more thrilling. As in the past, the best analogy is that we were a dedicated, deeply loyal band of brothers.

The daily turmoil did finally come to an end. After ten years of fighting, Intel settled with AMD for $1.25 billion, agreed to huge reforms of its marketplace behavior, and granted AMD rights to key microprocessor patents. On top of that, governmental regulators in the EU, Japan, Korea, and the United States levied fines on Intel that totaled more than $1.5 billion, and our case established bold new precedents for preventing abuse by firms with monopoly power in their markets.

PROGRESS ISN'T ALWAYS TIDY—OR LINEAR

That case was the hardest test of my professional life, but I can also tell you that I took the greatest relish from achieving victory in it. Besides proving, as if we needed more proof, that women have the courage and the skills to take on titanic challenges and prevail, the AMD case reiterated to me the importance of rebounding strongly and creatively when your work presents you with daily emergencies. The lesson is clear: sometimes progress is messy and uncertain; you must make progress anyway.

No doubt, I have talent for my work, as you do for yours. But the most important thing I brought to the AMD case was the well-honed set of tough but highly flexible skills I had developed over many years of taking on the hardest challenges and never quitting until I prevailed. Developing those skills, and the deep-seated confidence that goes with them, is what you need for dealing with life's trials—not just literal, legal trials like I've taken on, but those frustrating battles and hardships that can drag down any of us if we let them.

I didn't let them, and you can't either. If I can take on one of the world's most formidable companies for ten years and win, you too can climb the summits in your profession.

We are empowered. And we can use that power.

CHAPTER 17

REACH BEYOND YOURSELF TO LEAVE A LEGACY

"Never forget that you are one of a kind. Never forget that if there weren't any need for you in all your uniqueness to be on this earth, you wouldn't be here in the first place. And never forget, no matter how overwhelming life's challenges and problems seem to be, that one person can make a difference in the world. In fact, it is always because of one person that all the changes that matter in the world come about. So be that one person."

—BUCKMINSTER FULLER

- *Are you ready to seize the opportunity to use your talents, experience and kick-assets to make an impact far beyond your normal, professional work?*
- *Do you want to leverage your power and prestige to create a lasting legacy?*
- *Do you have the strength, the patience, and the passion to change the world?*

SIMPLY BY SUCCEEDING IN A MAN'S WORLD, YOU *already* have forged a legacy. You have harnessed your natural talents as a woman to dominate in business, not by leaning in or outmanning the men, but by capitalizing on your natural strengths. You have broken into the old boys' network, defied the male hierarchy, dismantled the misogynistic structure that dictates that only men can lead, and struck a blow to the patriarchy.

Your success has made you an invaluable role model. Brava!

Now I'm asking you to go further.

Yes, there are always higher mountains for you to climb. And yes, you should be vigilant in consolidating your gains and defending your current position from challengers.

But your success offers something else. Harriet Tubman said, "Always remember, you have within you the strength, the patience, and the passion to reach for the stars to change the world."

Success gives you the power and influence to do just that. It is a rare gift—the result of wielding your kick-assets and your smarts to become a force in your profession. When you reach the heights of your career, you have a platform from which you can fight for a passion or cause that you believe in—it's an opportunity to muster those same talents, experiences, and kick-assets to give back and make an impact far beyond your normal and outstanding professional work. You've made it to the top. Now it's time for you to make a difference.

Throughout my life, I've given time, energy, and money to charitable work, whether that meant helping Holocaust survivors file restitution claims, aiding asylum seekers in their bids to remain in the United States, or donating time to UNICEF. While I believe those efforts are worthy, if you want to leave a legacy beyond yourself, that implies doing something broader than mentoring, being involved in your church, or serving food at a soup kitchen. A legacy is created by leveraging your prestige and power to create a bigger impact.

In this chapter, I'm going to talk about some of the ways I've tried to do that with the pro bono (for free) legal cases I've taken on as a Big Law senior partner. Those cases have gone to federal appellate courts and the US Supreme Court to protect the right of *all* US citizens to vote, and to offer temporary protection from deportation for illegal immigrants who are the mothers and fathers of US citizen children. They have allowed me, channeling the massive resources of Big Law, to advocate for deeply held American values of equality and the protection of the rights of those who cannot speak for themselves.

USING YOUR POWER FOR GOOD

Once you have successfully established your authority and cemented your reputation, you have the ability, the freedom, and the power base to leave behind an even more impressive and fulfilling legacy.

My guiding theory of giving back is this: *to use what you're best at on behalf of those who need it most.* I developed an expertise in large-scale litigation—expertise refined through fire—so that's where I've directed my energy. Plus, I had the resources of my law firm at my disposal which provides a deep bench of attorneys for significant cases.

Similarly, you can use your particular brand of success as a springboard, building directly on your area of expertise, or on your stature at work and in the community. Perhaps your job success has given you access to a network of influential and receptive people. Maybe your experience allows you to connect with a board or association within your profession that provides aid, scholarships, education, job training, shelters, support, medical care, or something else that can directly help people in need.

It's critical that the cause is meaningful for you. There is an astounding variety of charities, nonprofit organizations, and disaster-relief efforts in virtually every field, from health (hospitals, substance abuse, disease research, mental health, crisis services) to social and public benefit causes (civil rights, civil liberties, community improvement, voter education and registration, life insurance providers, unemployment compensation organizations, pension and retirement funds, employee associations, and cemeteries). Within each broad category, there are specialized organizations that might dovetail with your expertise or your passion. There are women involved in supporting technology scholarship programs, shelters for women and children, refugee assistance groups, animal rights foundations, welfare, conservation and environmental preservation societies, and institutions for the performing arts. The list is inexhaustible.

Merely donating some money or volunteering a bit of your time will not satisfy your desire to give back. Every charitable and nonprofit group needs leadership expertise, strategic management, analytics, grant management and fundraising expertise, accounting and tax services, legal aid, or scientific research. The need is endless. And the need is *what you have.*

Choose *your* way to make a difference.

GIVING A VOICE TO THE VOICELESS

Once I had become a senior partner, I was in a position to choose my own way to make a difference. I now had the resources of Big Law at my disposal and could represent the needs and hopes of the millions of individuals—people of color, legal and illegal immigrants, the poor, the elderly—who face discrimination and cannot make themselves heard within our legal system. My most memorable large-scale efforts on their behalf came when I represented their voices in two cases, one about voting rights and the other about the rights of immigrants to the United States.

In the first case, my allies and I squared off against Kansas Secretary of State Kris Kobach, who made his career by blocking people of color and the poor from registering to vote. You may know him better as President Trump's "immigration czar" and the head of his commission on voting integrity. Preying on the fears of white America by using a potent combination of anti-immigrant sentiment and dire warnings about (virtually non-existent) voting fraud, Kobach convinced the legislatures of Kansas and Arizona to adopt voter-registration laws requiring that all citizens provide either an original birth certificate or a passport—a driver's license was insufficient—to register to vote.

People are often surprised to discover how many US citizens, particularly immigrant US citizens, people of color, the elderly, and the poor, lack those documents or the knowledge of how to get them. Civil rights groups have compared such voter-ID laws to the poll taxes, literacy tests, and other Jim Crow laws designed to keep blacks from voting in the US South a century ago.

After Secretary Kobach brought a lawsuit (*Kobach et al. v. United States Election Assistance Commission et al.*) with the aim of forcing federal officials to adopt the same requirements imposed by Kansas and Arizona, my firm joined the Mexican American Legal Defense and Educational Fund (MALDEF) and one of its toughest litigators, a woman named Nina Perales, in opposing Kobach. Many other public interest organizations, each with its own Big Law representation, also waded into the fight.

As the suit wound its way through the judicial system, Big Law expended tens of millions of dollars and thousands of hours representing public interest groups opposed to Kobach's discriminatory attempts to suppress these citizens' constitutional right to vote. There was no possible way any of these disenfranchised people could have individually brought this lawsuit. It required battling through dozens of rounds of briefing to address the intent of Congress in passing voter legislation, the meaning of its provisions, constitutional issues, states' rights versus the rights of the federal government, and all of the facts on the prevalence or lack of proof of fraudulent voting. And that's before we got to actually arguing all of those points before the federal district court and the Tenth Circuit Court of Appeals.

(A heads-up to women: the competition for supremacy among the Big Law attorneys representing the various public interest organizations was just as cutthroat as any I had seen in my major commercial cases. And our fierce competitors for the lead were all alpha males. In the end, my group secured the lead by applying exactly the approach I laid out in Chapter 14.)

The district court in Kansas found in favor of Kobach, but that decision was reversed by the Tenth Circuit in a lengthy and well-reasoned opinion. Kobach appealed to the United States Supreme Court, but the justices declined to hear the case, meaning that the Tenth Circuit ruling stood. Our hard work paid off: *millions* of disadvantaged Americans could now exercise their right to vote without meeting onerous ID requirements designed specifically to deny it.

In my second major pro bono case, again working with MALDEF, I represented three mothers who were living in this country illegally. It was a landmark case that directly affected their lives and the lives of their US citizen children. Our first challenge was how the three of them could even be heard, given that just disclosing their names could subject them to deportation. The court allowed us to file their true identities under seal and permitted them to proceed through the district court, the court of appeals, and the US Supreme Court as Jane Doe #1, Jane Doe #2, and Jane Doe #3.

The case started after President Obama issued an executive order putting into place a program known as DAPA (Deferred Action for Parents of Americans and Lawful Permanent Residents). DAPA permitted low-priority illegal immigrants—the parents of US citizen children who also meet other specific criteria—to remain in the country for three years without fear of deportation. DAPA did not confer any pathway to citizenship. It simply meant that a DAPA-eligible mom or dad could go to the grocery store or work or to church without fear that arrest, detention, and removal proceedings would upend his or her life and split the family apart.

In enacting DAPA, President Obama was following Congress's directive to the Department of Homeland Security (DHS) to prioritize "the identification and removal of [immigrants] ... by the severity of the crime." Since the DHS only has enough resources to deport half a million illegal immigrants per year and the total number of illegal immigrants in the United States is estimated at more than 11 million, DAPA focused on deporting the actual bad guys—drug dealers, "coyotes," and other criminals—rather than people who had lived peaceably in the United States for years, caring for their US citizen children, paying taxes, and contributing to their communities.

Twenty-seven states, led by Texas, disagreed. They wanted to get rid of all illegal immigrants, so they filed suit in federal court in Texas (*State of Texas et al. v. United States of America, et al.*) to prevent the government from implementing DAPA. The Department of Justice defended DAPA on behalf of the US government, but no one was representing the interests of the millions of illegal immigrant parents who were directly affected, living in the shadows under constant threat of deportation. The Court allowed MALDEF and Big Law to come into the lawsuit on behalf of those mothers and fathers.

For the next two years, we pursued the case through the district court, the Fifth Circuit Court of Appeals, and the US Supreme Court. Not only did the parties file dozens of briefs, but when we reached the Supreme Court, more than 100 senators, representatives, state legislators, mayors, sheriffs, states, business organizations, and trade associations weighed in on one side or the other by filing amici curiae (friend of the court) briefs.

The experience of walking into the United States Supreme Court is, for a lawyer, akin to going into the holiest site of your religion. Even for me, with all of my previous trials and arguments before federal appellate courts, it holds a special significance. After passing through a strict security protocol, you enter the solemn and majestic courtroom. The justices sit on an elevated stage in front of you, as if ready to pounce. During our argument, there were only eight chairs on the stage, as Justice Scalia had died unexpectedly and the Senate refused to consider any nomination to fill his seat.

The Justices were fully prepared, with stacks of briefs piled beside them, and the questions flew fast and furious in the hushed courtroom. Outside, thousands of illegal immigrants demonstrated, holding signs, chanting slogans, and cheering on speakers. The media was out in force. As soon as the argument concluded, the media set up a space called "The Scrum" covered with microphones and cameras where the lawyers for both sides made statements and took questions from the press.

Ultimately, the eight-person composition of the Court led to a 4–4 deadlock. The Court held the case over for many months, hoping for the appointment of a ninth justice. Finally, with no such appointment in sight, the Court issued a one-sentence opinion that left the 4–4 deadlock in place, meaning that the decision of Fifth Circuit to block DAPA remained in place. It was a crushing blow to the White House, to our defense team, and to millions of parents of US citizen children. Obama, speaking at the White House, lamented the ruling. "For more than two decades now our immigration system, everybody acknowledges, has been broken," he said. "And the fact that the Supreme Court wasn't able to issue a decision today doesn't just set the system back even further, it takes us further from the country that we aspire to be."

As frustrating as that decision was, along with the Trump administration's decision to do away with DAPA altogether, I would take that case again in a heartbeat. Even though we didn't win, my team and I knew that what we were doing *mattered.*

EXPAND YOUR REACH TO MAKE A DIFFERENCE IN THE WORLD

Success—and the power that comes with it—has given me the freedom to change a small piece of the world. I am an unlikely model for a selfless do-gooder: as you know from reading this book, I'm driven, highly competitive, and ruthless when necessary. I didn't earn the title The Meanest Woman Alive for nothing. I have no illusions that there's a halo over my head.

That said, once you've earned your success, you can wield that power and influence to effect change in the world, and do it on a large scale. Whatever cause or passion you choose, you are in a position to do *serious* good in the world.

You'll need all the expertise, kick-assets, and experience you've developed along the way to seize the opportunity and make a difference. Everyone's path is unique. Mine was to devise legal strategies, prepare briefs, and go to court; your opportunity to meaningfully contribute will take its own form.

I didn't get to lead those pro bono cases just by asking nicely. You have to be powerful and persuasive to talk a law firm into spending millions of dollars to help the voiceless. You have to have real standing and clout to broach the subject in the first place. Even when the powers that be say *yes*, you have to convince other attorneys to come on board and donate their time. And *then* you have to use everything you've got to take on all the complexities of a major multi-year federal court case that will affect the lives of millions of people.

But that's the point. Major change doesn't come easily—if it did, it wouldn't be major, and the rewards of being part of it would be far less sweet. Remember that each difficult step you take toward your personal success can also be a stepping stone for those who still struggle.

I'm far from done making my contribution. I'll never be done. I'm going to keep using my standing, my power, and my kick-assets to pave the way for other women and, as Harriet Tubman urges, "reach for the stars to change the world."

I hope that as you climb toward the stars, you'll do the same.

What legacy will you leave?

CHAPTER 18

WOMEN CAN SEIZE POWER RIGHT NOW

"It doesn't matter how great your shoes are if you don't accomplish anything in them."

—MARTINA BOONE, *Compulsion*

- *Do you have the confidence to jettison the societal norms of male domination and use an entirely different playbook written by women for women?*
- *Can you be bold and speak up with self-assurance; be fearless and take charge of difficult situations; show grit under pressure and in the face of uncertainty; and push back against those who deny you what you need?*
- *Are you ready to lead? Can you establish dominance by seizing and maintaining control of projects, convincing the men to follow you, and neutralizing competitors?*
- *Are you ready to use your unique advantages as a woman to climb as high in your profession as you choose?*
- *Are you ready to use your kick-assets to pave the way for other women?*

ON A SHELF IN MY OFFICE SITS A gigantic basketball shoe—a men's size twenty-five. It is truly enormous, close to a foot-and-a-half long.

I paid way too much for the shoe at a charitable silent auction (it was between the shoe and a small car). But this shoe is legendary: it belonged to basketball hall-of-famer Shaquille O'Neal, who used it to end a decade-long drought and bring the first of three NBA championships to Los Angeles.

To see me standing next to Shaq as he presented me with the shoe was a hilarious sight. I don't even come up to his waist. To watch me try to put on the shoe was even more ludicrous—both my petite feet fit into it with room to spare.

The shoe once bore Shaq's signature, but it's long since been worn away. I travel with it to keynotes and conferences, and often the giant shoe makes its way around an audience, passed from astonished hand to astonished hand. Over the years, the signature has been rubbed away by its passage, but it's not really about the signature—even without it, the shoe still generates awe in men and women alike, who marvel that it can fit *anyone*.

But that's the point. The shoe *doesn't* fit anyone.

There is no way I could perform in Shaq's shoe. Neither could you. It doesn't fit. It wasn't designed with either of us in mind, and the idea of filling that shoe is both daunting and ridiculous.

The absurdity of standing in that shoe epitomizes how I felt when I first arrived at my law firm. I felt like I didn't fit the firm's mold. I was a lone woman in a sea of professional men, and there was no one at the firm to provide a road map I could follow. The male-created mold wasn't designed with me in mind. I couldn't perform in it; the idea that I could was just as daunting and ridiculous as wearing Shaq's enormous shoe itself.

Unless I wanted to accept defeat, then, I had no choice but to fashion my own mold, to create my own shoes, and then fill them in my own way. So that's what I did.

It didn't happen overnight, or even in a year. But slowly, over time, I built a shoe, designed for me, by me, that *fits*—a shoe in which I can perform just fine. In fact, I can perform brilliantly.

In my shoes, I have stood before the leaders of some of the greatest, most powerful corporations of our time and commanded their attention. In my shoes, I have given strategic advice on bet-the-company litigation, where billions of dollars were at stake. In my shoes, I've argued before countless federal courts and courts of appeal. In my shoes, I've stood up to and stared down some of the meanest, most belligerent lawyers my profession has to offer. In my shoes, I've held juries spellbound as they waited to find out what I would do next.

At this point, I can look back at the legacy I've built and rest secure in the knowledge that, even with my petite size-six Manolo heels, I've left some pretty hot shoe styles for other women to fill. My hope is that each of you, regardless of your profession, can use my mold as a starting point, and design your own shoes. You can tweak them to fit your own style and personality, your strengths and weaknesses, and the nature of your work. You can adapt them to each challenge you face. In your own shoes, you can walk any walk you choose, and run any gauntlet you must.

That's the challenge and the opportunity before you: to fashion your own shoes and perform brilliantly in them. You can be who you choose to be. You can do what you want to do. The legacy is yours for the taking as you apply your unique talents, your true grit, and your kick-assets. You can make a difference.

//////////////

You now have all the ammunition in your arsenal that you need to shift the power dynamics in your career. Your weapons are locked and loaded. You are battle-tried and ready. Your mission is clear. It's time to go forth and conquer.

For decades, woman have been seeking equality with men. But seeking to be treated in the same way as men while playing by a male playbook is a losing proposition for women.

Instead, you now understand that women possess special advantages uniquely qualifying us for success. In order to get ahead, we need to use our kick-assets and play by women's rules—not men's—to gain an advantage.

We are singularly qualified to lead, and lead we will. No longer will we buy into the false narrative that men deserve to be the masters of the universe while we sit back and take their direction. Men's aggressive, competitive, and controlling natures have been regarded for millennia as the stuff that leadership is made of. But now we know better. We know that in fact women are superior leaders.

We can shine by using our uniquely feminine advantages while also selectively adopting masculine attitudes where and when they work for us. We can wisely forgo the masculine traits that leave men beating their chests, marking their territory, and warring for supremacy with potential allies. While the silverbacks waste their time on all of that, we will take the reins and run the show.

FIGHTING THE FIGHT

Yes, it's a tall order. But you're primed to take action. Here's what I want you to take away from this book:

- Women's lack of confidence perpetuates male domination. Men often advance on confidence alone, but women must show both competence and confidence or we'll be left in the dust. We also know that confidence can be acquired. Taking risks and actions generates a belief that you can perform with skill, which generates confidence, which in turn stimulates further action. The cycle continues.
- Researchers have demonstrated that women have superior emotional intelligence, now a universally recognized marker for leadership success. Three of women's abilities grounded in EI bestow stunning advantages: reading minds, playing well with others, and understanding how emotions influence decisions. These factors, which marry intelligence and empathy, magnify our capacity for analysis and our comprehension of interpersonal dynamics to help us excel as leaders. Using these kick-assets—and their increasing recognition by the business community—women can confidently move up the corporate ladder.
- Resilience is required. It's only by consistently delivering excellent work, even while you're taking your lumps, that you prove your worth.
- You can, and must, diagnose the onset of self-sabotage and negate its effects, confronting that harshly critical voice in your head that says, You're not good enough or You can't make it.
- You have field-tested methods for putting assholes in their place. You're prepared to establish your own rules of engagement, then decide how you'll communicate, what you'll put up with, what

you won't, and what the consequences will be for assholes who cross the line.

- Sexual harassment can damage your career, but you have a step-by-step approach so you know what to do, when to do it, and how to keep control of the agenda.
- As you rise in your career, you'll face increasing danger from snipers—not only men, but also rival women who use gossip and rumor to sow doubt about your professional competence, morals, or fitness to lead. You are now alerted and armed to deal with them.
- You know that true grit— a combination of mental toughness, courage, hard work, and the sheer stubbornness to keep going—will be essential for achieving your goals.
- As women, we have no choice but to use everything we've got—including our femininity—to our advantage by honing our ability to shape our persona in a way that fits the moment. We can be tough, decisive, strong, and smart "just like a man," yet also use our emotional intelligence to relate to people in a human, thoughtful way.
- You now have step-by-step methods for cracking the old boys' network, and for finding your essential mentors and sponsors.
- Sometimes in your career, you simply need to kick ass. You're now primed with many techniques for doing exactly that.
- You know how to make sure that you are heard and listened to—without interruption.
- You have my battle-tested techniques for taking on powerful, egotistical men when the circumstances call for it.
- When facing vital projects that will define your career trajectory, you have everything you need to establish and defend your dominance as you take control of them.
- You know how to use your feminine abilities to lead a team, overcome every obstacle, and bring home a win.
- You're well equipped to muster all your talents, experiences, and kick-assets to tackle whatever challenge is thrown at you next.

- You've been challenged to leave a legacy by wielding your power and influence to effect change in the world.

Through our individual successes, we can prove to ourselves and to all the doubters that women have the audacity and the talent to grapple with the toughest, most complex assignments and perform brilliantly. Women can seize and maintain control and be fiercely competitive, even as we create a far more collaborative and effective workplace—one that men and women alike want to work in.

IT'S UP TO YOU

Outmoded gender roles have kept women from achieving their full potential for thousands of years. That bias denies opportunities to individual women, but it also prevents our society from achieving the great prosperity and creativity it could if women's talents were appropriately valued and unleashed. That's why traditional roles must be abolished. To accomplish that, we must proactively seize every opportunity to demonstrate our value in society and change the way women are treated.

It's not just time; it's well *past* time to explode these old myths.

Women must harness their natural talents *as women* to dominate in business. Not by outmanning the men, but by capitalizing on our natural strengths as women. It's up to us, playing by women's rules, to make full use of our special advantages to create a new world.

I can't wait to see how we remake the world together. Go for it!

NOTES

CHAPTER 2— EMBRACE YOUR DESTINY TO LEAD

1. Jack Zenger and Joseph Folkman, "Are Women Better Leaders Than Men?," *Harvard Business Review*, March 15, 2012; Victor Lipton, "New Research: Women Consistently Outperform Men In EQ," *Psychology Today*, March 18, 2016; See also Bob Sherwin, "Why Women Are More Effective Leaders Than Men," *Business Insider*, January 24, 2014; and Geoff Colvin, "The Trait that Makes Women Better Leaders," *Fortune*, March 26, 2015.
2. Tomas Chamorro-Premuzic and Michael Sanger, "How to Boost Your (and Others') Emotional Intelligence," *Harvard Business Review*, January 9, 2017.
3. *Psychology Today*, March 16, 2016. ESCI is a tool developed by Daniel Goleman, Richard E. Boyatzis, and the Hay Group, a division of Korn Ferry. The 12 competencies are: achievement orientation, adaptability, coaching and mentoring, conflict management, emotional self-awareness, emotional self-control, empathy, influence, inspirational leadership, organizational awareness, positive outlook, and teamwork. See also Dana Landis, Jennifer Predolin, James Lewis, et al., "In case of emergency, break glass ceiling: Women C-suite executives show all the right skill sets. So why are they so rare?" Korn/Ferry Institute, November 2011.
4. See, for instance, Manfred Kets de Vries, "Are You an Alpha Male Leader?," INSEAD Knowledge, March 9, 2016.
5. Daniel Victor, "Women in Company Leadership Tied to Stronger Profits, Study Says," *The New York Times*, February 9, 2016, based on a study by Joelle Jay, Marcus Nolan, Tyler Morgan, and Barbara Kotschwar, "Is Gender Diversity Profitable? Evidence from a Global Survey," Peterson Institute for International Economics, February

2016. See also Marcus Nolan and Tyler Moran, "Study: Firms with More Women in the C-Suite are More Profitable," *Harvard Business Review*, February 8, 2016.

6. Nancy Carter, Lois Joy, Harvey Wagner, and Siriam Narayanan, "The Bottom Line: Corporate Performance and Women's Representation on Boards," *Catalyst*, October 15, 2007.
7. Darya Borisova and Olga Sterkhova, "Women as a Valuable Asset," McKinsey & Company, April 2012.
8. Leadership Research Institute, "Women Leaders and Profitability: Are You Playing with Half a Team?," August 12, 2016.
9. Portia Crowe, "6 senior women on Wall Street share their best career advice," *Business Insider*, September 1, 2016.
10. Center for Creative Leadership, "Empathy in the Workplace: A Tool for Effective Leadership," April 2007.
11. Jack Zenger and Joseph Folkman, "Are Women Better Leaders Than Men?," *Harvard Business Review*, March 15, 2012. See also Bob Sherwin, "Why Women Are More Effective Leaders Than Men," *Business Insider*, January 24, 2014; and Geoff Colvin, "The Trait that Makes Women Better Leaders," *Fortune*, March 26, 2015.
12. Herminia Ibarra and Morten T. Hansen, "Are You a Collaborative Leader?," *Harvard Business Review*, July–August 2011.
13. See Marcus Buckingham, "Leadership Development in the Age of the Algorithm," *Harvard Business Review* 90, no. 6 (2012); Bill George et al, "Discovering Your Authentic Leadership," *Harvard Business Review* 85, no. 2.
14. Karen L. Cates, "To Become a Better Leader, Be Aware," Bloomberg, June 12, 2014.
15. Gwen Moran, "5 Keys to Inspiring Leadership, No Matter Your Style," *Entrepreneur*.
16. Carmine Gallo, "Richard Branson: The One Skill Leaders Need to Learn," *Forbes*, June 29, 2011.

CHAPTER 3— VANQUISHING THE DEMONS WITHIN AND WITHOUT

1. Nancy Makepeace Tanner, "Hunters, Gatherers and Sex Roles in Space and Time," *American Anthropologist*, June 1983; Nancy Tanner and Adrienne Zihlman, "Women in Evolution, Part I: Innovation and Selection of Human Origins," *Signs: Journal of Women in Culture and Society*, Spring 1976.
2. Irwin Silverman and Krista Phillips, "The evolutionary psychology of spatial sex differences," *Handbook of Evolutionary Psychology*, 1998.
3. *Catalyst*, "Women in the Work Force: United States," August 11, 2016.
4. Cordelia Fine, "The Hidden Sexism of How We Think About Risk," *Nautilus*, May 18, 2017.
5. Harriet Alexander, "Donald Trump Says Megyn Kelly's Tough Questioning Was Due to Menstruation," *The Telegraph*, August 8, 2015.
6. Catherine Pearson, "Here's What Trump Has Done For Women In His First 100 Days."
7. Huffington Post, Apr 27, 2017.
8. Rutgers University Center for American Women and Politics, "Women in the U.S. Congress 2017," "Women in Statewide Elective Executive Office 2017" and "Women in State Legislatures 2017," accessed June 22, 2017.
9. Rhiannon Lucy Cosslett, *The Guardian*, Jan. 24, 2017.
10. National Women's Law Center, "The wage gap: the who, how, why, and what to do," September 2016.
11. Kathryn Vasel, "5 things to know about the gender pay gap," *CNN Money*, April 4, 2017.
12. Corrine A. Moss-Racusin et al., "Science faculty's subtle gender bias favors male students," Proceedings of the National Academy of Sciences, August 2012.

13. See Natalie Kitroeff, "Why are so many women dropping out of the workforce?," *Los Angeles Times*, May 28, 2017.
14. McKinsey & Co. and Leanin.Org, Women in the Workplace 2016, September 2016.
15. *Catalyst*, "Women In Law In Canada And The U.S.," accessed June 25, 2017.
16. Jena McGregor, "The Number of New Female Board Members Dropped Last Year," *The Washington Post*, June 23, 2017.
17. Libby Hill, "New Study Reveals Fewer Women Working Behind the Scenes in Hollywood," *Los Angeles Times*, January 12, 2017.
18. Henry J. Kaiser Family Foundation, "Distribution of Physicians by Gender" for April 2017, accessed May 15, 2017.
19. Figures cited in Samantha Shaddock, "The Slide Rule Sisters Would Be Proud: GE's Female Engineers Talk About Changing The Gender Ratio In The Workplace," GE Reports, February 8, 2017.
20. *Catalyst*, "Women In Science, Technology, Engineering, And Mathematics (STEM)," accessed June 26, 2017.
21. Beth Jarosz and Mark Mather, "Losing Ground: Young Women's Well-Being Across Generations in the United States," Population Reference Bureau, June 2017.
22. US Census Bureau, "Measuring America: An overview of women-owned businesses," December 2014.
23. Laurie Meisler, Mira Rojanasakul, and Jeremy Scott Diamond, "Who Gets Venture Capital Funding?," *Bloomberg*, May 25, 2016.
24. Dan Cassino, "Why More American Men Feel Discriminated Against," *Harvard Business Review*, September 29, 2016.
25. Caroline Knorr, "What media teach kids about gender can have lasting effects, report says," CNN, June 29, 2017; "Watching Gender: How Stereotypes in Movies and on TV Impact Kids' Development," Common Sense Media, accessed July 24, 2017.
26. Ross Todd, "5 Takeaways from Justice Sotomayor's Spirited Berkeley Appearance," *The Recorder*, March 10, 2017.

27. Ellen Hendriksen, "What Is Impostor Syndrome?," *QuickAndDirtyTips.com*, accessed 31 July 2017.

28. Lena Dunham, "The Lenny Interview: Sheryl Sandberg," *Lenny*, June 24, 2016.

CHAPTER 4—DIG DOWN AND SOLDIER ON, SNOWFLAKE

1. For an example of how millennial attitudes can be exaggerated, see the analysis in Kelly Pledger Weeks, "Every Generation Wants Meaningful Work—but Thinks Other Age Groups Are in It for the Money," *Harvard Business Review*, July 31, 2017.

2. Institute of Leadership & Management, "Ambition and gender at work," February 2011.

3. Will McGrew, "Gender Segregation at Work: 'Separate but Equal' or 'Inefficient and Unfair,'" Washington Center for Equitable Growth, August 18, 2016.

4. Angela L. Duckworth, Christopher Peterson, Michael D. Matthews and Dennis Kelly, "Grit: Perseverance and Passion for Long-Term Goals," *Journal of Personality and Social Psychology*, Vol. 92, 2007.

5. For more on the debate about "grit," see Iowa State University, "No evidence that grit improves performance, analysis finds," ScienceDaily, 18 May 2016; Austin Fossey, "The truth about grit," The Predictive Index, August 31, 2016; and Zorana Ivcevic and Marc Brackett, "Predicting school success: Comparing Conscientiousness, Grit, and Emotion Regulation Ability," *Journal of Research in Personality*, October 2014.

6. For more on this quotation, including its possible origin with another speaker, see Amity Shlaes And David Pietrusza, "Calvin Coolidge Persisted, in Deed If Not in Word," *Bloomberg View*, June 11, 2012.

7. See Falon Fatemi, "5 Roles Men Project on Women in the Workplace," *Forbes*, September 20, 2016; Chelsea Fagen, "21 Moments

Of Sexism Every Professional Woman Has Experienced (But No One Believes)," *thoughtcatalog.com*, September 22, 2014.

8. Carly Rivers and Rosalind C. Barnett, *The New Soft War on Women: How the Myth of Female Ascendance Is Hurting Women, Men—And Our Economy*, p. 201.

CHAPTER 5—GET OVER YOUR OWN BULLSHIT

1. Tonja Jacobi and Dylan Schweers, "Justice, Interrupted: The Effect of Gender, Ideology, and Seniority at Supreme Court Oral Arguments," 103 *Virginia Law Review*, March 17, 2017.
2. Janet E. Ainsworth, "In a Different Register: The Pragmatics of Powerlessness in Police Interrogation," 103 *Yale Law Journal* 259, November 1993.
3. Richard Eisenberg, "What Women Must Do to Ditch Bag Lady Syndrome," *Forbes*, March 6, 2015.
4. Shankar Vedantam, "Research Examines The Effects Of Gender On Stated Ambition," NPR *Morning Edition*, January 24, 2017.
5. For a helpful general discussion of self-sabotage, see Adam Sicinski, "Do You Sabotage Your Own Success? Here's How to Stop Self-Sabotage," IQ Matrix, accessed August 11, 2017.
6. Elizabeth Revenko, "6 Ways to Combat 'Bag Lady Syndrome,'" *NerdWallet*, April 5, 2016.
7. This concept was pioneered by Prof. Carol S. Dweck. See her *Mindset: The New Psychology of Success*, Random House, 2007.
8. Tomas Chamorro-Premuzic and Adam Yearsley, "The Downsides of Being Very Emotionally Intelligent," *Harvard Business Review*, January 12, 2017.

CHAPTER 6—FAKE IT UNTIL YOU MAKE IT

1. Katty Kay and Claire Shipman, "The Confidence Gap," *The Atlantic*, May 2014.

2. Jill Flynn, Kathryn Heath, and Mary Davis Holt, "Four Ways Women Stunt Their Careers Unintentionally," *Harvard Business Review*, October 19, 2011.
3. Linda Babcock et al., "Nice Girls Don't Ask," *Harvard Business Review*, October 2003.
4. Venkat Kuppuswamy and Ethan R. Mollick, "Hubris and Humility: Gender Differences in Serial Founding Rates," SSRN *Electronic Journal*, posted June 28, 2015.
5. Margie Warrell, "For Women To Rise We Must Close 'The Confidence Gap,'" *Forbes*, January 20, 2016. The research was originally published in Bleidorn, et al., "Age and Gender Differences in Self-Esteem—A Cross-Cultural Window," *Journal of Personality and Social Psychology*, 2016, Vol. 111, No. 3, pp. 396–410.
6. Cameron Anderson, Sebastien Brion, Don A. Moore, and Jessica Kennedy, "A status-enhancement account of overconfidence," *Journal of Personality and Social Psychology*, 2012.
7. Kay and Shipman, *The Confidence Gap*.

CHAPTER 7—EXPLOIT THE SILVERBACKS

1. Chris Moss, "Are Men's Lives Ruled by Testosterone?," *The Telegraph*, August 29, 2017; see also Joe Herbert, *Testosterone: Sex, Power, and the Will to Win*, Oxford University Press, 2015.
2. Daniel Goleman, "Aggression in Men: Hormone Levels Are Key," *The New York Times*, July 17, 1990. In the decades since Goleman's article was published, further research has reinforced the role of testosterone in aggression. See, for instance, Menelaos L. Batrinos, "Testosterone and Aggressive Behavior in Man," *International Journal of Endocrinology and Metabolism*, Summer 2012, pp. 563–568.
3. Testosterone plays a significant role in the arousal of these behavioral manifestations in the brain centers involved in aggression and on the development of the muscular system that enables their realization. There is evidence that testosterone levels are higher in individuals with aggressive behavior, such as prisoners who have

committed violent crimes. Several field studies have also shown that testosterone levels increase during the aggressive phases of sports games. In more sensitive laboratory paradigms, it has been observed that participant's testosterone rises in the winners of competitions, dominance trials, or in confrontations with factitious opponents.

4. Lisa Ryan, "Here Are the First Excerpts From Hillary Clinton's New Book," *The Cut*, August 23, 2017; excerpted from Hillary Clinton, *What Happened*, Simon & Schuster, 2017.
5. The film critic Laura Mulvey coined the term in this article: "Visual Pleasure and Narrative Cinema," *Screen*, vol. 16, no. 3 (Autumn 1975), pp. 6 –18.
6. Quoted by Jean Kilbourne in *Killing Us Softly 4: Advertising's Image of Women*, written by Jean Kilbourne and directed by Sut Jhally, Media Education Foundation, 2010; see Natalie Perkins, "Transcript: Killing Us Softly 4:Advertising's Image of Women," *Definatalie.com*, October 23, 2010.
7. Beginning in 2004, the Dove soap company commissioned a series of major research studies that generated these findings. For a summary and analysis of the results, see Lindsey Morel, "The Effectiveness of the Dove Campaign for Real Beauty in Terms of Society and the Brand," Syracuse University, Syracuse University Honors Program Capstone Projects, *Paper 480*, 2009.
8. See note 5.
9. Infectious Perfection, "Body Makeover in Photoshop," YouTube, October 8, 2011; Insidious Perfection, "Beyonce Photoshop Makeover," *YouTube*, May 17, 2016.

CHAPTER 8—INFILTRATE THE OLD BOYS' NETWORK

1. "Old Boy's Network," Urban Dictionary.com, accessed September 15, 2017.
2. Francis Dickens, "How to Handle the Old Boys Network," *minutehack.com*, April 19, 2016.

3. UC Davis News Service, "UC Davis Study Finds Good Old Boys Club Holds in Top Businesses," *The Davis Vanguard*, December 6, 2012; "2015–2016 UC Davis Study of California Women Business Leaders: A Census of Women Directors and Executive Officers," UC Davis Graduate School of Management, November 17, 2015; Michael L. McDonald and James D. Westphal, "Access Denied: Low Mentoring of Women and Minority First-Time Directors and Its Negative Effects on Appointments to Additional Boards," *Academy of Management Journal*, August 1, 2013.

4. J. C. Karremans, T. Verwijmeren, T. M. Pronk, and M. Reitsma, "Interacting with Women Can Impair Men's Cognitive Functioning," *Journal of Experimental Social Psychology*, July, 2009.

5. Scott Barry Kaufman, "Interacting with Women Makes Men Stupid," *Psychology Today*, May 18, 2009.

6. John Gray, *Men Are from Mars, Women Are from Venus*, Harper Collins, 1992.

7. Research backs this up. See, for example, Sylvia Ann Hewlett, "Threatened by Scandal, Women Need Support," *Harvard Business Review*, September 15, 2010, which summarizes research conducted by the Center for Work-Life Policy (CWLP). The article states: "CWLP research shows that sponsorship is *the* critical promotional lever for women stuck just below the top layer of management. However, fear of being even *suspected* of an illicit sexual liaison causes 64 percent of senior men to pull back from one-on-one contact with junior women; conversely, for the same reason, 50 percent of junior women are hesitant to have one-on-one contact with senior men." (Emphasis in original.)

8. Ashley Parker, "Karen Pence Is the Vice-President's 'Prayer Warrior,' Gut Check, and Shield," *The Washington Post*, March 28, 2017; Emma Green, "How Mike Pence's Marriage Became Fodder for the Culture Wars," *The Atlantic*, March 30, 2017.

9. Claire Cain Miller, "It's Not Just Mike Pence. Americans Are Wary of Being Alone with the Opposite Sex," *The New York Times*, July 1, 2017.

10. See Dickens, "How to Handle the Old Boys Network," and McKinsey & Co. and *Leanin.Org*, "Women in the Workplace 2016," September 2016.

11. Sylvia Ann Hewlett, Kerrie Peraino, Laura Sherbin, and Karen Sumberg, "The Sponsor Effect: Breaking Through the Last Glass Ceiling," *Harvard Business Review*, January 12, 2011.

12. Sylvia Ann Hewlett, "The Real Benefit of Finding a Sponsor," *Harvard Business Review*, January 26, 2011.

13. Hewlett, "The Real Benefit of Finding a Sponsor."

14. Sylvia Ann Hewlett, "The Right Way to Find a Career Sponsor," *Harvard Business Review*, September 11, 2013.

15. Heather Saul, "Justin Trudeau: The Rise of the Feminist and Pro-Choice Canadian Prime Minister Who Wants to Legalise Marijuana 'Right Away,'" *The Independent*, October 20, 2015.

16. See Tony Schwartz, "Overcoming the Confidence Gap for Women," *The New York Times*, June 12, 2015; and "John B. Veihmeyer – KPMG," *Diversity Journal*, accessed September 1, 2017.

17. Kyle Chayka, "Startup Investing for Sport and Profit," *The Ringer*, June 8, 2017.

18. Jessi Hempel, "Special Issue: Outsiders," *Backchannel*, March 20, 2017.

19. See "New Study: Women Judged More Harshly When Speaking Up Assertively," VitalSmarts, August 5, 2015, and the white paper it references: David Maxfield, Joseph Grenny, and Chase McMillan, "Emotional Inequality: Solutions for Women in the Workplace," VitalSmarts, accessed August 20, 2017.

CHAPTER 9—WATCH YOUR BACK

1. Belle Derks, Colette Van Laar, and Naomi Ellemers, "The Queen Bee Phenomenon: Why Women Leaders Distance Themselves from Junior Women," *The Leadership Quarterly*, Vol. 27, June 2016; Naomi Ellemers, Floor Rink, Belle Derks, and Michelle K. Ryan,

"Women in High Places: When and Why Promoting Women into Top Positions Can Harm Them Individually or as a Group (and How to Prevent This)," ScienceDirect, Research in Organizational Behavior, Vol. 32, 2012.

2. Gary Namie, The WBI U.S. Workplace Bullying Survey, Workplace Bulllying Institute, 2010.
3. John Baldoni, "Taking the Sting out of 'Queen Bees' Who May Be Out to Get You," *Forbes*, March 4, 2013.
4. See Cheryl Lock, "The Best Way to Deal With A Mean Girl At Work," *Forbes,* March 8, 2013; and "Mean Girls in the Office: How to Cope with Bullies and Workplace Harassment," *Women's Health*, September 30, 2009.
5. Jenna Goudreau, "The 10 Worst Stereotypes about Powerful Women," *Forbes*, October 24, 2011.

CHAPTER 10 — DO NOT TOLERATE INTERRUPTIONS

1. Jessica Bennett, "Hillary Clinton Will Not Be Manterrupted," *The New York Times*, September 27, 2016; Emma Gray, "Donald Trump Couldn't Stop Interrupting Hillary Clinton On Debate Night," *Huffington Post*, September 26, 2016.
2. On this point, Bennett referenced Nicole Torres, "Proof That Women Get Less Credit for Teamwork," *Harvard Business Review*, February 9, 2016.
3. Victoria L. Brescoli, "Who Takes the Floor and Why: Gender, Power, and Volubility in Organizations," *Administrative Science Quarterly*, February 29, 2012.
4. Sheryl Sandberg and Adam Grant, "Speaking While Female: Sheryl Sandberg and Adam Grant on Why Women Stay Quiet at Work," *The New York Times*, January 12, 2015.
5. Adrienne B. Hancock and Benjamin A. Rubin, "Influence of Communication Partner's Gender on Language," *Journal of Language and Social Psychology*, May 11, 2014; Kiernan Snyder, "How to Get Ahead as a Women in Tech: Interrupt Men," *Slate*, July 23, 2014.

6. Christina Cauterucci, "Watch Two Republican Men Shush Kamala Harris in a Senate Hearing," *Slate*, June 7, 2017.
7. Jenna Greene, "Girl (Senator) Interrupted: Women Litigators Feel Kamala Harris' Pain," *The Litigation Daily*, June 15, 2017.
8. Tonja Jacobi and Dylan Schweers, "Female Supreme Court Justices Are Interrupted More by Male Justices and Advocates," *Harvard Business Review*, April 11, 2017. See also Jacobi and Schweers, "Justice, Interrupted: The Effect of Gender, Ideology, and Seniority at Supreme Court Oral Arguments," *Northwestern Law & Economics Research Paper* No. 17-03, March 14, 2017.
9. Tonja Jacobi and Dylan Schweers, "Justice, Interrupted: The Effect of Gender, Ideology, and Seniority at Supreme Court Oral Arguments," *Northwestern Law & Economics Research Paper* No. 17-03, March 14, 2017.
10. See also Don Zimmerman and Candace West, "Sex Roles, Interruptions, and Silences in Conversations," *Language and Sex: Difference and Dominance*, 1975.
11. See, for instance, Susan Chira, "The Universal Phenomenon of Men Interrupting Women," *The New York Times*, June 14, 2017.
12. Rebecca Solnit, "Men Explain Things to Me," *Guernica*, August 20, 2012. (This version reprints Solnit's original 2008 essay with a new introduction.)
13. Zimmerman and West, "Sex Roles, Interruptions, and Silences in Conversations."
14. Charlotte Alter, "Google Exec Eric Schmidt Called Out for Interrupting the Only Woman on Panel," *Time*, March 17, 2015.
15. Juliet Eilperin, "White House Women Want to Be in the Room Where It Happens," *The Washington Post*, September 13, 2016.

CHAPTER 11—ISOLATE AND NEUTRALIZE ASSHOLES

1. Despite frequent attribution to William Gibson, the original quote appears to be the creation of Twitter account holder @debihope,

who posted it on January 24, 2010. See Quote Investigator, "Before You Diagnose Yourself with Depression or Low Self-Esteem...," October 25, 2014.

2. Dan Schawbel, "Bob Sutton: How to Deal with Difficult People at Work," *Forbes*, September 12, 2017.
3. Oliver Burkeman interviewing Aaron James, "This Column Will Change Your Life: Don't Let an Asshole Get to You," *The Guardian*, November 30, 2012.
4. Birgit Schyns and Jan Schilling, "How Bad Are the Effects of Bad Leaders? A Meta-Analysis of Destructive Leadership and Its Outcomes," *Leadership Quarterly* 24, no.1, February 2013; Al-Karim Samnani and Parbudyal Singh, "20 Years of Workplace Bullying Research: A Review of the Antecedents and Consequences of Bullying in the Workplace," *Aggression and Violent Behavior* 17, No. 6, November-December 2012.
5. Aaron James, *Assholes: A Theory*, Doubleday, 2012.
6. It's worth noting that Aaron James wrote a follow-up volume titled, *Assholes: A Theory of Donald Trump.*
7. Bob Sutton, "Latest Tips for Surviving Workplace Assholes," *Work Matters*, August 22, 2007.

CHAPTER 12—DEALING WITH MEN WHO THINK WITH THEIR DICKS

1. Sarah McCammon, "In The Wake Of Harvey Weinstein Scandal, Women Say #MeToo," *All Things Considered*, National Public Radio, October 16, 2017.
2. Jonah Goldberg, "Why Harvey Weinstein Was Fired (Hint: Exposure Mattered More Than The Allegations," *Los Angeles Times*, October 9,2017.
3. Jessica Bennett, "The 'Click' Moment: How the Weinstein Scandal Unleashed a Tsunami," *The New York Times*, November 5, 2017.

4. Jim Rutenberg, Rachel Abrams and Melena Ryzik, "Harvey Weinstein's Fall Opens the Floodgates in Hollywood," *The New York Times*, October 16,2017.
5. Stephanie Zacharek, Eliana Dockterman and Haley Sweetland Edwards, "The Person of the Year 2017, The Silence Breakers," *Time*, December 6, 2017.
6. Mary L. Boland, Sexual Harassment in the Workplace, SphinxLegal, 2005 (ISBN 9781572485273); Louise F. Fitzgerald, "Sexual Harassment: Violence against Women in the Workplace," *American Psychologist*, American Psychological Association via PsycNET, 48 (10), October 1993: pp. 1070–1076 (doi:10.1037/0003-066X.48.10.1070); Alanna Vagianos, "1 in 3 Women Have Been Sexually Harassed At Work, According to Survey," *Huffington Post*, February 19, 2015; Jillian Berman and Emily Swanson, "Workplace Sexual Harassment Poll Finds Large Share of Workers Suffer, Don't Report," *Huffington Post*, August 27, 2013.
7. Debbie S. Dougherty, "The Omissions That Make So Many Sexual Harassment Policies Ineffective," *Harvard Business Review*, May 31, 2017.

CHAPTER 13—SPEAK TRUTH TO POWER

1. Michael Dell with Catherine Fredman, *Direct from Dell: Strategies that Revolutionized an Industry*, HarperBusiness, 1999, p. xxv.
2. SEC Press Release, "SEC Charges Dell and Senior Executives with Disclosure and Accounting Fraud," July 20, 2010.

ACKNOWLEDGEMENTS

To all the women who have decided to harness their natural talents as women – their kick assets – to dominate in business and to shine as the leaders we are meant to be.

To my editors Tim Walker and Dan Clements for their incisive skill in helping me to create a work with "casual gravitas"—and for bearing with me through the trials and tribulations of an author birthing her first book.

To my talented, creative and ingenious team—Christina Gorchos, Dan Lopez and Sable Worthy—who are truly my "band of brothers."

And to the master coach who guided me every step of the way on how to write, publish and market a book, my friend and mentor Honorée Corder.

SPECIAL INVITATION

WOMEN WHO WANT TO UNLEASH THEIR POWER, USING their feminine abilities—their kick assets—to succeed in business and in life have joined together in an online community to share ideas, render support, and promote women's success. I'd like to personally invite you to join us at: **TheMeanestWomanAlive.com/Subscribe** and **Facebook.com/MeanestWomanAlive**.

When you become part of our community, you will receive a free copy of my top 11 remedies for conquering self-sabotage. You can connect with me personally on Twitter @MeanestWoman, or MeanestWomanAlive@gmail.com. I look forward to connecting and hearing from you soon!

ABOUT THE AUTHOR

LINDA SMITH IS ONE OF THE FEW WOMEN to reach the summit of the legal profession. She has represented the world's foremost companies in "bet-the-company" cases where everything is at stake.

During her 40-year career, Linda has often tangled with outsized male egos (Mick Jagger, Michael Dell, Sumner Redstone) and with sexual harassment without ever breaking stride. Her tenacity as a gladiator for her clients earned her the prodigious title of "The Meanest Woman Alive."

After mentoring women for decades, Linda has taken on a broader mission to empower ambitious women in all fields to harness their unique abilities—their kick assets—as women to reach their own pinnacles of success. Whether the challenge is defeating gender stereotypes, conquering self-sabotaging behaviors, dueling with difficult men, or attaining leadership positions, Linda draws on her own experiences and those of other highly successful women to show women how to get ahead, shine and come out on top.

98980938R00144

Made in the USA
Lexington, KY
11 September 2018